A Reason to Tell

50 Original and retold stories for Assemblies

written by:

Alison Gardner

First published
February 02 in Great Britain by

Educational Printing Services Limited
Albion Mill, Water Street, Great Harwood, Blackburn BB6 7QR
Telephone: (01254) 882080 Fax: (01254) 882010
e-mail: enquiries@eprint.co.uk web site: www.eprint.co.uk

ISBN 1 900818 04 3

Acknowledgements

These stories are a collection of original and retold ancient stories. My thanks go to my daughter who patiently read through the stories, giving me feedback and for encouraging me in my dry periods of creativity.

Introduction

The Reason to Tell assembly storybook is intended to provide a quick and simple assembly resource for busy primary school teachers. It is ideal to 'dip into'. The stories can be used in the classroom and for whole school assemblies.

The book provides

1. 50 Stories.
2. A prayer or reflection that accompanies each one.
3. A themetic index to aid teachers' searches and for appropriate stories.

The emphasis is on moral dilemmas. Each story has at least one moral/spiritual theme that can be discussed during assembly. The assembly stories are intended for the 4-11 age range. Some are original stories and some are retold ancient tales and myths. They are drawn from many different cultural sources and range in mood from the serious, thoughtful, exciting and wonderful, to the funny.

Collective Worship in England & Wales

The law requires

- ❑ All pupils in maintained schools must take part in a daily act of worship.
- ❑ This can be for the whole school or groups of children.
- ❑ The school may select the time for the assembly/assemblies.
- ❑ Collective worship is the head teacher's responsibility, or the governors in voluntary schools.
- ❑ Most acts of collective worship should reflect the broad traditions of Christian belief.
- ❑ Worship must not be distinctive of any particular denomination.
- ❑ The head teacher may submit request for a determination to be granted by local SACRE. The school is then responsible for providing appropriate alternative forms of worship.
- ❑ Both teachers and parents have the legal right of withdrawal.
- ❑ Worship must be appropriate to all ages, aptitudes and family backgrounds of all pupils.
- ❑ Worship should promote respect and understanding of those with different religious beliefs and practices.

Aims of Collective Worship

The 1988 Education Reform Act states that worship should be part of a balanced curriculum that promotes spiritual, cultural, mental and physical development of pupils.

There should be opportunities for pupils to:

1. Consider spiritual and moral issues.
2. Explore their own beliefs.
3. Participate and respond either through active involvement or listening and watching.
4. Develop community spirit.
5. Share in common ethos and values.
6. Have positive attitudes reinforced.

What is 'Worship'?

Worship is concerned with reverence or veneration being paid to a divine being or power. Collective worship should reflect something special or separate from daily school activities. It can relate to the day to day life of the school and it must give children time for reflection.

Information gathered from the 1988 Education Act and Circulars 1/94 (England) and 10/94 (Wales).

Collective Worship in Scotland

The law requires

- ❑ All pupils to take part in religious observance at least once a week.
- ❑ Religious observance is a time when 'something akin' to worship takes place. The school policy will decide the format.
- ❑ In non-denominational schools it should be of a broadly Christian character, not specific to one denomination. Other religious traditions should be incorporated into this time.
- ❑ Parents have the right to withdraw their children.
- ❑ Religious observance can take place in a classroom, in a whole school or on a stage.
- ❑ The themes should suit children's own experiences and understanding and there should be a variety in the methods of presentation. Opportunities should be built in for pupils to be involved.
- ❑ School chaplains may often take the religious observance; they have a responsibility to remember that the act is not the same as that to a congregation.

Aims of Religious Observance

Religious observance in schools should:

1. Promote pupils' spiritual development.
2. Increase their understanding of religious practices such as prayer and meditation, and the religious experience that underlies them.
3. Promote the ethos of the school.
4. Provide opportunity for individual reflection on spiritual and moral issues.

Information gathered from the HMI report 1989, SOED Circular 6/91 and Religious and Moral Education 5-14, SOED 1992.

Collective Worship in Northern Ireland

The law requires

- ❑ An act of Collective Worship in every grant aided school for all pupils, each day. How the school arranges this, is left flexible.
- ❑ Parents have the right to withdraw their child wholly or partly from attendance.
- ❑ Teachers may ask for their school to be wholly or partly excused from attending or conducting Collective Worship. This request must go to the Board of Governors of their school. The request must be made on the grounds of conscience.
- ❑ The Board of Governors can ask for external people to conduct the collective worship.

Aims of Collective Worship

Some suggested aims are:

1. Encourage the development of a Christian ethos within the school.
2. Help pupils to see worship of God as a relevant part of daily life.
3. Illustrate practically aspects of Christianity and the lives of Christians.
4. Encourage pupils to reflect on why they exist and to question life.
5. Develop a sense of community within the school.

Information gathered from the Education and Libraries (NI) Order 1986 and Transferor Representatives' Handbook (Transferor Representative Council, September 1994).

Assemblies at a Glance

The Story of Little Tavwots

Origin

This story is a tale from Indian tribes and has been retold from 'The Basket Woman' by Mary Austin. It attempts to explain why rabbits are small but have enormous feet.

Theme

This story tackles pride and boasting. Tavwots' pride causes a lot of problems for planet earth!

An Indian woman who had lived on a reservation all her life told this story to a small boy who lived with his family outside the reservation. They had got talking one day, and this is the story she told him.

Tavwots is a strange name, a strange name for a little rabbit. But, do you know that Tavwots was not always so little? Long, long, ago Tavwots was the largest of all the rabbits for miles in the area. He was a mighty hunter and was very successful. All the other rabbits looked up to him, he was not only large, but he was also the best hunter of them all.

He would go hunting every day, and every day he would see the track of a huge foot in the ground. He was puzzled and angry. He knew that he, and he alone, had the largest footprints in the area! He was proud of this.

"Who is this?" he cried, "whose feet are larger than mine and who hunts in my area." He was so, so proud.

His mother scolded kindly, "Shhhh, no-one is greater than you."

He still wasn't happy. Each day he would spot these huge prints, but he could never see the creature that had made them. Each day he got up earlier than the last, he was determined to find out who was making these prints. What a long stride the creature must have, he thought.

He decided to set a trap for the cheeky animal; after all, he was also the cleverest creature too, wasn't he? He used his bowstring and set it across the trail very late one night. He felt sure this would get the creature. He got up really early the next morning; he couldn't wait to see what had happened.

Do you know what he had caught in his trap? He had caught the sun, and the ground beneath it was turning black with the heat.

"Are you the one making those huge prints?" Tavwots shouted at him.

"Yes, it is I," bellowed the sun back at him. "Set me free or the whole earth will catch fire, quick, quick!"

Tavwots knew he had to do something quickly. He could see smoke starting to curl and rise from the ground. He took his hunting knife and went to cut the bowstring across the trail.

"Hurry! Hurry!" shouted the sun.

Tavwots tried to cut the string with difficulty, all the time the heat was searing through his body. The heat was so great that Tavwots had melted to half his size already.

"Hurry! Hurry!" shouted the sun; he knew he was burning everything near him.

Tavwots kept trying to cut the bowstring, it was tougher than he had realised. In no time at all Tavwots was reduced to a quarter of his size. He moved away, the heat was so intense.

"Hurry! Hurry!" shouted the sun.

He cut and cut, and this time the bowstring sheared in two. The sun disappeared high into the sky, free to light and warm the earth.

Tavwots had managed to lose his greatness; he had been melted to the size he is today. There is one thing left about Tavwots that is truly great, that is his enormous feet. Just look at the ground sometimes and you will be able to see the print of his enormous feet in the soil. If you look really carefully in the reservation, you can see how great his stride was when he caught the sun in his trap.

Prayer / Reflection

Some people look down on other people and boast about how good they are.
It's good to be proud of work you have done, but wrong to boast and put others down.

Think about this saying: **'Pride comes before a fall'.**

What do you think this means?

The Parable of the Marbles

Origin

Source for this story unknown. I have known this story since I was quite small, I have rewritten it, but hope the original spirit of the parable still exists.

Theme

This story shows why it is important to look after things, and how being selfish and careless can leave you in a pickle.

Once upon a time there was a young boy of about nine years old. He was a normal happy go lucky lad, always out playing. This boy had always proved himself to be foolish, one way or another.

Now this young lad had a huge bag full of the most beautiful marbles. There were small ones, large ones, misty ones and colours of the rainbow. In fact it was a really beautiful collection. He was really proud of his collection. In fact he was so proud that he wouldn't play with them. Quite often he would take them out of the bag, count them and admire them. All his friends would crowd round catching a look at the amazing collection.

In the same school there was a very wise boy. He had seemed very wise from a very young age. He loved looking at the bag of amazing marbles. He dreamed of owning such a collection. He worked hard in his spare time to earn extra money. So far he had only managed to buy a bag for some marbles. He used to take out his marble bag every now and again, and dream of the marbles he would have one day soon, hopefully. He longed to share them with his friends and play games of marbles.

The foolish boy loved his marbles but he was quite careless with the bag. He would toss it around and drop it on the floor when he was in a rush. Well, one day the marble bag developed a tatty hole, not too big at first, but as you know, holes just get bigger and bigger. He didn't notice that the hole was getting bigger, and slowly one by one the marbles were dropping through.

Can you imagine who kept finding these loose marbles dotted here and there? You've got it! It was the wise boy. One by one he found the beautiful marbles just sitting on the ground. One by one he picked them up and each day his collection got bigger. Quite quickly he had a beautiful collection of marbles in his bag. His dream had come true.

The wise boy played lots of games with them and shared them with his friends. He always took care of the marbles and the bag. He had saved hard for the bag and he knew the marble collection was brilliant.

What happened to the foolish boy? Well, he had been selfish and careless and because of that he had lost all his marbles and was left holding only a tatty bag with a hole in it.

Prayer / Reflection

Do you know what a 'hoarder,' is? - A person who just keeps things, but doesn't really use them. Think of all the money and possessions people hoard in a lifetime.

Do you know what a 'giver,' is? - Someone who gives for no return.

Which one are you?

Why is it good to be a 'giver'?

The Talking Fish

Origin

This story has been rewritten from another story of the same name in Armenian folk tales by N.W. Orloff (1946).

Theme

The story is an ancient Armenian tale, which looks at kindness and doing nice things for others.

Once upon a time there was a man who was very poor. He hadn't had work for ages, but at long last he found some. He was going to work on a fishing boat as a fisherman's helper. He was paid just a few fish a day but this was all he and his wife needed. They were grateful for anything.

On this particular morning he kissed his wife goodbye and left for work just as normal. After all, it was just a normal day, wasn't it? They went out far to sea and the weather was perfect. The first net he pulled up had a really marvellous fish in it, it looked perfect. He turned it over and over in his hands. Suddenly the fish spoke to him.

"Watch what you're doing. I was just playing with my friends and got caught in your net! Now here I am, probably dying."

The fisherman was so shocked he was speechless.

"Please throw me back, my friends will be searching for me. Please, please throw me back."

The fisherman stared at the fish in his hands. Could it really be happening? Do fish play and have friends? His mind was going round and round with lots of questions. He decided to throw the fish back.

"Go back to your friends, quickly, I don't want them worrying about you."

His boss saw him throw the fish back and was furious.

"You stupid fool! You're sacked!"

They got back to shore, neither men talking to each other. The fisherman walked sadly home. What would his wife say? What would they do for food?

Coming along the road towards him he saw a man with a cow.

"Good day to you, why are you so sad?" asked the stranger.

The fisherman told him about the amazing day he had had, but how it had ended in unhappiness.

"I'll help you. See this cow, well you can keep her for three years. She'll give you lots of milk. There is one condition though. At the end of the three years I will come and ask you some questions. If you get them right you keep the cow. If you don't, well there's a price to pay. If you get them wrong I keep you and the cow!"

The fisherman didn't want his wife to go hungry, so he accepted. Off he went, happy and full of hope for the future.

His wife was happy to see him and life went well for a few years. The cow gave enough milk for them to sell. They enjoyed a much better life. In the evenings the fisherman and his wife would think about the strange man who had given them the cow, what questions would he ask? They felt troubled but could do nothing about it. The end of the three years came quicker than they could have imagined.

One evening in mid winter, a young man knocked at their door and said, "I am really weary, may I stay the night?"

"Of course!" said the fisherman, "only tonight is a bad night."

They explained their unusual story to the young man. He said he wasn't worried about any danger to himself and that he would stay anyway.

At midnight on the dot, there was a loud knock on the door.

"It is I!" boomed the voice. "It is time to answer my three questions."

The fisherman's wife clutched her husband in fear. "We'll never be able to answer them," she cried.

The young man stepped towards the door saying. "Don't worry, I'll answer them for you."

"Where are you from?" asked the man.

"I'm from the other side of the sea," answered the young man calmly.

"How did you get here?"

"Riding a lame flea."

"The sea must have been immensely small?"

"No way, even an eagle would have trouble doing the distance!"

"The eagle must have been a mere fledgling?"

"No, his wings were wide enough to cover a whole city!"

"The city must have been tiny."

"No, even a hare couldn't run from one end to the other."

The man was running out of questions. What could he ask? He stood outside silently for a while. Still he could not think of any more trick questions to ask. After a while the fisherman realised he had disappeared. They were overjoyed and had a little celebration of hot coffee and biscuits.

The young man celebrated and chatted with them for hours. Soon the sun started to rise and he said he was leaving.

"You can't go yet, you saved our lives," the wife cried. "Tell us who you are, we need to thank you properly."

The young man smiled and looked across at the couple.

"A kindness is never lost, even if you throw it into the water. I am that talking fish you threw back!"

They looked back in astonishment, and in that moment he disappeared forever.

Prayer / Reflection

Listen to this role from the eighteenth century John Wesley, a Christian who tried to live by it.

Do all the good you can,
By all the means you can,
In all the ways you can,
In all the places you can,
At all the times you can,
To all the people you can,
As long as ever you can.

The Spider and the Honey Tree

Origin

This story is an ancient folk tale from Liberia.

Theme

It focuses on being selfish and greedy. The girl in the story is a lot smarter than she appears.

There was once a young girl who lived in a tiny village in Africa. She had a very special talent. Her talent was most unusual. She was able to find the very best foods in the countryside. When she found oranges, they were sweeter than all the others, when she found bananas they had more taste than any others. Everyone in the village wondered where she found these delicious foods; they never seemed able to find them. Nobody ever asked her, that is, nobody asked her after they heard the story of the spider and this young girl.

Here's that story!

One day a spider asked Kayle, this young girl, to help him look for food. He was terribly lazy and didn't want to look for himself. He knew he could trick this young girl into sharing all her secrets. What he didn't know was, how clever Kayle was!

"Little girl, your fruits are always the tastiest, will you take me with you when you next go into the countryside looking for food?" cooed the spider.

"I've never taken anyone with me before," she said.

"It would mean the world to me if you could, just this once, pleeease..."

Kayle gave it a little thought and then decided to do it just this once.

"Do you promise to keep my secrets?" Kayle asked.

"You can trust me," said the lazy spider.

Kayle told the spider that her favourite foods were oranges and kiwi fruits. Spider told her excitedly, that his were plums and bananas.

"I especially love honey though," added the spider, licking his lips.

"I think I can help you," grinned Kayle.

Spider couldn't believe his luck, she really was stupid.

Kayle took spider far into the countryside, moving off a path, trudging over rough fields. Spider wasn't worried, all he was thinking about was filling his stomach with his favourite foods, and...... discovering all her secret places for finding food. He'd never have to hunt hard for food again.

Kayle stopped under a small straggly plum tree.

"This plum tree doesn't have much fruit so everyone walks on by, but its fruit is the sweetest I've ever tasted," explained Kayle.

Now, spider was also very, very greedy. His mouth was watering; he couldn't wait to eat them. He pushed Kayle into the bushes, climbed the tree and sat and ate every single plum on the tree. He didn't even say, "thank you!"

Spider rubbed his tummy and thought of bananas, yes, he'd like some bananas now.

"Do you know where there are any bananas?" said spider, now being friendly. Kayle smiled and said, "Okay."

"She must be very foolish," he thought to himself.

Kayle walked for a few minutes, getting into the much quieter areas. No one usually walked this far! "Over here are the best bananas ever," shouted Kayle.

Once again, his mouth started watering; he pushed her away and grabbed as many bananas as he could, shoving them in his mouth. He didn't stop until he had eaten every last banana. And still.....no thank you! He was so, so full, but he hadn't finished yet.

"This girl is so foolish," he said to himself.

Kayle looked at spider and asked really politely if he'd like some honey. He would never say no to honey, so off they set even further into the countryside. No one ever came this far!

"Over here," she beckoned. "It's a very special tree. Deep inside a small hole is the most delicious honey."

Now I don't know if you've realised it yet, but Kayle was not as foolish as the spider thought. She watched his mouth watering, saw him coming to push her aside, and do you know what? She just let him push her!

He squeezed into the hole and drank every last drop of golden honey. And again not a thank you!

He was full now, and ready to go home. He squeezed and squeezed, but his stomach was so big that he was well and truly stuck.

"Help me, I'm stuck!" he shouted.

"You wouldn't be stuck if you hadn't been so selfish," scolded Kayle.

"I'm sorry, I am really," spider begged.

"I'm not as foolish as you think. You're not sorry, you're only sorry you're stuck in the tree."

The spider protested his innocence, but in his heart he knew she was right. He'd loved all the food, and enjoyed tricking her!

"Please call for help, I am trapped."

Kayle smiled and agreed to do what spider asked. So..... she cried for help, but as softly as she could.

"Help. Help! Somebody please come and help this greedy spider."

Of course no one could hear. They were too far away from the village and all the people.

Kayle looked up at the spider stuck in the hole, grinned, and said, "Bye spider, I'm going to get some oranges now, huge ones for my family. If you want to eat some, just follow me."

She waved as she skipped happily on her way.

Prayer / Reflection

Think about this saying from the Bible.

"We bring nothing into the world and can take nothing out." (Timothy 6, 6-10).

What does 'bringing nothing in' mean?

The Boy Who Disappeared!

Origin

This is an ancient fairy tale from Bohemia. It is adapted from a story called 'The Lost Child' from Folk Lore from Foreign Lands by Catherine T. Bryce 1913.

Theme

This story is a classic fairy tale that looks at compassion and kindness, in particular, the effect on others of kind words. It also tackles bravery in circumstances of poverty.

Many, many years ago there lived a very important rich man. He had a gorgeous baby son. Something very odd happened to this man the night before his son was born. He had a dream, a most peculiar dream. In his dream, his son could only grow to be a man if the boy's feet didn't touch the earth until he was 12 years old.

He took this dream very seriously and hired the best nurses in the land to look after him. He was constantly watched and carried around by the nurses. Sometimes the rich man's servants carried him in a special chair. The young boy's feet never went near the ground. Time went by very quickly and soon the boy was twelve years old.

The young boy got more and more excited as his birthday neared. His father planned a big party with amazing food. One day, they were preparing for the party when a dreadful noise echoed through the castle. It was a piercing scream. The nurse carrying the young boy dropped him in terror and ran to the window. The noises had stopped. She turned round to pick him up and do you know what had happened? He had completely disappeared. She realised instantly that his feet must have touched the floor and now he was gone. Oh what trouble she was in!

All the servants in the castle had heard her screams and came running. The rich man followed.

"What on earth has happened, where's my son?"

The nurse cried while she told her story. The father was distraught. He sent servants to hunt all over the castle and in the grounds. He promised big money to anyone who could find his son. No news at all!

The man grieved for many years. After a few years one of the servants told the rich man that they had all heard footsteps and groans in one of the bedrooms. Each time they looked, no one was there. The rich man wondered if this could have anything to do with his son. He offered to pay a big reward to anyone who would stay an entire night in this room. Many tried but by midnight they were so scared, they left.

The rich man was desperate. He new of a very poor family near by, perhaps they would help? The eldest daughter decided to try and stay in the room, she knew how much they needed the money. Her mother was really worried but knew it would help them all if her daughter was successful. The rich man was amazed by her bravery.

"Will you really be able to stay a whole night?"

"I'm willing to try, I only ask for a little food to keep me going through the night," she said.

The rich man made sure she had plenty to eat, plenty of wood for a fire and a candle for light. She lit the fire and made herself comfy. Quite soon she heard horrible screams and moans. She couldn't see anyone at first until suddenly a young man appeared as if from nowhere.

"Who's all this food for?" he asked.

"For me," she uttered, quite startled.

"Who's the table set for?"

"Me!"

"Who is this lovely warm fire for?"

"For me, to keep me warm," she said, still surprised at his questions.

She looked into his face and saw tears in his eyes, and then as suddenly as he appeared he went.

She tried to sleep a little, but felt too excited to sleep properly. In the morning she told the rich man what had happened. She left out the tears, fearing that may upset him. The rich man paid her and was extremely grateful for any news of his son. The next day the middle daughter went and offered to stay the night in the room.

She had lots of food, wood for the fire and she made herself comfy. As the night before, the young man appeared as if from nowhere.

"Who's all this food for? Who's the table set for? Who is this lovely warm fire for?"

She answered for herself, to all the questions. Just as the night before tears came into his eyes. She told the rich man what had happened in the morning. On the third day the youngest daughter decided to try and stay in the room.

She entered the room just like her two sisters, lit the fire and settled in for the night. As the clock chimed twelve she heard footsteps, groans and cries. At first she couldn't see anyone, then, as if from nowhere, a young man appeared. She looked into his big sad eyes and completely forgot the answers she was meant to give.

"Who's all this food for?"

"For me, unless you'd like to join me."

"Who's this lovely warm fire for?"

"For me, but you're welcome to join me."

He smiled and said he would join her, but first he had to thank the friends who had looked after him.

At that very moment, a large hole appeared in the middle of the floor and the young man took her hand and together they seemed to float to the bottom. She saw a whole new world open up before her eyes, a river flowing with gold, meadows and thousands of beautiful flowers. The young man took the girl through a forest of gold trees. All the time, the young man seemed to be talking to the birds. The young daughter snapped off a small twig of gold as a keepsake and hid it in a pocket.

They eventually reached a forest of silver, sparkling its beauty. Animals crowded round the young man, the young man communicating with them all. She quickly picked off a silver twig to keep. Eventually the young man had said goodbye to all his friends. They rose through the floor of the room back to the warm fire. The hole was gone! They sat together and ate the supper.

"That was delicious, now it's time to rest," said the young man, contentedly.

Very quickly he was sleeping beside her.

Early in the morning the rich man was eager to hear the youngest daughter's story. She didn't appear and he started to feel impatient. In the end he decided to go into the room for her. What a shock he had when he went in. There on the bed was his son sleeping, and in the chair the sleeping girl. He was so happy; words couldn't describe how he felt.

The young man awoke and saw the twigs. "These branches will be our home."

And with that the young man tossed them out of the castle window. Do you know what happened? It was amazing, a magnificent palace made of gold and silver appeared. The young man and the girl married and lived happily in this palace forever. The father was overjoyed at the return of his son and his happy marriage.

Prayer / Reflection

Help us to be kind, friendly and helpful to others.
Teach us to use nice words to help others when they are upset, and to cheer up others.

The Popular Classmate

Origin

This story has been written by Alison Gardner.

Theme

This story focuses on real friendships. What is it? Are we real friends to anyone? Who are our real friends?

Just how popular was Louise? Very!

Every year her classmates voted her the favourite student. She had not lost one election yet. She was fun in the classroom; she could make all the others laugh. If someone wanted to spring jokes on a supply teacher, Louise was first to volunteer, and really she was the only one brave enough to do it. They all admired her and looked up to her, didn't they?

She had far more friends than anyone else in the class. At playtimes she was always surrounded by friends, friends wanting to laugh and joke with her, friends wanting to share their snacks, friends wanting to plot some fun with her.

One day, the ten-year old was caught passing notes in class, not just any old class, Miss Jenkins' class - MUSIC! She lost her break-time as a punishment. Miss Jenkins was very strict and did not want any messing around in her music lessons. Staying in, in this school, meant you had to help to do something 'useful', like picking up litter, washing the paint pots.

Now Louise's school had just started a new scheme, a scheme to encourage kindness and friendship. Once a month you could swap your punishment with someone else. If you had some punishment on that day of the month, you could ask a friend to stand in for you. Of course, you had to return the favour, within the same month. Otherwise the favour cancelled itself out.

As it happened, on that very day Louise had to stay in, Mr.Bries was doing the cricket trials. Louise was brilliant at all sports and she loved cricket. She knew if she went to the trials, she would be selected for the team. It was a great team; all the matches were played in school time, so you missed loads of lessons. The cricket's good too though!

Louise knew this break-time was her only chance. Mr.Bries was going to make a decision on the team members straight after the trials at break. Oh why had she played up today? Today of all days. Louise needed someone to stand in for her. That was a problem though. It was the last day of the month, so anyone who helped her would be doing it out of pure friendship. The favour would be cancelled. Who was she going to ask?

No problem. She had loads of friends, didn't she? She immediately went to look for Rhian, her 'best' friend.

"Oh no, Louise, I can't do it, I'm tidying the library for Mrs. Groves."

She then launched into describing her job in detail. You could tell she was really proud to be a library monitor.

"Manjit, will you do my break for me please?"

Manjit was happily playing netball, shooting goals into the net.

"To help Miss Jenkins? I wish you'd told me earlier. I've got to practise my netball, my teacher asked me to."

By now Louise was beginning to doubt if even one of her friends would agree to stay for her. But, she tried again. This time she asked three of her friends together. These three had often supplied her with ideas for tricks; they were always around when needed. Of course no one said 'no' outright. They were all great friends. Each one had a 'reason' why they couldn't help that break. "Couldn't they do it another day? If only it were another day."

So, off Louise trooped, back to Miss Jenkins, no cricket trials. She was close to tears when she went in the classroom. Miss Jenkins noticed and asked her what was wrong; after all it was only one break! Louise told her about the cricket trials and how she really, really wanted to be on the cricket team.

Now Miss Jenkins was a very strict teacher, but she was also very fair. She postponed the punishment until next break so Louise could go to the trials. Louise ran along as quickly as she could, though, not as happy as she had been that morning.

"Some popularity I have," she muttered to herself. "I may have many friends, but in reality I have none!"

Prayer / Reflection

Dear God,

Thank you for the friendships I make at school and at home.

Please help me too, to be a good friend to others.

Amen

It was an Accident

Origin

This story has been written by Alison Gardner

Theme

It is a story about making choices, and being able to say 'sorry'.

It was the beginning of the school holiday. They had a whole week at home, Joseph and Victoria. Joseph was older so he always made the decisions on which computer game to play, which TV programme to put on, etc. Joseph nearly always got his own way, but Victoria figured that one brother was better than no brother at all. At least she had someone to play with, sometimes.

Today, their mum had hired a video for them to watch. She was in the kitchen making popcorn. Joseph could already smell the gorgeous smell oozing through the kitchen door.

She shouted, "Popcorns ready!"

Joseph leapt up from the settee and jumped right over Victoria's head. It wasn't hard to do, she was only little. He wanted to be the first one to get popcorn!

Victoria tried to move out of Joseph's way, but TOO LATE! He didn't jump high enough and his big ugly toe poked her right in the eye. He tumbled onto the floor and just sat there for a second. He was hoping against all hope that she wouldn't cry.

Now as you all know, little sisters tend to cry at anything. Well, she did. She cried at the top of her voice and between the blubbers she shouted, "Mum! Joseph - Kicked - Me - In - The - Eye."

Joseph knew he was doomed, and he didn't even think about being sorry.

Next moment, their mum came running into the room and saw Victoria crying. The tears were streaming down her face by now.

"What did you do to her?" she asked Joseph.

"Nothing," he said, "it was an accident."

Victoria, still crying spluttered, "He kicked me in the eye on purpose!"

"It was an accident, she moved," Joseph protested.

His mum was having none of it. She was already fed up with their arguments and it was still only the beginning of the holiday. "Go to your room, Joseph," she ordered.

Joseph knew it was useless trying to argue. This always happened when Victoria cried. He hated his little sister sometimes, especially now!

A little while later the house seemed a lot quieter, Victoria had stopped crying. His mum knocked on his bedroom door and came in to talk to him. This always happened as well.

"All right young man," she said, "what did you do?"

"Nothing, I didn't mean it. It was an accident."

"Nothing! Victoria's got a black eye appearing in there. That's not nothing!" Joseph looked a bit sheepish, a black eye? What would his dad say?

"You seem to have accidents all the time, and they always seem to make your little sister cry. Her eye is swollen up like a raspberry."

Joseph didn't know what to say.

"You need to stay in your room until you have something to say to your sister," his mum said, as she left his bedroom.

He could still smell the popcorn wafting under his bedroom door. He wondered if Victoria had started watching the film without him, and eating all the popcorn! He started to think a little more, he was a lot bigger than Victoria, a black eye! He argued and muttered to himself.

"It was only an accident. I don't know what all the fuss is about."

Suddenly CAPTAIN CHANGE zoomed into his room and sat on his bed. He'd only ever been once before and Joseph was never sure if he had dreamt it or not.

"This is a job for CAPTAIN CHANGE," he shouted. "I'm here to help you make the right choices."

"Hey! How did you get in here!" screamed Joseph.

"I'm a superhero, I can do anything," Captain Change said.

"What do you want?" Joseph asked.

"I'm here to help you make better choices."

Joseph felt a little indignant. What was wrong with the choices he made?

"If you're talking about poking Victoria in the eye, well, it was an accident."

"Accident or not, you still hurt your little sister."

Joseph started to watch the door while he was talking to CAPTAIN CHANGE. Wouldn't his mum have heard all the shouting?

"It's not fair to be punished for an accident," argued Joseph.

"You need to show your sister that you didn't mean it."

By now Joseph felt really guilty. It was just too hard to apologise. He didn't know why it was so hard, it just was. He looked up to tell Captain Change that he was going to apologise, but he was gone. There was no sign of him, only a dent in the duvet where he had sat. He couldn't have imagined it, could he?

He opened his bedroom door and peeked out. He could see a large bowl of popcorn on the table, untouched! Victoria was playing with her Barbie; he could just make out her black eye. It looked painful.

"I'm sorry, it was an accident, honest, Victoria," he said sheepishly.

"Come on," his mum said, "we're waiting for you to start the film."

Joseph smiled and sat next to Victoria, giving her just a quick hug, only a quick one mind!

Prayers / Reflection

Dear God

Please help me to know when I am in the wrong.

To help me to say sorry when needed.

Thank you for my family.

Amen.

The Tailor-Bird and the Cat

Origin

This story originated from Bengali folklore.

Theme

It is a story about flattery.

In West Bengal the plants and birds are very different to here. They have the strangest of names and the plants grow huge. This story is about a Bengali bird called a 'Tailorbird', and a plant called a brinjal-plant.

To the rear of this large house, there was a yard, a yard full of plants. The brinjal-plant had large leaves that felt very soft. A tailorbird started collecting the leaves to make a nest. The nest was in a tree at the back of the yard. The tailorbird was hurrying around, knowing that her chicks would be born soon. By the end of the day her nest was finished, ready for her chicks.

By the end of that week, the yard wasn't so peaceful anymore. Three chicks had been born and were constantly chirping very loudly for food. They were so tiny that they couldn't fly or open their eyes. They could only open their mouths and cheep.

The family that lived in the house had a very wicked cat. The cat spent her days thinking, "I'd like to eat that tailorbird's chicks."

One day the cat stood underneath the nest, watching and waiting.

"Hello, little bird, what are you doing?"

The tailorbird had thought of a plan. She knew this cat was dangerous.

"Humble greetings, Your Majesty," she said, bowing until her head touched the branch beneath the nest. This made the cat very pleased, she felt very important. Off she went, tail high. She came like this every day, and every day the tailorbird bowed down before her and called her Your Majesty. The cat would always go away very happy. She stopped thinking about catching the chicks and just thought about how important she was.

The tailorbird's chicks ate and ate, getting bigger and stronger each day. They grew beautiful wings and their eyes were now wide open. The tailorbird said to them. "Children, do you think you can fly?"

"Yes, mother we do." They all chirped with excitement.

They had been trying to flap their wings for days now, but there wasn't enough room in the nest.

"Well," said the tailorbird, "let's see first, whether you can go and perch on a branch of that palm tree."

The chicks all flew off at once, they couldn't wait to try flying. Then the tailorbird laughed and said. "Now let's see what happens when the wicked cat comes."

After a while, the cat emerged from the house. The noise of the chirping had woken her up and she wanted to see what was going on.

"Hello little bird, what are you doing?"

Now normally the tailorbird would bow and call her, Your Majesty, but today was different. "Go away, you good-for-nothing cat," she chirped, flying teasingly around the cat's head.

The cat saw red, and darted towards the tailorbird, trying to catch it each time it came near. She spotted the chicks now flying after their mother; she wasn't fast enough to catch any of them. She flew at the tree trying hard to get higher; the thorns of the brinjal scratched her and stopped her from trying any harder. The scratched cat, tired from the chase, slunk back into the house, tail between her legs, feeling very silly indeed.

Prayers / Reflection

Dear God

Please help me not to boast,
nor to brag about my things.
Help me only to praise people when I mean it,
not to just get something.

Amen

The Salmon of Knowledge

Origin

An Irish legend.

Theme

Explores trust, kindness and thinking before taking an action.

Long, long ago in Ireland, there was a tale about a famous salmon. The Salmon of Knowledge. Rumours and stories about its existence abounded and everyone wanted to be the first to catch it. All the stories talked about its skin shining like silver and the first person to taste it would be able to see into the future. An old poet called Finnegas had been told the story many years ago by his grandfather and he firmly believed that this fish existed.

He lived in a small hut by the River Boyne. He spent most of his time writing poems and occasionally he tried fishing for the salmon of knowledge. He kept on hoping that he would be the one to catch it and taste it. Many people came to fish in the Boyne, but they would all return to their homes sadly.

One day Finnegas was sitting outside his hut trying to write. He saw a fair-haired boy running towards him.

"Who are you?" asked Finnegas. "Why are you running?"

"My name is Fionn," said the boy. "My father has been killed in battle, now his enemies want to kill me too."

"Do not be afraid," said Finnegas kindly. "Stay with me and I will look after you."

And so it was. Finnegas was a kindly man and he grew to love Fionn like his own son. Fionn helped Finnegas, who was getting on in age and needed a little help. In the daytime Fionn would help clean the hut and cook some meals. Finnegas would tell him wonderful stories and read him his new poems.

One day Finnegas went out fishing as usual. He still fished for the salmon of knowledge, but only ended up with supper. After a short time he came rushing to the hut, shouting.

"Fionn! Fionn! Quick!"

Fionn rushed out, he thought there was something terribly wrong. There stood Finnegas holding an enormous silver fish wriggling in his arms.

"I've caught the salmon of knowledge, can you believe it! Now I'll have great knowledge."

They set to work, making up a huge fire on which to cook this fish. Finnegas was trembling with excitement. He had spent his whole life dreaming of catching the salmon of knowledge. Soon the fish was cooking, but it was so large the fire was running low.

"Look after the fish while I go and get some more firewood," ordered Finnegas. "But you are not to taste it," he warned Fionn.

Fionn sat watching the salmon cook. He knew this was a very special day. He remembered all the stories Finnegas had told him about the salmon of knowledge. He watched fascinated, the heat from the fire making a huge blister appear on the salmon. It was getting bigger and bigger. He couldn't resist pressing his thumb on the blister; he wished he hadn't straight away. He shrieked as a burning sensation spread through his thumb. Without thinking he put his thumb in his mouth to relieve the pain.

He realised straight away what a terrible mistake he'd made. He could taste the salmon in his mouth and knew that he was the first to taste the salmon of knowledge. What was he going to say to Finnegas? He'd let him down dreadfully.

When Finnegas came back he knew straight away that Fionn had tasted the salmon. Somehow he could tell that Fionn had the power of the salmon. He was very sad.

"It was an accident, there was this blister and ......"

He could tell it was useless making excuses.

"You will now be able to see into the future, you must go and become leader of the Fianna, you must use these powers for the good of your people," said Finnegas to Fionn.

And that is what happened, Fionn was a good, kind and wise leader, he always remembered not to misuse his powers, Finnegas had taught him well.

Prayer / Reflection

Dear God

Please help me to love others, to appreciate people who help me.
Please help me to do as I'm asked.

Amen.

A Very Special Egg

Origin

This story has been written by Alison Gardner.

Theme

A story about the relationship between grandparents and their grandchildren.

Harry loved visiting his grandma; she always spoilt him, as grandparents do. He only had to mention being hungry, and as if by magic all his favourite things would be on offer. He loved going shopping with her, he would help her choose her groceries, and carry them! That was the hard part, she always seemed to buy so much and the bags seemed to get heavier each time.

Each time he went to the local store with his grandma, he got a free cookie from the lady in the bakery. He never knew why that was, it had always just happened. He'd munch his biscuit straight away, it was always gorgeous, filled with chocolate drops or smarties or other delicious ingredients.

After he'd finished eating, he'd always help grandma with her shopping list. He'd run around and find things and fill up her basket. He always found things that weren't on her list, gran always said yes, how could she resist his smile and pleading eyes?

He especially liked picking out the eggs and filling a box. Today, Harry noticed an unusual egg in the back of the stack. It was larger than the other eggs and had the tiniest blue spots on it. He picked it off gently and put it with the others in the carton. The lid only just closed.

When he got back to his grandma's house, he couldn't resist having another look at it. There it was, he knew what he had to do. Hatch it! He would hatch it himself! He'd seen chicks hatched out at school and knew he needed a warm place for it. He thought of the oven. Too hot! The airing cupboard? Too cold now grandad had put a cover on the tank. The hairdryer? Too noisy. Sit on it himself? He couldn't sit still for that long. He knew that was impossible.

He had the perfect solution! His furry Dougal on the bottom of his bed. That was so soft and warm, and it never moved. He placed the egg gently underneath, and he waited, and waited for it to hatch. It was strange that his grandma never asked why there were only five eggs in the box. He could only assume she hadn't noticed.

He waited .... and waited .... and waited .. and.

Suddenly Dougal jumped in the air and landed on the floor. It happened so quickly. Harry couldn't believe his eyes. There sitting on the bottom of his bed, surrounded by pieces of broken shell, was a baby dragon.

He looked at Harry and blowing purple smoke, smiled a little smile.

"Wow! My very own dragon!" shouted Harry.

"Wow! My very own boy!" shouted the dragon.

"I'm going to call you Spikes," said Harry.

"I'll call you Specs," said the dragon.

"My name's Harry, not Specs," shouted Harry indignantly.

"And my name's not Spikes! It's Brady," shouted the dragon back to him.

"How can you have a name already, you've only just hatched," asked Harry puzzling.

"I don't know, but I can talk, breathe fire and be a dragon, I hatched like it."

Harry looked a little upset; he wanted to be able to name HIS dragon Spike. "Oh I suppose I understand," said Harry very reluctantly. "My grandma wouldn't understand, you must pretend you're a toy when she's around."

"That's silly," snorted Brady.

Harry spent quite a while explaining about grown-ups to the dragon, especially about grandparents!

"Shhh," Harry suddenly hissed. "She's coming, remember what I said."

Grandma came in with some pop for him and asked if he was hungry yet. Harry was starving and his lips started to water when gran said she had made a cake.

"What's that you're playing with?" she asked, as they went into the kitchen.

"Just my toy dragon brought from home," he said, holding Brady high in the air.

Harry got a little nervous as his grandma moved a little nearer for a closer look. He didn't mean to, but he couldn't help it. He squeezed Brady with nerves, a little too hard and a little puff of purple smoke came out through his nose.

"Wow! How did you do that?" asked gran.

Harry started to stammer a little, he wasn't sure if he'd given Brady away.

"It's easy, you just squeeze him a little."

He was so nervous by now that his hands were sweating. And can you guess what happened? He squeezed again, way too hard and all the fire that Brady had was squeezed in that moment right up through his nose and out.

Brady looked like he was laughing, Harry was terrified, how was he going to get out of this one? He realised the fire hadn't burnt anything, what a relief! Grandma was nowhere to be seen. He thought she must have been scared and had run into the kitchen.

"We're for it now," he shouted angrily at Brady. Brady was still giggling, Harry couldn't understand him at all.

"I'm in the kitchen," called grandma, really calm.

Harry carried Brady in and found his gran sitting at the table with a cake, not just an ordinary cake, a cake with a candle on it.

"I'm sorry, grandma. I found this egg at the shops when I was with you, and I hatched it myself. I hope we haven't scared you too much."

"Happy birthday Brady," his gran said, as she lit the candle.

Harry watched as she winked at Brady.

"Don't you realise Harry?"

He moved closer.

"Grandmothers always know what their grandchildren are up to. Now blow out your candle Brady."

Prayer / Reflection

Dear God

Thank you for our family.
A special thank you for Grandparents.
Who love us and spoil us.
Look after us and think we're special.

Amen

The Grateful Crane

Origin

An ancient Japanese tale retold.

Theme

A tale of greed and broken promises.

Once upon a time, a poor man lived in the tiniest of houses. It was all he could afford, but still, he was glad to have somewhere to live. It was wintertime in Japan and winters are very cold. The snow was falling silently on the ground, a shining white sheet of winter.

One day, after finishing work, the poor man set off on his long walk home. He loved listening to the crunching sound his shoes were making in the snow, although his feet were starting to get a little wet. He heard strange noises, strange groaning sounds. Wondering where the sound was coming from, he followed his ears into some fields nearby. He jumped the gate and carried on following the groaning sounds.

What he found made him sad. He found a crane moaning on the ground. An arrow had speared its wing. He tried to comfort the bird and decided the only thing he could do to help the crane was to pull the arrow out. He gave a sharp tug whilst talking and calming the crane, and out it came. The wound looked as if it would heal and the crane started to struggle to free itself from his arms. He let it go and it flew away and vanished into the sky.

The poor man carried on his journey home. He was very lonely and nobody ever visited him. But, on this one night, very late, a caller tapped gently on his door. He jumped up in surprise, wondering who would visit on such a wintry evening, and at his house! He opened the door and saw the most beautiful young woman. She was lost and begged him to let her stay. He felt sorry for her and of course he let her stay. She was delightful company and she stayed the next night, and the next night after.

Finally he plucked up courage to ask her to marry him. He had fallen hopelessly in love. She agreed and although they were very poor, they were very happy together. Still, the winter was long and cold and on a very cold weekend they realised they had no money and no food.

The beautiful wife decided to weave a piece of cloth and her husband got the loom ready. Before she started weaving she said. "While I am weaving, you must not come in and look!"

The husband promised her that he wouldn't. She shut herself in the back room and started weaving. She was weaving for one night, two nights, on the third day she brought in her work. How tired and hungry she must have been.

He looked at it in amazement. It was the most beautiful piece of cloth he had ever seen. The husband travelled as quickly as he could to the nearest town to sell it. He was able to sell it for quite a lot of money. He returned home and they were able to survive most of the winter quite happily.

Right towards the end of the harsh winter they ran out of food and money again. The beautiful wife told her husband not to watch or come into the room, and she would spin some cloth again. On the fourth day she emerged with a piece of cloth, more gorgeous than the last one. He sold it easily for a huge amount of money.

His wife made him really happy and with her weaving, life was a lot more comfortable, but he started to want more and more money. The neighbours also started asking very awkward questions.

"How could she weave such beautiful cloth but never buy thread?"

He, too, started to wonder. He wanted some more money, so he asked his wife to weave some more cloth. She said that they had enough money now, but he kept on and on until she agreed. She reminded him not to watch her, and reluctantly he disappeared.

By now he had hatched a plan, he really wanted to know how she did it. He forgot about his promise and gently opened the door just a crack so that he could see in. What he saw made him nearly faint. Instead of a wife a crane was sitting tearing out its feathers one by one and weaving the most beautiful piece of cloth. Now he understood. The crane had noticed the door opening and before his eyes, she changed back into a human being.

The young wife then told him her story of how she was the crane he had saved, she had become a human wife to pay back his generosity. But, since he hadn't kept his promise to her, and now he knew the truth about her, she would have to go, forever. He was so, so sorry, but it was too late, he had broken the trust. His desire for more and more money had robbed him of true happiness. She turned into a crane and disappeared that very day, forever.

Prayer / Reflection

Dear God

Please help me to appreciate what I've got, to not be greedy and want more.
To keep any promises to others.

Amen

Cracking Mountain

Origin

An ancient Japanese tale retold.

Theory

A story about a wicked badger and the price of revenge.

Once, there was an old man and an old woman. The old man worked very hard, sowing seeds and singing in the fields. He always sang the same song. "One seed becomes a thousand seeds."

And everyday when the old man came to work a badger came, he sat near the field and he sang. "One seed is one and I'll eat every one."

The old man came back each day and each day there was nothing left. The badger had eaten every seed. So the old man and his wife carried on being very poor.

It went on like this for weeks and months, and the badger didn't have the decency to leave even one seed. One day, the man got really angry and decided to catch whatever was eating his seeds. As usual he worked really hard all day, sowing hundreds of seeds by hand. He sang his song as always, and watched the badger approaching. The badger neared and started laughing at him.

In a twinkling of the eye, the old man lunged at the badger, caught him and tied him up. He carried the struggling badger home to show his wife. He got to the front of his house and shouted to his wife.

"Look! I've caught the thief! Lets have a badger stew tonight."

He left the bundle and went back to the fields to finish planting all the seeds.

His wife started to grind the rice to make rice cakes; they were her husband's favourites. The very sneaky badger said to her, "It's too much work for you, untie me and I will help you."

The old lady hesitated, she knew she shouldn't untie him, but she was tired and thought the badger's offer was genuine.

The badger got straight to work; he picked up the pestle and started to grind the rice. Or so she thought! As quick as a flash, he hit her on the head and fled to the mountains. The old man returned from the fields, looking forward to his meal. On opening the door, he found his wife dead, killed by the badger. He sobbed and sobbed, when a hare approached him and asked him why he was so upset. The hare felt so sorry for the old man and said.

"I will get revenge for you! Trust me."

The hare was in the mountains the next day, looking for dry wood, when who should he see, but the badger! He asked the hare why he was collecting firewood. He said it was going to be a very hard winter, so he was going to store it. The badger decided to collect wood as well and they both collected huge piles of wood together. They loaded it onto their backs to carry it down the mountains.

"It's so heavy, I can't manage," complained the hare over and over as they began the long journey down. The badger took the bundle off him and started to carry both bundles. The hare skipped happily behind him, collecting small pieces of flint along the way.

Crack! Crack!

The badger could hear the sound of flints but didn't know what the noise was.

"What's that noise?" asked the badger.

"It's the Cracking Birds from the Cracking Mountain."

The badger carried on down, trusting his new found friend. Hare carried on striking the flints together and eventually managed to set the wood on badger's back alight. The wood was so dry it burst into flames and made a whoosh noise.

"What's that?" asked badger, a little alarmed at the noise.

"Don't you know? It's the sound of the birds flying; they call this mountain, Whoosh Mountain."

Badger carried on down the mountains until he could feel his back on fire.

"Ouch!" shouted the badger, but hare had already disappeared. He rolled and rolled until the flames went out.

The next day hare was picking red chilli peppers and bumped into badger again. He was angry and shouted over, "Because of you I was burnt badly, yesterday!"

The hare pretended he didn't know what he was talking about, and said, "Hares from Cracking Mountain are hares from Cracking Mountain. Hares from Red Pepper Mountain are hares from Red Pepper Mountain, I don't understand what you are talking about."

The badger thought, and then realised it was true.

"Have you any medicine for my burns?" asked badger.

"I've just made some that's really good for burns." And he put lots of the powder on badger's back. At first badger didn't feel anything, and then his back began to sting and sting and sting! The hare was nowhere to be seen.

The next day the hare was in the mountains cutting down some trees to make a boat and whom should he bump into? The badger, of course.

"I nearly died at Red Pepper Mountain because of you!" shouted the badger.

The hare acted as if he had never met the badger before in his life. "Hares from Red Pepper Mountain are hares from Red Pepper Mountain. Hares from Cedar Mountain are hares from Cedar Mountain, I've never met you before."

Once more, the badger believed the hare.

"Why are you making a boat?"

"It's for fishing in the river."

Badger wanted a boat too, so they spent the day building boats together. Hare said to him, "As my fur is white, I'm building a white boat with this cedar wood. As your fur is black, you should make your boat out of the earth, so the boat is black."

Badger did as the hare suggested and when the boats were finished, hare suggested they take them on the river. They paddled out together, but not surprisingly, badger's boat started to fall apart in the middle of the river. "Help! Help!" the badger shouted, but hare was nowhere to be seen.

"Think of the poor old woman who died because of you," was all badger could hear. He shouted help over and over, but in vain.

The hare raced back to tell the old man that he had killed the badger, but the old man was not pleased. "Revenge won't bring my wife back!" he shouted at the hare. He wished he had never told anything to the wicked hare now.

Prayer / Reflection

Dear God

Help me to forgive people who upset me, not to keep bad thoughts.
Help me to always forgive and get on with life.

Amen

Min-na-wee (Why the Crocodile Rolls)

Origin

An ancient Aboriginal story handed down through the generations

Theme

Explores troublemakers and their effect on other people.

One night, there was a beautiful red-pink sunset, which swept majestically over the sweeping coastal plain. All the local girls from the village were out playing and having fun together. The boys were all out with their fathers, watching and learning how to be an adult. The boys had to learn how to hunt, build houses, catch fish, etc.

The women in the village were working hard preparing food for the evening meal. They knew the men and boys would be tired after a hard day and were cooking fresh fish on the coals. It was starting to smell delicious. The men had caught mud-crabs and mussels the day before and this was going to be tonight's meal for them all.

All the villagers were happy, this year had been a good year for them all. There had been no shortages of food and the seasonal weather had been kind to them. Only one person wasn't happy, Min-na-wee. Min-na-wee was different; she was always causing arguments among the girls. She would cause mischief, in the hope that a fight would start. If ever there was trouble, Min-na-wee was never far away! She had a constant sulky look on her face, she **WAS TROUBLE**!

Sometimes the mothers' of the girls would fall out because of Min-na-wee's trouble making. She managed to create quite bad atmospheres at times. All the older people in the village tried to warn Min-na-wee's mother and told her that if her daughter didn't stop her troublesome ways, then something terrible was bound to happen to her.

Years passed and Min-na-wee grew into a young woman. Even though she was now an adult, she still liked to cause trouble. One day, all the young women had to gather together for a day of 'Bride Selection'. The older people in the village would decide on this day, who would marry who, a strange way but it seemed to work.

Min-na-wee stood in a line with all the girls from the village. They were all really excited and wondered who their husbands would be. When the ceremony had finished, guess who was left standing, with no man chosen for her? Yes! Min-na-wee. All the elders in the village decided that until she was nicer, then they could not possibly find a husband for her, it was some sort of punishment.

Min-na-wee was very angry and she approached the other girls to cause a fight. The men in the village had seen this happen many times before, so they raced over and grabbed her. As they tried to stop her she was rolled round and round in the mud, she kept on struggling, struggling to get out and fight someone.

She managed to escape and ran into the waves of the sea. It is here legend says, that she called on the evil spirits to change her into a vicious animal so that she could attack her tribe. She wanted revenge. In an instant, Min-na-wee was changed into a very large crocodile and she hid in the shallow muddy waters waiting to attack the villagers.

The people in the village started to forget about Min-na-wee and the arguments and the fighting had stopped, village life was a lot calmer without Min-na-wee. The men went searching along the muddy banks looking for mud crabs. Min-na-wee spotted one of the men who had stopped her from fighting. She seethed! She slid slowly out of the water and grabbed him, rolling him round and round as he struggled, just like she had been rolled round and round in the mud.

Eventually she let him go and he fled back to the village, bleeding, but glad he was still alive. To this day the villagers believe that Min-na-wee's spirit stays with the crocodile, and that is why every time a crocodile catches its prey, it rolls it round and round in the water.

Prayer / Reflection

Think of this rhyme as I say it:

Soloman Grundy,
Born on Monday,
Christened on Tuesday,
Married on Wednesday,
Ill on Thursday,
Worse on Friday,
Died on Saturday,
Buried on Sunday,
That was the end
of Soloman Grundy.

Are you making the best of your life at home and school?

The Village Fool

Origin

Retold from Malaysian folk tales.

Theme

Looks at being a daydream, and putting others before yourself.

Once upon a time there was a daydreamer called Paj Pandir. He was known as the village fool. Everyone liked him, but he just didn't listen to anything. He was always daydreaming. In his dreams the world was a good and happy place.

When he was a young boy, his teachers despaired of him. In lessons he'd drift off into his own world and get a glazed look in his eyes, as he stared out of the windows. He never managed to learn anything, in the end his teachers gave up.

When he was older he had a beautiful wife called Mak. She loved him dearly, but would love him to stop daydreaming and look after her and his children a little better. One day she said to him. "Please go and get a buffalo, so we can plough our rice fields. The rice is nearly ready."

"What's a buffalo?" asked Paj.

The family laughed. They knew what he was like. Paj had many neighbours with buffaloes, but because he was always daydreaming, he didn't really know what one was.

His son told him. "A buffalo eats grass."

Paj pretended he knew and felt a little embarrassed that his children knew more than he did. Mak gave him a gold chain to exchange for a buffalo, and off he went. He sang as he went. "A buffalo eats grass, a buffalo eats grass." When he came to a field he stopped and watched the farmer cutting the grass with a scythe.

"That thing is eating grass," thought Paj, "it must be a buffalo."

He approached the farmer and asked if he could buy the scythe. Now he knew all about dreamy Paj, and decided to take advantage of him.

"Of course, what have you to exchange for it?"

Paj showed him the gold chain.

"Not bad, here you are then."

Paj thanked the man and went off thinking how lucky he was to have found a buffalo so quickly.

"What a beautiful world!" he sang to himself.

When he got home, he rushed to show his wife the fine buffalo.

"Where is it?" she asked, sounding a little surprised.

"Isn't it a fine buffalo?" Paj said, with pride.

The children laughed, but Mak was upset. She knew he had been tricked. Sometimes she despaired of her husband.

The next day she decided to cook a special meal. She asked Paj to go to the Good Genie's house and fetch him to have dinner with them. Everyone knew where the Good Genie lived, except dreamy Paj! Mak told him.

"Go straight through the village, when the path forks, take the left path. The left path takes you straight to the Good Genie's house. Whatever you do, don't take the right path. It leads to the Evil Giant's house."

He sang the instructions to himself as he went, but after a while the words got muddled up. He couldn't remember whether to turn left or right. As you can imagine, he took the wrong path. He knocked on the door of an enormous house.

The evil Giant said. "What a surprise!"

'Please come to my house for dinner tonight, my wife is cooking a really special meal," asked Paj.

"Oh, lovely. I wanted to have all of you for dinner, and your kind offer sounds wonderful."

That evening the giant came. Paj's family was shocked! Halfway through the meal Paj realised that his visitor wanted to eat them all.

"When did the Good Genie turn evil?" he thought to himself. He suddenly started to really worry for his family. "Come with me to get my friend and his family, they only live across the river," he asked the visitor.

The giant thought immediately of more people to eat, and was delighted to follow him.

They got into a boat and Paj started rowing hard. He knew there was a leak in the boat and he intended to sink the boat in the middle of the river. He knew he might drown too, but it was the only way. As he thought, the boat started to fill with water; the evil giant fell into the river. They both started flapping around, the giant begging to be saved.

"I'll never eat people again, I promise!"

The villagers couldn't leave them to drown. They got into their boats and rescued them both.

"You are a fool!" they shouted at Paj.

Surprisingly, the evil giant became a good giant. He had really admired Paj's courage.

"He may be a fool, but he was very brave and very clever when his family were threatened," said the giant. He could not help but admire that.

Paj thought the world was a beautiful world again. But he could be forgiven; after all, he had shown he wasn't quite the fool they all thought he was!

Prayer / Reflection

Think of this saying

"Tomorrow is another day."

Do you make the best of each day?

Think of one thing you could do today that will put someone else before yourself.

The Mystery of the Mermaid

Origin

Ideas taken from ancient folklore in Spain.

Theme

Examines laziness and love.

Once upon a time there was a man and a woman who had a very lazy daughter. They all lived on the bank of a stream. They had taught her nice manners, but as for work - she just tossed her beautiful hair and laughed when asked to do anything. She spent her days playing and dancing with her friends.

One morning the mother looked so tired that even the selfish girl felt she had to offer to help. The mother was surprised, but really happy for any help. She asked her to take the fishing net out to the riverbank to fix, it was full of holes.

The girl took the net and worked really hard for once in her life, not a hole was left. It took her many hours. Just as she finished, she heard a splash. A big fish was jumping through the air. As quick as a flash, she grabbed the net and caught it.

"What a beauty!" she cried.

"You had better not kill me, if you do, I will turn you into a fish yourself," the fish croaked.

The girl laughed and ran home with the big fat fish. The mother was so pleased, they decided to cook it for dinner that very evening.

"Didn't I say it would be delicious?" she asked her mother.

Before the mother and father had time to taste the fish, the girl's eyes started to look odd, her head got flatter, her legs and arms stuck to her sides and she started gasping for breath. With a mighty jump she threw herself through the open door and fell straight into the stream. That was better, and she swam away towards the sea.

It was quite a long way to the sea, but when she got there she was welcomed by lots of other fish. They all pressed around her so they could hear her story.

"I'm not a fish at all," she started to tell them. "I was a girl a few minutes ago."

"Come with us and see our queen," shouted all the fish excitedly.

They all swam together for what seemed like hours, she was really tired, she wasn't used to all this swimming. Under the sea she swam past mountains and valleys, and finally into a deep valley. There, she could just see the palace of the queen of the fishes. The walls were made of pink coral and all around the windows were sparkling pearls.

They entered the palace and the girl recounted her sad story to the queen.

When the girl had ended the queen told her: "I was a young woman once too, a princess. My father was king of a great country. On my wedding day my father, the king, put a crown on my head and told me as long as I wore it, I would be a queen. I was so happy. Then one day as I was walking in my gardens, a giant snatched the crown from my head. He gave it to his daughter and she took my place! I was so miserable I threw myself into the sea, as did all my servants. Instead of dying, a wizard turned us all into fishes. He allowed me to keep the face and upper body of a woman."

She then told the girl that they would have to remain fishes until someone brought her crown back.

The girl shouted. "I will bring it back, if you tell me what to do."

The queen explained how she must go back on land; go to the top of a high mountain, to the giant's castle. There you'll find him crying, as his daughter has died. Her husband, my husband, is now king. The giant has the crown.

"I'll give you the power to change yourself into any animal that will help you. You cannot become human."

The girl tried it out. She tapped her forehead and shouted out the name of a deer. In a moment she stood on the riverbank, a beautiful beast, quivering to be gone. Off she ran, leaping over all obstacles in her way. The king's son was out hunting, the deer dashed across his path.

"Don't kill me, for I have much to do," cried the deer.

The deer's eyes enchanted the prince. He knew it must be wizardry and that the deer must be a human. He vowed to find her and marry her one-day.

As she reached the castle, she saw the towering smooth walls. She changed very quickly into a tiny, near invisible ant, scaling the wall. At the top, she could just see a tree right by one of the windows of the castle. Before you could see, she had changed into a monkey, swinging straight into the giant's room. There he was, snoring away. She then decided to be a pink and grey parrot, so that she could talk to him.

She said very boldly that she had been sent for the crown, he leapt out of bed with an angry roar. He shouted and shouted, then struck a bargain. He asked for the collar of blue stones from the Great Arch, in exchange for the crown. She knew about these famous stones, and although it seemed an impossible task, she agreed. She made her way to the window and off she flew, quickly transforming into an eagle.

It took her ages to dig out the stones with her beak. She strung the stones together and hung them around her neck, flying back as quickly as she could. The parrot appeared before the giant and his eyes glistened with greed.

"These aren't as good as I thought, get me a bag of stars from the sky. Then I will give you the crown."

She knew he was a trickster, but she had no choice but to try and complete the task. She turned into a toad and hopped into a deep, clear pool. The stars were sparkling in the water. She filled up the bag she was carrying with the shining water and as a parrot flew quickly back to the giant.

This time he knew he was beaten and flung the crown at her. She didn't wait for him to change his mind and changed pronto into a monkey and swung out of the window. She scaled the wall as an ant, still clutching the crown. It was lucky that each time the crown shrunk as well as her!

The fishes had long given up. They thought that she had been gone so long; the giant must have killed her. Suddenly a voice was heard.

"The crown! I've got the crown!"

She placed it on the queen, and do you know what happened? A wonderful thing! Her tail dropped away, her legs appeared and the scales vanished. This didn't just happen to the queen, it happened to all of them.

They swam quickly to the surface and raced to the queen's palace on land. The queen's husband, now king, recognised her at once. The little boy she had left behind was all grown up and she hugged and hugged him. The son told her at once of his sadness as well as his happiness at seeing her again. He told her he had fallen in love with a beautiful deer.

The queen knew at once who this was.

"She's here in my palace. She saved my life and brought the crown back to me."

She sent for her at once. When the girl approached the prince, she whispered in his ears.

"Do you remember looking into my eyes in the forest?"

He knew those tender eyes, and knew it was his love. They married three days later and of course, the queen saw to it that the missing blue stones in the arch were found and restored.

Prayer / Reflection

In the Bible, laziness is seen as a person's failure to use their gifts.

What gifts do you have?

Do you use your talents?

The Six Seeds

Origin

Retold from the ancient Greek legend of Persephone.

Theme

Looks at why the seasons exist, relates it to seasons in life, seasons of birth and death.

In the beginning there were no seasons. There was light, dark, sun, rain, heat and cold. The year didn't go in any order. Demeter, goddess of the earth, looked after all the things that grew.

Demeter had a daughter called Persephone. She was a most beautiful creature. Her favourite place in the entire world was a Greek island called 'Sicily'. Here she played with her friends, the nymphs. When it was hot they would sit in the shade, laughing and singing. Down, deep in the underworld there were none of these things, no light, warmth, or laughter. The king of the underworld was called Hades, and he remembered the light, warmth, and happiness of the world above.

Three brothers had divided creation, light and life to Zeus, the sea to Poseidon and Hades the underworld. Hades hated it and was very jealous of his brother Zeus. Hades would sometimes come out in anger, dressed in black, riding black horses. He would ride across the earth. He went to Sicily and saw Persephone playing happily with her friends, and her beauty filled his heart. He wanted her as queen for his underworld kingdom.

He swept over and took Persephone, like a fleeting shadow. She screamed and screamed for help. Only her belt, embroidered with flowers, was left on the grass. She cried and cried in the underworld. She didn't want Hades' love; his touch was icy cold, his people ghosts.

Over the time, she got used to Hades. She started to see how lonely he was, she began to love the people in his kingdom. Her heart still ached at times, for flowers, light and warmth. She knew she had a job to do here, to give the people life and hope.

What she didn't realise was, that for her mother and the people she had left behind, there was only despair. Demeter wandered the world calling her daughter's name. All the plants and living things had been forgotten, everything was dying. A famine came next, the people prayed to Zeus for help.

Zeus heard, he knew his brother had Persephone, but he also knew about all the good she had done in that world. He sent for Demeter and told her.

"Your daughter is a queen in the underworld. She has eaten six pomegranate seeds. For each seed she has eaten, Persephone must stay one month each year in the underworld, ruling with her husband Hades."

That is what happened. For six months a year Persephone ruled each world. When she is away it gets colder and colder until she comes back to bring things to life. And so it is in both worlds. The Seasons began!

Prayer / Reflection

Think for a moment about the seasons in a person's life, from birth to old age.

Can you think of one thing you like about the British seasons, Summer, Autumn, Winter and Spring?

The Chief was No Fool!

Origin

This story is retold from old African tales, handed down through the generations.

Theme

This story looks at how 'feeling important' can cause people to boast. It also tackles truth and lying.

"Help me!" begged the old man. "My neighbour has stolen from me."

Ayra, the old man was talking to the chief, the chief of all his tribe. The chief was listening very carefully. He loved being asked for advice; it made him feel really important.

"My neighbour stole my goats. I'm poor, how am I going to replace them?"

The chief arranged another meeting to sort out this trouble. Both Ayra and his neighbour turned up, both sat glaring at each other.

The chief told the neighbour what Ayra had said.

"I don't know what he is talking about," answered the neighbour.

The chief knew this was not going to be an easy problem to solve. He would have to rely on his wisdom. He enjoyed tough problems.

"I have a test for you," announced the chief.

"Whoever passes this test will own the goats."

Ayra and his neighbour leaned forward to listen.

"Go home and only come back when you can answer my question. I want to know what is the fastest thing in the world?"

The two men left shaking their heads. How were they going to find the answer? Who would they ask to help?

When Ayra got home he sat down and puzzled and puzzled. He couldn't think of any answer that would please the chief. His daughter Ziah asked what was wrong. He explained what had happened, and the question posed by the chief. Right away she whispered an answer into his ear that he knew would please the chief. He'd always known she was as beautiful as she was wise.

Ayra couldn't wait to see the chief the next morning.

"You have an answer already?" the chief said in surprise, when he saw Ayra.

"Yes," replied Ayra. "It wasn't difficult".

"And what is the fastest thing in the world?"

"Time," answered Ayra confidently.

"We never have enough of it, it always goes too fast. There is never enough time to do all we want to do."

The chief was amazed. What a brilliant answer!

"Who helped you?" asked the chief with curiosity.

Ayra then decided to lie, he didn't really know why.

"No one helped me, I thought of the answer myself."

The chief looked long and hard at him. "If you are not telling the truth I will punish you."

Ayra felt he could lie no more and owned up to the truth.

"It was my daughter Ziah, she told me the answer, and she is a very wise woman."

"She must be!" thought the chief. "I would like to meet this woman."

The chief invited Ayra and his daughter to visit. When they came, the chief was captivated by her beauty and asked her to marry him.

Ziah accepted happily. Although the chief was pleased, he was also worried about having such a clever wife. He didn't want her helping him, he enjoyed being asked to sort peoples' problems.

"Everything in the house is yours," declared the chief. "I have one rule for you. You must never involve yourself with the problems brought to me. If you break this rule, I will send you from my house."

Things went well for a while. One day the chief gave one of his troublesome puzzles to two boys who were arguing over a sheep. One of the boys cried to Ziah and she felt she had to listen to him.

"The chief asked for something impossible. He gave us an egg and said whoever could hatch the egg by tomorrow would own the sheep."

Ziah knew she shouldn't help, but she liked the boy and felt sorry for him. She told him to take some rice to the chief, tell him to plant it today, so that in the morning you have rice for your chicken. She told the boy that he would know that is as impossible as the task he gave you.

The boy ran to the chief with the rice and did exactly as he was told. The chief exploded with anger.

"Who told you to do this? This is too clever for a young boy."

The boy lied and said it was his own answer. The chief warned him he would punish him if he was lying. The boy felt really scared and shouted.

"It was Ziah, she told me!"

The chief was more than furious. He called her and told her to go back to her father's home as she had broken the agreement.

"Before I go, can I make you one final meal?" asked Ziah.

Ziah set to work preparing his favourite meal.

When the chief had eaten he fell asleep through all the wine he had drunk. Her family helped her to carry him to her father's home and place him on a bed.

In the morning the chief's voice boomed through the house.

"Where am I? What am I doing here?"

Ziah walked in the room and smiled. "You said I could take whatever I wanted from your house, and I wanted you."

"You certainly are a wise and clever woman," smiled the chief.

He knew he'd be a fool to ever let her go, and whisked her away back home.

"You are no fool!" whispered Ziah to herself.

Prayer / Reflection

It's always best to tell the truth.

Can you think of a time when you told lies to get yourself out of trouble?

Did it get you into more trouble?

Why is honesty the best policy?

Why the Sea is Salty

Origin

This story is taken from Korean tales handed down through word of mouth.

Theme

This story explained a natural phenomenon before scientific explanation. The story tackles the issue of stealing.

Many hundreds of years ago, there was a king who had a very unusual stone hand mill. You could put stones in it and grind them down to powder. It wasn't an ordinary stone mill; this mill had very special powers. All anyone had to do was say what you wanted and turn the mill.... and hey presto... out it would come! If you asked for gold, out it would pop, if you asked for rice, rice would pour out. Whatever you asked for, the mill would make it.

A very nasty thief heard about this mill and decided to steal it. He couldn't stop thinking about it, and how it would make him rich. For days and days he thought about how he could steal it, but he wasn't a very clever thief, so he didn't come up with a plan. Thinking about it drove him mad. How he wanted that mill.

Then one day he dressed like an educated man and set off to see an official. This official worked in the palace. The thief greeted him and chatted about this and that, and finally the thief said, "I heard that the king buried his strange hand mill in the ground because he doesn't trust the people who work for him."

"What's that?" said the official in surprise. "He doesn't trust his workers? Where did you hear these things?"

"That's what they say in the countryside," retorted the thief indignantly.

The thief could see that the official was now really interested in talking to him.

"They say the king dug a really deep hole and buried it far down, just so no-one could steal it."

"Absolute nonsense!" shouted the official. He'd worked for the king for many years and couldn't believe what he was hearing. He'd always liked and trusted the king.

"And anyway, the king's hand mill is beside the lotus pond in the inner court of the palace. I've seen it myself."

The thief was really excited by now. His half thought up plan was working. "Oh, is that so?" said the thief sarcastically.

"No one would ever dare to steal it, lots of people are around the lotus pond each day. It's always been safe there."

"Yes, I suppose you're right," said the thief, trying to hide his excitement as he left.

He was so happy now. He knew exactly where the special hand mill was kept. Now all he had to do was to find a way to steal it. He watched the palace for a while, to see when it was quiet near the lotus pond. One very dark night he climbed the high palace walls, crept towards the pond, and quickly stole the hand mill. He scaled back over the walls before anyone noticed anything.

He felt triumphant with his treasured possession, but also he felt scared, scared of being caught. He carried the mill on a deep inside pocket. When anyone at all walked by him in the street, his heart skipped a beat. Did they know he'd stolen the king's mill?

He couldn't stand the strain any longer, so he decided to find a way to travel home to the island where he grew up. He felt he would be safer there. He had to steal a boat, but he had done that many times when he was a child.

Once at sea, he relaxed. No one would catch him now. They'd check all the roads in the city, but not the boats at sea. He laughed to himself. He began to sing with happiness when he thought about how rich he would become. He started to daydream about what he would ask the mill for. He didn't want to ask for something that nobody needed. He thought and he thought.

"Salt! Salt!" he suddenly shouted to himself. "Everyone needs salt. I can sell it and become a rich man. I'll be the richest man in the country."

He started to turn the hand mill, shaking with excitement. He sang. "Salt! Salt! Make me some salt."

The hand mill kept turning and turning, and turning and turning, salt spilling everywhere. The thief didn't notice, he was too busy thinking about being rich and planning what he was going to buy.

The boat became so heavy with all the salt that it started to sink. The thief didn't notice until it was too late. The boat, the thief and all the salt disappeared below the waves. No one knew how to tell the mill to stop turning and to this day it is still turning, which is why the sea is salty.

Prayer / Reflection

Think about your conscience. It's like a quiet voice inside telling you when not to do bad things.

When do you feel your conscience working?

Can you think of a time this week?

The Good Turn

Origin

Written by Alison Gardner.

Theme

This story shows examples of being selfish and boastful. It also looks at friendships and doing good turns.

Every time Charlotte walked down the lane where she lived, some neighbour or the other would remark that the 'spoilt kid' was off to some place. The six-year-old was an only child and she was very, very spoilt. Even when she was a small child, her parents never refused her anything; she had absolutely everything she wanted. And she, in turn, made sure she got everything she wanted.

One day, Charlotte's mum suddenly noticed that Charlotte did not share anything with her friends. She didn't share books, toys, sweets, anything. She watched her daughter for a few days and discovered something else as well. Most of the children in the lane did not like to play with her daughter. She was nearly always alone. Mrs. Benson approached a small group playing skipping and she asked them straight out, why they didn't play with Charlotte. She didn't like their replies! They all said that Charlotte bossed them and made them cry.

Charlotte's mum went home and felt really sad and worried. She realised that it was their fault that Charlotte was behaving like that. Hadn't they spoilt her by giving her everything and anything she asked for? Was Charlotte able to share and make friends? They would soon know for sure. Next week Charlotte was going into Year One and was joining the Brownies.

Her teacher at school had told her parents how clever she was, but she had also said that Charlotte didn't have many friends, just Vicky. Vicky was new to the school and to the area; she was very shy and happy to be looked after by Charlotte. Well, bossed around really. But at least she had someone to play with.

One day the teacher got rather cross with Vicky for not concentrating whilst doing her maths. She hated maths and just couldn't understand any of it. She did try, but her teacher got fed up explaining the same thing over and over again to her. Vicky burst into tears, she was so fed up with these sums. She watched some of the children in the class sniggering at her and she felt even worse then.

Charlotte told her mum about Vicky crying in class.

"Why don't you try to explain the work to her, she likes you and it might help her to understand?"

"Mummy I don't have time to waste. I can't help it if she's not clever," said Charlotte.

"But Vicky is your friend and if you don't help her, who will?" scolded her mum.

She could see that Charlotte wasn't budging; she had no intention of helping Vicky. Her mum suddenly thought of a way to get Charlotte to understand. She decided to tell her the story of, 'the ant and the dove'.

One day an ant fell into a stream and was desperately trying to save itself. A dove was sitting on a tree overhanging the water. The dove pulled off a leaf, and let it fall into the stream close to the ant. The ant managed to climb on the leaf and floated safely to the bank. A little later, a bird catcher came and stood under the tree, ready to throw a net over the dove. The dove had no idea at all about what was going to happen. The ant had spotted the bird catcher and stung him in the foot. Big ants can bite really hard if they want to. The bird catcher yelled out in pain and the noise made the dove fly away.

"Did you understand the story Charlotte?" asked her mum. "It means if you do a good turn, someone will do a good turn back."

"What a silly story, said Charlotte. "It's for little children, I'm big."

Charlotte's mother then decided enough was enough.

"If you don't help Vicky, I won't let you watch cartoons for a week."

Very reluctantly, Charlotte helped Vicky. And wonders of wonders, Vicky understood and did much better in all her maths. The teacher was really pleased and gave Vicky a gold sticker for the week. Vicky was so happy, she told everyone what a good friend Charlotte had been. Charlotte preferred to forget about it; she'd only helped because she'd been forced to.

Meanwhile Vicky was looking for a way to repay her friend. The opportunity came sooner than she thought. Charlotte was in the middle of a group of girls arguing at playtime, she accidentally lost her temper and pushed one of the girls who fell and bruised her knee. Charlotte was sent to see the Head teacher; she gave her a very hard time. Her punishment was to stay in at break-times and pick up all the rubbish on the floors, in each and every classroom!

Charlotte was heartbroken and embarrassed. How was she going to face anyone again after this? She wanted the ground to open up and swallow her. At the first break she was left to start on Mrs. Hodgkin's classroom, everyone knew this was the untidiest in the school!

She was sniffling away to herself, picking up crayons, paper etc. This is how Vicky found her, sniffling, the odd tear running down her face. She had already asked her teacher if she could stay in and help Charlotte and that is what she did. Charlotte remembered the story of the ant and the dove and from that day on, she and Vicky were the best of friends.

Prayer / Reflection

Think about this proverb from the Bible.

'People show what they are by what they do.'
(proverbs 20.11)

How do you show who you are?

Is it good things?

A Caterpillar's Voice

Origin

This story is an ancient story from the Masai tribe in East Africa.

Theme

This story shows how jumping to conclusions can be a bad thing. It is a story of trickery.

Once upon a time there was a hare. A hare's a bit like a rabbit, but it can run really fast. He had this lovely house he had made in a cave. Well, this one day when the hare had gone out, a caterpillar crawled inside and made himself at home.

When the hare returned home, he noticed new marks on the ground going into the cave. He called, "Who's in my house?"

The caterpillar boomed out in the loudest voice he could.

"It is I! Yes, I who crushes rhinos to the earth and tramples elephants into dust!"

The hare was slightly scared when he heard the loud voice. He hopped about a little, crying to himself. "What can a small creature like me do with a creature who crushes rhinos and tramples elephants into dust?"

He hopped away, but soon he met a jackal. He suddenly had a thought!

"Can you talk to the terrible creature who's taken over my home? Get him to leave, pleeaase........."

The jackal agreed, he was a fierce beast, and he wouldn't be scared.

When they reached the hare's house, the jackal barked loudly, "Who's in my friend the hare's house?"

The caterpillar's voice rocked the earth. "It is I! Yes I who crushes rhinos to the earth and tramples elephants into dust."

The jackal listened, his fur twitching with each booming word the caterpillar shouted.

"Certainly, I can do nothing against such a creature."

Off he went in a hurry.

The hare went to visit his friend leopard, a fierce creature. He begged him to help.

"No trouble at all, just lead the way."

When the leopard arrived outside the cave he stretched his claws in the sand, growling he said. "Who's in my friend hare's house?"

The caterpillar replied in his booming voice. "It is I! Yes I who crushes rhinos, and tramples elephants into dust!"

The leopard took a step back alarmed, and thought to himself, "If he crushes rhinos and elephants, what will he do to me?" Then rushed away as if on an important mission.

The rhinoceros next, thought the hare, he's huge.

"I am the most fearsome of beasts," grunted the rhino. He marched straight up to the cave; his massive steps could be heard echoing for miles.

"Who's inside my friend hare's house?"

The caterpillar answered in his usual booming voice, "It is I! Yes I who crushes rhino and elephants!"

"What! He can crush me! I don't like the sound of that." And the rhino thundered away, feet banging and crashing through the trees.

The hare was desperate by now. Was he ever going to get his house back? He hopped up to the elephant, stared straight into his big doleful eyes and begged him for help. "Please, please help me."

The elephant came along, trunk swinging happily; confident he would be able to help. As soon as he heard the caterpillar's voice, he was off. He didn't intend to be trampled underfoot.

The hare was close to tears, what was he going to do? He asked a frog passing by if he could help. The frog very bravely hopped right up to the entrance to the cave and asked who was inside. He listened to the reply but didn't hurry off like all the other creatures. He went nearer to the entrance and shouted. "I, who am the strongest of all, have come at last. I am the one who tramples underfoot those who trample elephants and rhinos."

The caterpillar trembled with fear, all his hairs standing to attention. He sensed the shadow of the frog coming nearer and nearer.

"I'm only a little caterpillar," he said. He tried inching along the edge of the cave, trying to escape without being noticed.

All the animals that had helped hare had gathered outside, they spotted the caterpillar and grabbed him.

"**What you!**" they all cried in sheer disbelief.

"I would never dream of having a house in a cave like that," said the caterpillar, with his nose in the air. "An echo like that is not for a gentle creature like myself."

He wriggled away changing colour from yellow to orange, with embarrassment.

All the animals laughed at all the trouble he had caused them.

Prayer / Reflection

Think about a time when you jumped to a wrong conclusion.

Did you apologise for being wrong?

How did apologising make you feel?

How do you think the other person felt?

Monkey Lies

Origin

Written by Alison Gardner.

Theme

This story talks about the love of books and trying your best. It would be a good story to read to youngsters to encourage them to join a library.

Kayleigh was a very helpful girl, and today she was helping in the local library. It was Saturday, no school and she just loved books, books with stories, books with pictures, and all kinds. The assistant said she could watch the front desk, while she put some books away. Kayleigh felt very important standing behind the counter, she could only just see over the top.

Well, today was going to be a very unusual day. Her first customer was a monkey.

"Can I borrow a book please?" asked the monkey.

"You need your library card," said Kayleigh helpfully.

"Oops! I forgot my card," the monkey said woefully.

Kayleigh felt sorry for him, she knew how much she'd wanted some new books today.

"That spider over there can be a witness as to who I am," said monkey, pointing to a spider in the corner.

Kayleigh thought about it, and it seemed quite fair. She handed monkey the book he wanted.

"Make sure you bring it back next week, it's been ordered by a little boy," Kayleigh said with importance. She knew she had to do a really good job on the counter.

Next Saturday Kayleigh was helping out again and the monkey came in. He was looking at all the new books that had come in that week.

"Have you remembered to bring the book back?" asked Kayleigh very politely. The assistant was working just behind her and she wanted to impress.

"We need the book today."

"Who, me?" said the monkey in surprise. "I have never seen you before in my life," said the monkey very indignantly.

Kayleigh didn't know what to do. She knew it was the same monkey, and she couldn't work out why he was lying. The assistant had overheard what had happened and asked Kayleigh what the monkey had borrowed and what he had said.

"Mr. Monkeydew promised to return the book today," Kayleigh stammered, nearly crying. "He said he would borrow it and bring it back today, and he hasn't."

The assistant asked the monkey a few questions. This was a most unusual happening.

"No! It never happened, I tell you!" shouted the monkey, looking a little anxious.

"I never took the book like she said. I never said what she said I did, I never saw the little fur ball in my life!"

Kayleigh was so shocked, why would he lie so, she'd never be allowed to help out again. Suddenly she remembered the spider and whispered those details in the assistant's ear. The monkey stood, twitching his tail.

"Mr. Monkeydew, did you happen to see anything or anyone unusual when you were talking to Miss Priceless last Saturday?"

Mr. Monkeydew answered. "I've already told you. I did not talk to Miss Priceless last Saturday!"

The assistant then got more serious, "You didn't talk to Miss Priceless? Then I suppose you didn't notice that there was a witness to the scene? A spider."

The monkey snorted in disgust. "A spider? That's the most ridiculous thing I've ever heard."

"A spider that heard everything? Who heard you promise? A spider on your hat?"

The monkey laughed and laughed. Kayleigh was near to tears again.

"That shows how much you know! The spider wasn't on my hat, it was on that book in the corner over there!" The monkey stopped immediately he'd said that.

"Ah ha, now we have the truth," the assistant chuckled.

She knew she had tricked him into telling the truth.

The monkey looked at the floor, ashamed of himself. He knew he had been caught out.

"I lied, I lied about the whole thing, and I only wanted to borrow a book."

The assistant told him how he could join properly and borrow any books he wanted, but only if he brought the other book back.

He promised, and apologised to Kayleigh. She knew he was telling the truth this time. Maybe she would be allowed to help out again after all.

Prayer / Reflection

Thank you God, for all the different books written and for all the different stories I've read.

Amen

Thukeri

Origin

An ancient Aboriginal story handed down through the generations.

Theme

This story focuses on greed, to be satisfied with what we have got.
This is a story about two boys who lived on the edge of Lake Alexandrina. They belonged to a tribe of people called the Ngarrindjerri people. They were great friends and they loved to go fishing together.

One day they decided to go fishing and they got their canoe ready. It was a very special canoe; they had cut down a tree and made this canoe together. They were very proud of it. They paddled across the calm waters until they came to their favourite fishing place, called Loveday Bay. They thought this was the best place to catch the most delicious bream fish. Their tribe called bream fish, 'Thukeri'.

They found a spot to sit between some reeds, with a little shelter from the midday sun. They had made their own fishing lines from the reeds themselves, and the hooks were made from very sharp bird bones.

They were excited as they sat down to fish. They knew that some of their friends in the tribe were collecting vegetables to cook and eat with the fish. They were very successful, catching more and more fish as the day went on, lots of juicy Thukeri. They knew the canoe was nearly full of fish, but they just kept on fishing, catching more and more, and filling the canoe up more and more.

They paddled back rather slowly, keeping their fingers crossed that the weight of the fish wouldn't sink the canoe. As they neared the shore, they could see a stranger in the distance. He seemed to be walking straight towards them. The two boys looked at each other, and then looked at all their lovely fish. What if the stranger wanted some of their juicy Thukeri?

They quickly covered up the fish with woven mats so that the stranger wouldn't see the fish. The stranger smiled as he neared the two boys and said.

"Hello, brothers. I haven't eaten anything today, could you spare me a couple of fish?"

The two boys looked at each other, then at the mats hiding the fish.

"I'm sorry friend, but we've only caught a few fish today and we have to take them home to our families for dinner, they are depending on us."

The stranger stood there for a while and then started to walk away. He stopped and suddenly turned around.

"You lied, I know that you have plenty of fish in your canoe."

The two boys looked ashamed and their faces glowed with embarrassment. How did the stranger know? They thought to themselves.

"Because you are so greedy, you will never be able to enjoy those Thukeri ever again, said the stranger.

The two boys just stood in silence, and watched the stranger walk away into the sunset. They shrugged their shoulders and began to get the fish ready to carry back to their tribe. They put all the fish into a pile and began to gut them. You have to take the head off and get the insides removed to be able to cook and enjoy fish.

The Thukeri shimmered in the night-light; they used their sharp knives to make a start. When they cut open one Thukeri, two, three, four - they found that they were all full of the tiniest sharp bones. They couldn't eat these; they'd choke on them.

"What are we going to do? We can't take these home to cook, they'll choke on them."

The two boys checked a few more fish, but they were all the same. They had to return to their tribe with the bony fish and explain what had happened. They walked into their village full of shame, and told their story.

The elders in the tribe explained to the two boys that the stranger wasn't really a stranger, he was really a Great Spirit called Ngurunderi. He had punished them for being so greedy. Now all the Ngarrindjerri people would be punished forever, because the two boys were so greedy.

And even today, whenever people catch a bream that turns out to be full of tiny sharp bones, they are reminded of long ago, when the Great Spirit taught them a lesson, a lesson about greed.

Prayer / Reflection

Think about this saying from the Bible.

'To be wise is better than having gold'.
(proverbs 6 - 16)

What does this mean?

Can you think of a time you were greedy?

The Very Sad Dad

Origin

Written by Alison Gardner.

Theme

This story looks at being happy with what you have got, being contented.

Dad was a dad of many. He had a huge family, children everywhere, a wife, grandma, animals galore and a lively farm to look after. He was always working, up at the crack of dawn; he very rarely found time for a rest. The farmhouse was very cramped, no room to move. There was no room to eat porridge, barely room to read a book, barely room to even put on your pants!

All this made the dad sad. He couldn't seem to solve the problem, so he decided to go and ask the, 'Old Wise Woman' for some advice. He said.
"Oh wise woman, there is no room in my house for all my family. It's bad, very, very bad.

The wise woman thought for a minute, then said very thoughtfully.

"Here is my advice, go back and bring all your animals into your house."

The dad went back to the farm a lot happier; he was more than keen to follow her advice. He set to work bringing all the animals in. The problem was worse, now there was no room at all. Less room to eat porridge, less room to read a book, and less room to put on pants. This made everyone in the house mad, the wife, the children, and the grandma. It made dad very, very sad.

The very, very sad dad went back to the wise woman. He said. "Oh, wise woman, now there is even less room. It's terrible."

The wise woman looked thoughtful and said. "Here is my advice, go back and take the chickens out of the house."

The sad dad went back to his farm, happy to follow her advice. He couldn't wait to have more room. He got rid of the chickens the minute he got back. They went straight back into the yard, pecking away at the ground, happy to be in the fresh air. There was definitely more room, but still not enough to eat porridge, read a book and put on pants. Everyone was still mad, mad with each other. The dad was still very, very sad.

The very, very sad dad decided to go back again to the wise woman.

He said. "Oh wise woman, it's still bad, there is no room to eat porridge, to read a book, to put on pants. The wise woman answered wisely.

"Here is my advice, go back and take the goats out of the house."

The sad dad agreed rapidly and rushed back to let the goats into the first field. They leapt about, butting the fence, he wouldn't miss those horns!

There was more room, he couldn't deny that, but.........well, he still couldn't eat porridge, read a book, or put pants on. They still tripped over each other and the animals. They argued over the smallest thing. He decided to go and see the wise woman for one last time.

Off he set that very morning, to solve this problem at long last.

"We still haven't enough room, to eat porridge, read a book, put pants on."

"This is my advice. Take all the animals out of the house."

"Thanks for your advice," said the sad dad, a little happier, although he wasn't completely sure if the advice would work, but...he was willing to try.

He marched back; a spring in his step, getting more and more confident that it would work as he neared the farm. As soon as he got there he chased every last animal out of the house. They seemed to love being in the fields.

And now, even though there was barely room to eat porridge, read a book, or put on pants...........it was not so bad.

"It could be worse," he said to himself.

And with that, he jumped up and down on the spot, hugged all his family, every last child...........and then they all danced with joy, happy with their home and each other.

Prayer / Reflection

Think about this well known saying,

'You don't know you're born'

What do people mean when they say it?

Do you appreciate the good things in your life?

The Talking Yam

Origin

Written by Alison Gardner.

Theme

This story talks about helpful reminders, about being untidy and forgetful.

Have you ever heard the story of the talking yam? Well Shona listened to the story in the school library. The story came from West Africa, from the Ashanti people. Her teacher had brought in a yam especially to show everyone and they had all passed it around.

When Shona found it in her lap, she picked it up dreamily and turned it back and forth in her hands. She said to herself quietly. "I wonder what this yam would say if it could really talk."

Suddenly the yam slipped out of her hands and plopped noisily on the floor.

"Oops!" Linda said, as she hurriedly picked it up. "Sorry."

"Hey! Next time be more careful!"

"Who said that?" whispered Shona shocked.

"I did," piped up the yam, as it rocked on the floor.

"Aaah!" cried Shona, dropping the yam as she ran to find her friend Carl.

When Shona found Carl, he was hunting for something. He was looking under bags, coats, in his desk, under the bookshelves.

"Hey, Shona, have you seen my football socks? I know I left them here somewhere."

But Shona said. "Carl! yam! The yam talked!"

"I don't think so," said Carl.

"Yams can't talk!"

Carl pulled his football socks out from under a heap of books in his desk.

"There you are," he said.

"I thought you'd never find me," said the socks, "I'm so glad."

"Aaah!" cried Carl. He dropped the socks in shock.

The teacher came in, and Carl told her excitedly about his talking socks. Shona kept interrupting to tell the teacher that the yam talked.

"Calm down, only one of you can talk at once," she said calmly.

Just as they were running through their explanations, David came bounding in clutching his new pencil case.

"It talked Miss! It talked."

"This can't be happening," cried Shona.

"Oh yes it can. **HE** left me on the floor!!" the pencil case rattled.

"My socks talked to me."

"The yam talked to me."

"My pencil case talked to me."

"Take it easy, you know socks, pencil cases and yams can't talk."

"They can! They can!"

"Who's that talking?" shouted Carl impatiently.

"I am," said the classroom. "And the room needs a good tidy."

They all looked at each other, not sure what to say or do. They looked first at the socks, then the yam, and then the pencil case. The teacher asked them to stop and think for a minute.

"The talking objects were all being helpful, reminding you of things, don't you see?"

"Really," said Shona, Carl and David in unison.

"Then again, it might just be our imaginations," piped up Carl, ever practical.

"That's it, it's just our imaginations," decided Shona, turning the yam round and round in her hands. David threw his pencil case into his desk, just to make sure he didn't lose it again, and ran out to play.

The teacher asked Carl and Shona to help tidy up, by taking the tape recorder back to the library for her. As they walked along the long corridor back to the library, Shona said to herself, "A storytelling lesson can be quite exciting, can't it?"

And the tape recorder buzzed and said. "It can! It can can't it? You'd better believe it!"

Prayer / Reflection

Dear God

Help us to remember all the things we should.
To not need reminding all the time.

Amen

What a Trap!

Origin

This story has been adapted by Alison Gardner and taken from 'How a Child Saved His Mother's Life,' from Congo Life and Jungle Stories, 2nd edition by Reverend John H Weeks. (1922).

Theme

This story looks at hard work and trickery.
To understand this story you need to know a little about a plant called Cassava. This strange tale happened in Brazil, a country where Cassava is grown, up to eight feet high. The root is used to make thin cakes called Cassava Bread.

Once upon a time a man and his wife had a farm, where they grew lots of food to eat. They had carefully planted Cassava and were looking forward to a new crop. His wife made the most delicious Cassava Bread, how they loved the smell of freshly baked bread.

Well, it came to the time to pull out their new crop, it was really hard work but they knew their efforts would be rewarded. They walked down to the bottom fields, quite a long walk. As they neared the Cassava field their eyes widened in horror! The wild pigs had visited the crop before them and nearly all the roots had been pulled out, chewed and trampled. It seemed as if they had nothing left to show for all their trouble.

They sat down, very upset, talking about what they could do. The husband decided to dig a really large pit. If any wild animals decided to steal their crops, they would fall into the pit and be trapped. They were both really pleased with their plan and started work on it straight away.

The next day, the man was digging away, sweat pouring down his face, when an Imp - a nasty, mysterious creature of the woods - jumped out from the trees.

"What are you doing?" questioned the Imp.

"This trap is to catch all the wild animals who want to eat my crops, I'm fed up with them eating all the food we plant."

"Are you now? Well that's interesting. I will help you dig the pit if you share the animals with me," the Imp said, licking his lips and smiling.

The man was scared of the Imp, he had heard lots of stories about Imps and none of them were good. He decided he would have to agree with the Imp, he couldn't risk more trouble.

"All the male ones that fall into the trap will be yours, but all the female ones will be mine."

The man agreed. That deal didn't sound too bad, did it? They worked hard all day and by evening the trap was finished. They both went their separate ways, the farmer back to his wife and the Imp, well, back to wherever Imps go in the woods at night!

The next morning they met up at the pit, there was one male pig. The farmer took it back to his farm, just like the agreement. Every morning they went to look at the hole and it was the same. Some days there'd be male pigs, some days antelopes and some days even buffaloes, never female, always male.

The farmer was pleased each day. He laughed and said to the Imp. "You were foolish to make such a bargain. Didn't you know that it's the male animals that go hunting for food?"

The Imp just smiled and disappeared into the woods.

The farmer had lots of animals at his farm now, and his Cassava was growing tall and strong. Soon the new crop would be ready for bread making. Mmnnnnn he could smell it already. The farmer and his wife decided to cut some Cassava roots tomorrow; they could wait no longer for their delicious bread.

So the next morning, the wife set off, carrying large knives to cut with and huge baskets to carry the roots back in. Her husband stayed to look after the animals. The farmer fed the animals and then set off to help his wife, it would be hard work cutting all those roots. As he neared the field he could hear the Imp.

"Oh my. Oh my, at last I have a female animal in the trap."

The farmer neared the trap and asked the Imp why was he dancing and singing. He laughed when the Imp told him, all that fuss over one animal. He wasn't laughing a minute later when he looked into the pit and saw his wife.

"You can't have my wife, she's not an animal!" cried the farmer, still in shock.

They argued and argued over whether a woman was an animal or not.

The Imp was not going to change his mind. What was the farmer going to do? Suddenly an idea sprang into his mind.

"I've had lots of animals, how can I begrudge you just one?"

The Imp grinned and leapt into the pit to claim his prize.

No sooner had he done this, than the farmer called out. "There's a male animal in the trap and IT is mine."

When the Imp had jumped into the pit, he had forgotten the agreement, males for the farmer, and females for the Imp. He had been tricked! He was furious.

The Imp had only one way to save himself, he had to give up the woman and then the farmer would let him go. The farmer lifted his wife out first; just to make sure he wasn't going to be tricked again. The Imp vanished the minute the farmer hoisted him out.

"What a trap!" said the farmer to himself.

Prayer / Reflection

Think about a time you put someone first.

What did you do?

Did you feel sad or happy afterwards?

The Class Swot

Origin

Written by Alison Gardner.

Theme

Can friendship be bought? What is true friendship? Do we all need to 'fit'?

Mandy was the class swot! The usual sort of swot, always finished first, top in every subject, always given the 'Good' jobs etc. Every class has one and Mandy was 5G's. Everyone knew it, including Mandy. There was a time she didn't mind, in Year 1 for example. Mrs Dray gave her all the interesting jobs and always asked her the answers to the really important questions.

Year 2 was different, in Year 2 she was taunted with 'Teachers Pet'. In Year 3 it was 'Brain'. Year 4 brought much worse names, swot, nerd, creep. It wasn't so good anymore. At times she tried to hide how clever she was, she would daydream so that she couldn't always answer the questions, or tried to look blank like Tommy. He got away with it, so why couldn't she?

Her parents seemed to think that being clever was brilliant, they were really proud of all her achievements, even making matters worse by showing off to relatives and friends. She cringed inside everytime. What did they know anyway? Adults always seem to think they are right, well, they most certainly aren't.

Being a swot was becoming less than a novelty. She desperately wanted friends, just one would do. She decided on a new tactic, one that would hopefully find her some friends. She raided her piggy bank and counted what she had. It was enough, just enough for her plan. Sweets! And lots of them. She brought them to school each day and gave them to the popular girls each break time. They flocked around her, chatting away. They greeted her in the mornings and asked her to join in their games. She had never been this popular, ever.

It couldn't last, and she knew it. She was running out of money, only enough for another two days. She gave out the sweets and watched each one disappear quickly into hungry mouths, knowing each sweet was one of the last. She didn't enjoy the chatter at all on the last of the 'sweet days'. All she could think of was tomorrow. What would happen tomorrow?

When Mandy got home she checked everywhere in her bedroom for loose change, no luck. Her heart sank, she had got used to the friendly chats in the morning, the skipping games, being picked for teams in Games lessons. Her parents had noticed a change in her too. They kept asking her who her new friends were, asking Mandy to invite them home for tea.

The following morning Mandy left for school very reluctantly, she even tried the 'I feel sick mum.' But no, not even that was going to work today.

Mandy arrived at the school gates, Anne, Monica and Letisha all ran to greet her, asking her to join in their game. She knew it wouldn't be long before they stopped playing with her. Break time wasn't far away . . .

The morning seemed to fly by and very quickly she heard the morning break bell.

Mandy tried again, 'Miss I don't feel well, Miss can I do any jobs for you?'

Again, nothing worked. Filled with dread, off Mandy went towards the playground.

Anne was the first to ask, 'Got any sweets for us today?'

Then Letisha, 'Come on Mandy hand them over!'

Mandy nearly choked on her own words; she could feel tears close behind. 'I haven't got anymore, sorry'.

Anne and Letisha ran off to play with the others. Just for a brief moment Mandy felt all alone, then she realised that Monica was still standing by her.

'I haven't got anymore sweets! OK!' she shouted rather rudely at Monica.

'I only wanted to play,' whispered Monica very quietly. She had been quite shocked at Mandy's outburst.

After a break time of fun with Monica her sadness was soon forgotten. She realised that she couldn't buy friendship, it didn't matter how many sweets you had.

The day passed quickly, Mandy looked forward to each break knowing Monica would be there to play and chat with.

Anne and Letisha occasionally made nasty comments as they walked by, but Mandy couldn't care less. Not now she had a real friend - Monica.

Prayer / Reflection

In the Bible, Proverbs 24, 1-1 it says:
Do not try to make friends with unpleasant people, as all they do is cause trouble and hurt people.

What does 'unpleasant people' mean?

Everyone needs good friends; we would be very lonely without them.

Remember to have a good friend, you must be one!

Why Zebras Have Stripes!

Origin

Adapted from old Kenyan tales.

Theme

This is a story to explain the stripes on a zebra. It looks at the rights of working animals. Are human beings right to work animals such as horses?

Many, many years ago in Kenya, men had only managed to tame dogs. They wanted to tame donkeys, but had not managed it yet. They could see that donkeys would be very useful to the village.

One of the hunters from the village set off for the day to hunt for food for his family. Off he went into the bush, it was a long tiring day, tracking animals on foot, and usually failing to catch them. He eventually managed to hunt and trap an animal, but struggled to carry it through the bush. It was taking him ages, dropping it, picking it up, stopping for rests. He stopped, sat down, and tried to think of a way of carrying his prey without dropping it again.

Just as he was deep in thought, a donkey passed nearby in the bush. That was it! The idea sprang straight into his head. He could put the prey on the donkey's back; it would be strong enough to carry it easily.

The donkey didn't attempt to run away, so, he loaded up his family's meal. He led the donkey gently back to his village. He couldn't believe the donkey carried it without complaining. He unloaded the donkey then fed and watered him straight away. The donkey ate hurriedly, happy to be fed. He'd deserved it! The man found a place to keep the donkey, until he needed his help again, and that was the end of the donkey's freedom.

The story spread really fast around the village about this donkey that would carry really heavy loads. The man told them how easy it had been to tame the donkey. Lots of the villagers wanted a donkey so that they could see for themselves. The donkeys in the bush were totally unaware about what had gone on. They started to realise that some of their friends were disappearing and not coming back to the bush. They hid deeper and deeper in the bush, but it didn't work, still they were disappearing.

The donkeys were really worried. Lots of their group had been captured by now and the rumours they heard were terrible! Rumour had it, that these donkeys were being captured and worked too hard, and had only just enough food to keep them going. This was very frightening for all the donkeys.

The very next morning, one of the donkeys went to see Hare. Hare was only too willing to help. Hare asked the donkey to round up all his friends and bring them to him the next morning. They felt relieved; they knew that somehow Hare would come up with a plan. When they arrived at Hare's the next morning, there he was with a very large tin of white paint.

They couldn't imagine how white paint was going to help them! Hare tried to explain, but no one would be the first volunteer. Finally, a brave donkey stepped forward to be a volunteer. Hare set to work. He started to paint stripes of white over the donkey's hide. Soon, this very brave donkey was painted with black and white stripes, no more plain grey.

The other donkeys started to admire him. They all started to want the stripes. They were all so keen that they were fighting to be second, third, etc. Quite a few had been painted when one rather tubby donkey pushed forward to the front, stepped in the white paint bucket and all the paint poured out. That was the end of everything. Hare had no more paint. The remaining donkeys couldn't be painted. They were the 'unfortunate' ones.

Hare told them that he couldn't help them any more, the paint was spilt, and there was nothing more he could do. The donkeys that were painted were safe from mankind; they changed their name from donkeys to zebras. The unpainted donkeys were left grey, and destined to work hard for man. They were less fortunate and had to keep their name of 'donkey'.

Prayer / Reflection

Think for a moment about animals that people use to help them, guide dogs, horses, and donkeys.

Is it right to use them in this way?

Are they treated kindly?

The Generous Poor Man

Origin

Adapted from old Kenyan tales.

Theme

This story focuses on being selfless and generous. The story shows someone giving for no return.

Once upon a time there lived a very poor man. He had no family and no friends. His parents had died when he was a young child. Everyone in his village looked down their noses at him because he was so poor. He was very unhappy living there, so one day he decided to leave. He got together some food, some meat, honey and water, all in a fried gourd ready to carry. He set off on a long journey to make his way in to the world and find happiness.

He walked for hours, travelling for many miles. He was worn out. He stopped to rest under a small tree, to hide from the sun and have a little food. He pulled out some corn and in an instant a little weaverbird perched on his shoulder and said.

"Give me some of your corn and I will help you one day."

The man put some in his hand and fed the weaverbird. After the bird had eaten, it thanked him and flew away.

The man carried on with his journey after the short rest. Darkness started to come, so he climbed up a tree and slept. He started his journey as soon as the sun came up. After a few hours of walking he got very weary. He sat down and pulled some meat from the gourd. He ate the meat and then spotted a hyena sitting, quietly watching him.

"Could I have the bones to eat, I'm really hungry," growled the hyena.

The man gave them to him willingly. The hyena chewed and chewed until they were all gone.

"I will help you some day," he said as he left.

He walked all day, slept, and rose early again the next day. He walked until the sun was too hot for him. By now he was suffering from sunburn and needed a long rest. He found somewhere shady to sit and got the honey out.

As he started to taste it a bee started buzzing around him.

"Can I have some honey, I'm hungry," it buzzed.

He gave it some honey and off it flew, saying something about helping him as it went.

He walked again for a while, and then sat again to drink some of his water. He was so, so thirsty. A very dusty crocodile crawled up to him and asked for some water. The kind man, as always, helped the crocodile and shared his water.

"As you have helped me, I shall help you one day," he spluttered as he crawled away.

The poor man neared a new land, a land with a different king. He met a stranger on his journey, who only stopped long enough to tell him that he was near the king's palace and that the king had a very beautiful daughter. He also said that the king would marry his daughter to anyone who could pick her out in a large crowd, and give them his kingdom.

The poor man decided to visit the palace and see what was going on. He arrived looking very dirty and ragged. Hundreds of people were gathered together, the men ready to pick out the princess one end and the crowd the other end. The poor man joined the large crowd and waited.

He heard a buzzing around his ears, looked up and saw the bee he had met, sitting on his ear.

"I am the bee you helped. I'll pretend to fly round and sting the princess, then you'll know who she is."

The bee flew off towards some beautiful women. The poor man watched as a lady in the crowd started throwing her arms in the air. The poor man took her hand and went straight to the king.

The king thought the poor man looked very dirty and raggedy. He didn't want him marrying his daughter. The king then pretended that, that was the first task only. He told him there were more tasks to perform. The poor man felt very disappointed.

When nightfall came, the king sent for the poor man. He showed him a pile of mixed up seeds, three different types. It was a huge pile. He gave the poor man one night to sort the millions of seeds into separate piles. The king knew this was impossible. The poor man sat in front of them and started thinking hard. How was he going to do this impossible task? The weaverbird suddenly landed on his shoulder and chirped. "I'll fetch all my friends and we will help you complete this task."

He flew off and arrived back minutes later with lots of other weaverbirds, and sure enough the task was completed by morning.

The king was shocked. "This evening you must do another task for me," he said with authority.

The king got hold of a huge cooked bull and instructed the man to eat all of it by morning, leaving only the bone. He could never eat that much, there was enough for a hundred men. He tried a little, and then gave up. He suddenly heard a rustling behind him and out of the darkness emerged the hyena.

"I'll get all my family and we'll help you do this task," growled hyena.

Sure enough in the morning, only the bones were left. The king was furious. He decided to give the poor man one last task, a much more difficult task.

"Across this wide river there is an ostrich feather. Cross the river and bring the feather to me. If you do that, you can marry my daughter and have my kingdom."

The king smirked to himself, thinking of all the hungry crocodiles in the river. He instructed the poor man to start the task at lunchtime and the entire town came to watch.

The man looked at the huge crowd gathered and started to near the water's edge. He had a very worried look on his face. As he started to venture in with his feet, the crocodile he had helped popped up through the water's surface. The poor man jumped with surprise.

"Just wait there a moment while my friends create a bridge for you," spluttered the crocodile through glinting teeth.

Each crocodile held the head and tail of another crocodile, forming a very bumpy but effective bridge.

The poor man walked proudly to the other side, found the ostrich's feather and walked back to loud cheers from the townspeople. The crowd gave him a hero's welcome and there was no way the king could do anything. He had promised and everyone had heard. The king gave the poor man his daughter's hand and they lived happily ever after, king and queen in a new land.

Prayer / Reflection

Think about a time when you did something for someone, just because you wanted to.

How did you feel?

The Tortoise and the Lizard

Origin

Adapted from an ancient Bantu story

Theme

This story is about the importance of salt. It also explores greed. Are finders, keepers?

Tortoise loved putting salt in all his meals, he liked it so much that he overdid it each time, and always ran out of salt. His next meal tasted bland, he couldn't stand eating food without salt. He decided he would call on his brother and ask if he had any spare.

"I can't eat my food without salt, everything is so tasteless without it," wailed Tortoise to his brother.

"I've got plenty spare, but how will you carry it all the way home?"

"Can you wrap the salt in a piece of bark cloth? Then I'll put the string over my shoulder and drag the parcel along the ground behind me."

"A splendid idea!" exclaimed his brother.

He carefully wrapped the salt in some fresh bark cloth, tied it tightly and gave it to his brother. Tortoise positioned it behind him, got comfy, and set off.

The bundle went bump, bump, bump along the ground, as it was dragged behind him. Suddenly he pulled and nothing happened. He nearly went flying with the jolt. He looked back over his shoulder and saw a large lizard sitting on his parcel, staring hard at him. He stared back in anger.

"Get off my salt!" he exclaimed.

"It's not your salt!" replied the lizard.

"How do you expect me to get this all the way home if you are sitting on it?" said Tortoise.

"It's not your salt!" shouted the lizard. "I was just walking along this path when I saw this bundle lying here, I took it and now it belongs to me."

"What rubbish you talk!" said Tortoise, now annoyed at the time he was wasting. "You know it is mine, I'm holding the string that ties it!"

The lizard still carried on insisting that the bundle of salt was his. He just wouldn't get off it, so Tortoise could not go anywhere.

"I'll only get off it if we go together to the elders and get them to decide in court," muttered the lizard.

Tortoise had no choice but to agree. Off they set, together, to see the elders in court.

When they got there, Tortoise put his case first. He explained that, as his arms and legs were so short, he had to carry bundles by dragging them behind him. The lizard then explained that he had found the bundle lying in the road.

"Surely, anything that is picked up on the road belongs to the person that picks it up!" cried the lizard indignantly.

The elders discussed the case between them for quite a long time, giving it a lot of serious thought.

Many of the elders were related to the lizard family, they thought they might get a share of the salt, and so they were persuaded to make a decision. They decided the bundle should be cut in half, each animal keeping one half each. Tortoise was very disappointed. He knew it was an unfair decision. All he could do was sigh heavily and watch as they cut the bundle in two.

The greedy lizard immediately seized the half that had the biggest amount of cloth. Poor Tortoise was left with a parcel with escaping salt pouring out. He watched as it spilled onto the ground, he tried in vain to gather the grains up. It was useless! His hands were too small and he didn't have enough cloth to wrap it in. Eventually he had to set off for home, dragging the scrappy parcel behind him. He tried to rewrap it using leaves but had little success. The greedy elders scooped up what was left on the ground and took it home, very pleased with themselves.

When he got home, Tortoise's wife was very disappointed. She had expected a lot more salt. He told her the whole story and she was very angry at the way he had been treated. The long, slow journey had tired him and he needed a few days rest. While he was resting he spent many hours trying to think of a way to get even with the lizard. He was quite a clever Tortoise and eventually he came up with a cunning plan.

The very next morning he set off, refreshed and ready. He said good-bye to his wife and plodded along the dirt track towards lizard's home. He spotted the lizard, sitting enjoying a meal of flying ants. The lizard hadn't spotted him though! Slowly and silently he came up behind the lizard and put his hands on the middle of the lizard's body.

"See what I've found!" shouted Tortoise loudly.

"What are you doing?" asked the very puzzled lizard.

"I was just walking along the path when I found something lying here," explained Tortoise. "So I picked it up and now it's mine."

The lizard started to wriggle, trying to free itself from the Tortoise's grasp. "Set me free! Set me free!" screamed the lizard.

Tortoise insisted that they go to the elders for a decision; lizard had no choice but to agree. The elders listened attentively to both sides of the story, and then one said.

"If we are to be perfectly fair, we must give the same judgement as the salt."

The elders nodded their heads in agreement.

"We cut the bag of salt in half, therefore we must cut the lizard in two. Tortoise shall have half.

"That sounds very fair," replied Tortoise.

The lizard looked round for a way to escape, but as quick as a flash, Tortoise seized a knife from one of the elders and sliced the lizard in two. That was the end of the greedy lizard!

Prayer / Reflection

Do you know what the 8th commandment says?

"You should not steal."

When you lose something, how do you feel?

Thunder and Lightning

Origin

Adapted from an ancient Nigerian tale.

Theme

This story is about a natural phenomenon. It was a story told to explain the origin of thunder and lightning, before scientific explanation. It focuses on anger and how it can upset others.

A long, long time ago, both Thunder and Lightning lived on this earth, among people. Thunder was in fact a mother sheep and Lightning was her son, a ram. Neither animal was popular with any of the people. It's easy to see why.

If anyone dared to upset Lightning, he would fly into a furious rage, and burn anything near him. He didn't care what it was. He would burn huts, crops, and even large trees. Occasionally he killed people who got in his way, his temper was that bad!

Thunder would find out what was happening and she would raise her voice to shout at him as loudly as she could. She was very angry, and very, very loud. All the people would get upset. They lost crops through the damage, lost their homes, and sometimes their lives. The villagers complained to the king many times. At last he got fed up of the complaints and decided to do something about it.

He sent Thunder and Lightning to live at the very edge of the village. Even this didn't do any good. Lightning could still see people as they walked round the village, and as usual he picked fights with them. The king received many more complaints, so this time he sent for both Thunder and Lightning.

"I have given you a chance to mend your ways and stop annoying and upsetting the people in my kingdom," boomed the king. "But it's useless. From now on you are both banned from my kingdom. You must live in the wild bush away from people. We do not want to see your faces here ever again!"

Thunder and Lightning weren't happy, but they knew they had to obey the king. They left the village, shaking with anger, angry at all the complaining people in the village. The villagers didn't know what was in store for them next. Thunder and Lightning weren't finished. Lightning was so angry that he had been banished to the bush, that he set fire to all the plants and bushes there! There hadn't been any rain for months and the fire raged quickly. He watched it spread very, very quickly, heading towards the small farms on the outside of the village.

Many farms and many houses burnt down to the ground. The farmers were in despair. They could often hear the mother sheep's mighty voice telling her son off, shouting at the top of her voice. But, it was always too late; it was always after the damage had been done.

The king called a meeting, a meeting of all the important people in his kingdom. He talked with them about Thunder and Lightning's behaviour. They discussed how many chances they had been given to behave. After a lot of talking they came up with a plan.

They decided to banish Thunder and Lightning from the earth forever, they could give them no more chances. They decided to send them to live in the sky where they all hoped they couldn't do any more damage. The king made a proclamation and instantly Thunder and Lightning were sent into the sky forever. Things didn't go quite to plan though. Lightning still loses his temper from time to time and when he does he sends down fire to the earth in temper. The people can still hear his mother shouting at him in her loud rumbling voice. Still, it's not too often!

Prayer / Reflection

Think about this from the Bible.

'Don't let the sun go down on your anger'
(Ephesians 4.26)

What might this mean?

How do you control your temper?

The Story of the Sparrows and the Tiger

Origin

Folklore from the Bengali tradition.

Theme

This story tackles the issue of bullying. What can the bullied do?

Once there was a wife who kept a beautiful large cooking pot, hanging from the low ceiling in the corner of her house. It was so large that she hadn't used it for a while; she had lots of other cooking pots, a little smaller. As it had been left empty for so long, a sparrow and his wife had made a home inside the pot. They had flown in twigs and made a really comfortable nest inside.

One day the sparrow said. "Wife, I wish we had some sweet cakes I could eat, I really feel like eating some."

"Bring me the ingredients for sweet cakes and I'll make some."

"What do you need?" asked the sparrow.

"I need flour, treacle and bananas. Oh! Don't forget some milk and more firewood to cook them on," replied his wife, trying hard not to forget anything.

"All right," twittered the sparrow, keen to go and get everything. He could already taste those sweet cakes! Mmmnnn.

"I'll bring you everything, you just wait there."

Off he flew into the forest. He started to snap off the tiniest twigs. He looked down and saw a huge tiger, but this wasn't a problem for the little sparrow because the tiger had always been friendly to these two sparrows.

"Why are you snapping off the tiniest of twigs my friend?" asked the tiger.

"I'm getting firewood so that my wife can make sweet cakes," said sparrow happily.

"I've never eaten sweet cakes," said the tiger. "You must give me some."

The sparrow decided to be very cute here.

"Only if you bring us the ingredients," said the sparrow.

"What ingredients do you want?" asked the tiger.

Sparrow ran the list off to him. He repeated it just to be sure that the tiger wouldn't forget anything.

"All right. You go home and I'll bring you everything."

The sparrow flew off home clutching the little twigs in his beak. He felt really pleased with himself.

The tiger went lolloping off to market. When he got there he just stood still and roared. It worked every time. All the market traders screamed when they heard his roar.

"Help! Help! Tiger! Run! Run!" they would shout, whilst running as fast as they could.

The stalls were empty and it was easy for tiger to help himself to anything he wanted. He collected flour, treacle, bananas, butter, pots, and pans and delivered them straight to the sparrow's home.

The wife set about the cooking. She mixed and mixed all morning. She couldn't wait to eat them either; her mouth was watering at the thought. By noon, the cakes were ready, the smell was delicious. The two sparrows set about eating as many as they could. They ate and ate until they could eat no more.

"Quick! We forgot the tiger and there's only a couple of cakes left," whispered sparrow to his wife.

He knew that tiger would smell the cooked cakes and be here soon.

They came up with a plan. They laid out a few cakes for the tiger on a leaf on the ground. They were so full now that they settled in their pot for a sleep. The tiger, as expected had got the waft of sweet cakes and was following his nose and his stomach. He put the first one in his mouth.

"Ummmnn, delicious."

He started to nibble the second one. "This isn't so good, it tastes of flour." As he tried the third one, he started choking a little. "Yuk, this tastes horrible."

He spat the remains onto the ground and picked up the fourth one to try.

"It smells of dung! I can't eat this!" he roared.

He now realised he had been cheated by the sparrow. He knew they'd given him cow dung cakes. He was absolutely furious.

"You're a villain! A cheat!" he roared again and again.

He couldn't get rid of the horrible taste in his mouth.

In the cooking pot were sitting two very scared sparrows.

"Wife! Wife, I'm going to sneeze, I can't help it," spluttered sparrow, trying to keep quiet, but not succeeding.

"Ssh, Ssh," scolded wife. "You can't sneeze now, quiet!"

He managed not to sneeze at that moment, but a minute later was screwing up his nose trying to stop the sneeze again. He just couldn't stop it coming.

"Wait till I find that sparrow, I'll chew him up and swallow him," retched the tiger, still trying to get the bits of dung out of his mouth.

"Aah-choo!"

The tiger jumped right into the air. The sneeze had echoed so loudly in the pot, it sounded like a giant sneezing. His jump had knocked the pot from its hook and down it clattered sparrows and all!

The tiger was so shocked by it all, he hadn't realised what had fallen on his head. He wasn't sure if it was thunder and the sky falling in. He was so scared he didn't wait to find out. He ran in terror as fast as he could into the forest, his tail between his legs. He didn't stop and look back, not even once, only feeling safe when he reached his lair.

Prayer / Reflection

Think about this old saying:

'Two wrongs don't make a right'.

What does this mean?

Can you think of an example?

The Blind Men and the Elephant

Origin

A traditional Indian tale - looking at things from a different viewpoint.

Theme

This story could be told as an introduction to looking at a new faith.

India is a long way away and is quite a hot country. Most people live in small villages, not towns and cities as in Britain. In this one particular village there were six men all of whom were blind. All the villagers helped to look after these men and they worked hard in the village doing helpful jobs.

Often the six men would sit together and talk, talk for hours about all kinds of things. One day there was a great fuss in their village. They knew that an elephant had been brought to the next village to help move large logs of wood. They were far too heavy for the villagers to move.

"What is an elephant?" asked one of the men.

"Let's go and find out," his friend replied.

They all agreed to go together to the next village to find out what an elephant was. They went slowly, picking along a path they had taken many times before. They didn't want to get lost.

When they got to the next village they shouted for the mahout. That's the man who looks after the elephant. He took the blind men to where the elephant was tethered with food and water, under the shade of a large tree. All the six men were standing right by the elephant, but remember, none of them can see.

The first man put out his hand and touched the elephant's trunk.

"Ah ha," he said. "An elephant is like a snake, long and bendy."

The second man put out his hand and touched the elephant's tusk.

"Ah ha," he said. "An elephant is like a knife, hard and sharp."

The third man put out his hand and touched the elephant's ear.

"Ah ha," he said. "An elephant is like a big leaf, smooth and thin."

The fourth man put out his hand and touched the elephant's leg.

"Ah ha," he said. "An elephant is like a tree, round and strong."

The fifth man put out his hand and touched the side of the elephant.

"Ah ha," he said. "An elephant is like a big wall, high and wide."

The sixth man couldn't wait to feel the elephant. He had waited very patiently and was very confused by all the comments. He put out his hand and felt the elephant's tail between his fingers.

"Ah ha," he said. "An elephant is like a rope, long and swishy."

The men stood arguing with each other for ages. Each man was convinced that he was right.

"No, no you are wrong."

"No, no YOU are wrong."

And so it went on for ages. None of them appeared to be talking about the same thing, like a snake, like a rope, like a wall! How could this be?

Then the mahout, who had stood very quiet up until then interrupted and said. "Excuse me. You must stop arguing, you are all right."

"We can't all be right," argued the six men.

"Yes you are. Listen! The elephant has a trunk that is like a snake, tusks which are like knives, ears like big leaves, legs like tree trunks, a body like a wall and a tail like a rope. See, you are all right."

Prayer / Reflection

Think about this really old saying:

'Don't judge a book by its cover'.

What might this mean?

Narahari Das

Origin

A story from the Bengali folklore tradition.

Theme

This story looks at growing older and the steps we need to take. It looks at the importance of what adults tell us. Do they want the best for us?

The fields stretched for miles, then the forests spreading at the base of high, high mountains. The mountains were capped with snow, sparkling in the distance. At the foot of these mountains there was a cave, and in this cave there lived a little goat. He was only young so his mother wouldn't ever let him roam out of the cave. He just wasn't old enough yet.

He begged and begged his mother each day.

"Please let me go out and explore, it looks so exciting."

"No you don't! The bear will catch you, the tiger will take you, and the lion will eat you up."

The little goat got quite frightened when his mother told him these sorts of stories. He would stay quite quietly in the cave, waiting for her to come back.

He got bigger and bigger each week. As he got bigger and bigger, he got braver and braver. Whenever his mother went out to get food, he would peep out of the cave.

One day he got really brave and he stepped right out of the cave. He felt very grown up and started to wander, only a little.

There was a large ox munching away on grass not far from the cave. The little goat had never seen an animal that big before. He was much bigger than his mother. He looked at its horns and then decided it must just be a very large goat, so large because it had lots of good things to eat.

"Hello there, what do you eat?"

"I eat grass," said the ox.

"My mother eats grass and she hasn't grown as big as you."

"I eat lots more grass than your mother does," said the ox. "And much better grass too."

"Where is this grass?" asked the little goat.
He thought he might like to try some. He would love to grow big and strong.

"Over in that forest," said the ox.

"Will you take me there?" pleaded the little goat.

The ox agreed and took him along. It was quite a long walk. The little goat's legs got tired, he had never gone anywhere before.

When they got inside the forest the grass was soft and very green. It tasted delicious. The little goat ate until his stomach was so full, it would take no more. He felt so full he couldn't move. When it started to get a little dark, the ox said.

"Come on, let's go home now."

The little goat tried to get up but was still too full.

"You go, I'll go in the morning."

So off the ox went. The little goat knew he wouldn't be able to go far until his meal had digested. He was starting to regret eating so much now. He longed for the warmth and comfort of the cave. He saw a hole nearby and crawled into it, it was better than nothing. The hole belonged to a jackal. The goat was black so when the jackal came home it couldn't see him in the dark. He could only see a dark fearsome shape.

The jackal decided it was a monster and asked with a quivering voice.
"Who is in my hole?"

The little goat was quite a clever goat and he answered.

"My beard is long, I shake it too and fro, and my name is Narahari Das the strong, and I swallow fifty tigers in one go!"

"Help! Help!" yelled the jackal, as he ran off.

He ran and ran as fast as he could to his friend's house, the tiger. The tiger was very surprised to see him. The jackal had only just left his house and now he was back.

"What's up? Why are you back so soon?"

"A terrible thing has happened, a monster called Narahari Das is in my hole. He says he can swallow fifty tigers in one go!"

The tiger was furious. What nonsense he thought to himself.

"Come on, let's go and see this fearful monster," said a very angry tiger.

The jackal didn't want to go back. He was really scared.

"If the monster comes out and snaps us up, you can run away, I won't be able to escape," cried the jackal.

"What do you mean? I would never leave without you," said the tiger to his friend.

"Tie me to your tail, then we can flee together if we need to."

The tiger agreed, tied the jackal firmly to his tail and set off.

The two arrived at the hole. They tried to creep up quietly, but the little goat had spotted them.

"You stupid fool - be gone! Be gone! I gave you money for ten tigers, but you've only roped up one!"

The tiger jumped out of his skin with fright. He was sure that the jackal had tricked him and brought him to the monster to eat. He was so scared he raced off, the jackal still tied to his tail. He raced through the trees, scraping against bushes and plants, and branches in the way. The jackal was bounced and battered all over the place.

"Ouch! Stop!" shouted jackal.

The tiger just thought he was screaming because Narahari Das was chasing behind them, so he ran even faster.

He ran all night until he was as far away as possible. In the morning the little goat made his way home. It was a long way and he was looking forward to his comfy cave and seeing his mother again. The jackal had had a terrible time; he was extremely bruised and could not run properly for weeks. He was so angry at tiger that he never ever forgave him.

Prayer / Reflection

Think about this proverb:

'People who want to grow in knowledge want to be told when they are wrong. Hating correction is stupid'.

The Crane's Walk

Origin

Retold from Aesop's Fables.

Theme

This story looks at how being different is good. We are all special

A large family of crabs lived on the shores of a giant blue sea. The waters were crystal clear and the beaches a soft glimmering sand. The family played in the sands, hiding behind small dunes, chasing each other. They lived on mussels, clams and other small sea creatures. They had plenty of food and a wonderful place to live.

One day the mother crab saw a beautiful crane walking about along the sands. She couldn't take her eyes off it. It walked in such a graceful manner, it was a delight to watch, a straight graceful walk in its long reed-like legs.

"How graceful that crane looks," she muttered to herself.

Just at that moment she caught sight of her son waddling towards her. She felt irritated as she watched him. He looked so awkward and clumsy. He moves like a heavy sack, she thought to herself.

"Why do you walk like that!" she snapped.

He waddled nearer looking a little shocked.

"Instead of walking one-sided, use your ten legs to walk straight, straight and GRACEFULLY," she ordered.

"How do I walk straight? I only know how to walk like this," said the little crab very sheepishly. He was very confused and didn't really understand what mother crab was so upset about. Mother crab insisted and insisted. She tried to explain over and over. The little crab tried and tried, he just couldn't get it right.

"Come on, you're not really trying," she scolded.

"Can you show me mother, I just can't do it, no matter how hard I try."

"You must try harder," she said, still not really helping him at all.

"If you show me the straight way, I'm sure I'll catch on."

Mother crab went over and tried to do the straight walk. It was much harder than she had ever imagined. She tried and tried, toppling, tripping, her legs just didn't seem suited to walking straight.

"This is useless. It's impossible," she hissed tiring from all the effort. "I give up," she panted, after several more unsuccessful attempts.

"Forget it child, I don't think nature intended us to walk like the crane, we're just not built for it!"

Prayer / Reflection

Thank you, God for making us all different.

Thank you, for each one of us being special.

Four Eyes

Origin

Written by Alison Gardner.

Theme

A story about tolerance and bullying.

Mr. Martin was our teacher for this term. Our usual teacher, Mrs. Davis, had gone off to have a baby. As a class we loved her and were sad to see her leave, but Mr. Martin was great fun, and he loved history.

Today we were going to have a lesson on Black History. Lots of us had brought in things from home to show in class. We were looking forward to this lesson. I'd brought in a picture of my grandparents when they'd first come to this country. I was really excited about show and tell, in this lesson.

Mr. Martin taught about 'Our Black Heritage' and how it is all about going back to the glory of our ancestors, to help us build a better future. It is important for people of all colours and religions to know that black people gave the world great civilizations and inventions. Our black heritage tries to teach us to respect other people no matter how different they are to us.

I was listening, but then, as usual I drifted off. I could hear Jason, Loresa and Chris asking questions, they always asked lots of questions. Chris asked the most questions, he had brought in loads of pictures from home and had question after question for Mr. Martin. I started to think about break time, my stomach was rumbling and today, today I had jaffa cakes.

Mr. Martin was still talking, but all I could hear was blah, blah, blah. This happened a lot to me. History's not that important is it anyway? Chris, my best friend, well, he loves to learn. It doesn't matter what the lesson is, there he is, all ears. He annoys me sometimes. He keeps saying that he wants to be a teacher, just like Mr. Martin. I can't think of anything worse!

I started to think of whom I would play with at playtime. I looked over at Loresa, yes; I'd play with her today. Then I looked at Jason, he was still wearing his new glasses. He looked really stupid, and the thing is, he thinks he looks cool! The bell went and we all raced out into the playground.

"Jason, your glasses are too big for your face. You look really stupid." I said, laughing as I walked by.

"Yeah four eyes!" yelled Tek.

Tek was the boss, he decided who could play in the football games. If you were too slow or didn't know all the rules, or he didn't like you, well, you couldn't play. You could bribe him sometimes with your morning snack, especially if it was a cake, homemade that is. He was a sucker for cakes.

"Yeah four eyes," I said joining in. He really did look funny. Jason didn't seem to like the jokes, he scowled at me.

"You shouldn't disrespect someone for the way they look," piped up Chris, as he ran behind us. "That's what we learnt today isn't it?"

Later Jason was at Chris' house and he still looked sad. Nothing Chris did would cheer him up.

"What's wrong?" asked Chris.

"I didn't like all the teasing at school today."

"Oh, don't worry about that, no one meant it," comforted Chris.

Nothing worked. Jason was not going to cheer up, not today anyway. I felt a little guilty, but I hadn't meant anything. Jason would know that.

"You've really hurt his feelings," Chris shouted at me when Jason had gone home.

"I didn't mean to, I just thought it was funny."

"Who cares if he wears glasses, that doesn't give you the right to crack jokes about it."

Chris was going red in the face. That meant he was really angry! I felt tears stinging my eyes. I knew he was right. I knew that first thing tomorrow morning I would apologise to Jason. Would he forgive me and still be my friend? I hadn't been a very good friend so far.

The next morning before lessons, I spotted Jason playing with his yo-yo in the corner of the playground. I raced over but he didn't want to know. He turned his back on me and carried on practicing for the yo-yo competition next week.

"You shouldn't make fun of people just because of how they look. Just because people are fat or tall or black or white doesn't mean you can make fun of them." Jason said, with anger in his voice. I didn't know what to say for a moment.

"I'm sorry and I'm wrong. I'm sorry for making fun of your glasses. I'll never do it again."

I didn't know what else I could say. I felt terrible. I didn't realise I had upset him that much.

He turned to face me, still spinning his yo-yo. He was never going to win.

"Come on, I'll show you some tricks on the yo-yo, we've got to beat Tek next week."

Prayer / Reflection

Think about a time at school when someone was nasty to you in the playground.

How did you feel?

Do you think the other person knew how you felt?

Krishna and Sudama

Origin

Retold from The Story of Krishna. This story comes from the Hindu faith

Theme

This story deals with how to treat other people and the effect of our behaviour on others.

Krishna was King of Dwarka. He was really popular and had loads of friends to play with. Everyone enjoyed his company and wanted to be his friend. As they turned into teenagers, various friends moved away. They moved away to get married or look for work.

They didn't have telephones or the postal service, so Krishna never knew what had happened to his friends. He used to miss them, and he would sit daydreaming, wondering what had happened in their lives.

One of his very best friends had been Sudama. He had got married and had a lovely daughter. Sudama doted on his daughter; there was nothing he wouldn't do for her. Sudama had become a teacher, but he wasn't paid a lot. Often he didn't have enough money to buy food for his family, he tried, but he just didn't earn enough.

Sudama's wife had heard all about Krishna from her husband. She knew he was a kind friend. She suggested to Sudama that he go and visit his friend and ask if he could borrow some money. Sudama didn't think he could ask the King of Dwarka for money, even though he was his friend. He hadn't seen his friend for quite a few years, and asking for something didn't seem quite right.

Sudama's wife realised her husband had a lot of pride, so she sat and thought what to do. She came up with a good idea, or so she thought anyway. She suggested to Sudama that he take some puffed rice to his friend King Dwarka, as a gift. She remembered that Sudama had told her how they both loved puffed rice when they were younger. So off he set with a small bag of puffed rice.

It was a long way to the palace and he found the walking very hard. He hadn't eaten a proper meal in a few days and felt exhausted. He walked for hours and hours. When he got to the palace he collapsed on the steps. He hadn't the strength to tackle the long steps up to the palace door.

Krishna spotted him and rushed down to help him. He picked him up and carried him into the palace. He put Sudama in a big room and left him to rest. As soon as he woke up, Sudama saw his friend, he was so happy, he had so missed him. The king gave him as much food as he could eat and they talked and talked about old times. They ate and talked for days, there was so much to catch up on.

Sudama kept the puffed rice, feeling it was not a good enough gift for a king. He didn't mention how poor he was, he felt embarrassed. When they were talking, Krishna spotted the bag of puffed rice.

"How wonderful! I haven't had puffed rice since we were children. Fancy you remembering I loved it!"

They sat together talking, the king really enjoying the treat of puffed rice. During that time Krishna found out where Sudama and his family were living.

Krishna had realised that Sudama was in trouble, but he didn't say anything. In secret, he sent some of his best workers to Sudama's village and they built a new house for Sudama. They left lots of good healthy food for Sudama and his family. All this time Sudama had been recovering in the palace. When he was strong enough to walk, he set off for home.

He had loved seeing his friend again. He walked with a little sadness in his step; he knew it might be a long time before he saw his friend again. He started to walk a little faster, thinking now of his hungry family at home. Little did he know!

Prayer / Reflection

Thank you God, for all our friends.
Help us to remember the effect we have on others.
To treat others with kindness and respect.

Amen

The Magic Pot

Origin

A Caribbean tale retold

Theme

This tale explores how greed can be harmful, in more ways than one.
Anancy, sometimes man, sometimes spider, is a trickster in Caribbean folklore. Many stories have been told about him.

Anancy had a farm and he worked really hard each day. The rain had stopped coming and his fields were looking really dry. Each day he went to look at his crops, and each day they looked more withered. The drought looked like it was never going to end.

One morning, Anancy went through the forest to the river. He wanted to see if the river had nearly dried up. Perched on the edge of the river was a beautiful pot. He went closer and saw that it had strange symbols on the outside, it was like writing, but he couldn't read it. He turned it round and round in his hands. The inside of the pot was super smooth, just like the worn pebbles in the river.

"I wonder what these symbols mean?" he said to himself.

"Fill the pot!" boomed a voice from somewhere inside the pot.

"Fill the pot!" Anancy repeated in shock.

He looked and saw a most delicious meal, chicken stew, his favourite. He munched until the pot was absolutely clean. It didn't need washing. Before he could pick the pot up, it was refilled with more of his favourite food. He managed to eat it all, until he was far too full.

"Gosh! This is great!" he gushed. "How often can you do this?" he then asked. "Whenever you like, and wish for whatever you like. Just say the words fill the pot, but whatever you do, don't wash the pot or it will wash the magic away."

Anancy hid it in some bushes and went home.

The next day he took the same path through the forest to the river. He couldn't wait to get back to the pot and its magic. As soon as he got to the bushes, he shouted.

"Fill the pot, fill the pot, pork and beans."

Immediately the pot was full of pork and beans. Anancy ate and ate until he could eat no more. In bed that night he couldn't stop thinking about the food he would order the next day. He ran down the path the next day, burning with eagerness.

"Fill the pot, fill the pot, pea soup."

And it was, full to brimming.

Anancy ate before anyone would find him, even licking out the pot. Anancy returned home to his wife and children. They only had a few vegetables each night. Anancy ate his portion too, so not to arouse suspicion, although it was a little obvious that he was getting a lot plumper.

He had a clever son called Takko. He was very suspicious of his father. They were all getting thinner and Anancy was getting fatter. He told his mother that he thought his father was up to some tricks. He knew him well. Anancy's wife began to keep a closer eye on him.

The next morning she followed her husband down the forest path. When she caught up just behind him, she saw him eating from the pot. She went home and cooked the vegetables as normal. They all sat down to eat and not a word did she say!

The next morning, she got up before her husband and rushed down to the river to have a better look at the pot. She looked at the strange writing, then inside. It was filthy disgusting! She took it to a shallow part of the river and gave it a jolly good wash. She then decided to take the pot to a market to sell. They really needed some money.

Anancy woke and found his wife gone. He assumed she had gone to look for vegetables for tonight's meal. He went straight down to the river, just as he usually did. The pot had vanished! He tore up all the bushes in his rage; it had vanished into thin air. Finally, he had to give up searching and go home.

When he got home, his wife was busy planting seeds. Nearby were three chickens. He was really surprised.

"Where did all these come from?" he said.

"In my dreams last night, I saw a pot filled with food, hidden, not far from here. I got up early to look for it and I found it!"

"The pot! The pot! Where is it?" he screamed.

"Well I gave it a wash and sold it at the market."

He couldn't speak for anger. His wife just couldn't understand what was wrong. The seeds grew into lovely vegetables and the chickens laid lots of eggs. Anancy didn't speak or eat for days. His legs and arms went very skinny. He looked really strange, because do you know, to this day, his stomach stayed podgy and fat with all the food he had eaten.

Prayer / Reflection

Dear God

Help us to be kind towards others, to be loving and sharing.

Amen

The Most Precious Thing in the World

Origin

A Dutch legend from the Province of Friesland.

Theme

Some of the most precious things in the world might not be the most obvious. The story explores greed and selfishness too.

"Pardon, my Lady?" the old sea captain wasn't sure if he'd heard right first time.

Lady Staveren was the richest and proudest person in Staveren. He was amazed she'd come over to talk to him in the first place.

"Can you say it again please? My hearing's not that good, you know, old age an all."

The Lady was pacing around, seemingly annoyed and very impatient.

"I said, I want to hire you and your ship. I want you to find and bring me the most precious thing in the world."

"I don't know what the most precious thing is, or where to find it," the captain said, very shocked by her outrageous command.

"I am paying you to find it and bring it to me!" she shouted at him. She was not used to people not doing what she demanded, immediately.

"But what is the most precious thing? I haven't got a clue."

"Don't you think I'd already have it if I knew what it was. Now here is the payment, and I expect the job done. I will not take no for an answer."

The captain repeated again that he didn't have a clue what the most precious thing in the world was.

"Look! I need to beat all my rival merchants, this will be one thing they can't copy me on." She was not going to take no for an answer.

He decided to have a go. She had given him lots of gold.

She parted with a very serious comment. "If you fail, you will never find work in Staveren again!"

He set off the next morning, in search of ..... well, he wasn't sure what yet! He sailed for months, looking, never finding anything that seemed good enough. Back in Staveren, the Lady had boasted that she would soon have the most precious thing in the world. Everyone was wondering what it would be.

"A most magnificent gown."

"No! A marble hand carved statue."

"No! Some precious metal."

She loved all the attention. Many months later she watched as the ship pulled into the harbour. All the townspeople ran down to the dock, they couldn't wait to see what she had got.

"My Lady, I have brought you what you wanted."

"What is it? What is it?" she shouted excitedly.

"The most precious thing in the world, just as you asked," the captain said, very calmly.

"But what is it?" she shouted impatiently.

"I've been to many ports all around the world, I've seen the most amazing things, but in the very last city I visited I found what you wanted."

"What? What have you found?"

"Wheat! My ship is filled with wheat!"

The Lady of Staveren looked furious. She went white then red. She could hear the crowd muttering.

"Wheat? Wheat?"

"What could be more precious? We all need bread, without bread, we would starve!"

She went very silent. She could hear some of the crowd laughing. She did not like being a laughing stock.

"All this wheat is mine?" she said very calmly.

The captain knew she was hiding her fury.

"Can I do what I like with it?" she asked.

"Of course," said the captain, wondering what on earth she was getting at.

"Pour it into the harbour, all of it!" the Lady ordered.

The captain was flabbergasted. All that wheat! It had taken months for him to find the treasure! The crowd was murmuring in shock.

"There's enough here to feed a city!" shrieked the captain. He was horrified. He asked if he could give the wheat to the poor instead.

The Lady of Staveren had never been hungry, never been poor. She flung a ruby ring from her finger into the harbour, shouting. "I don't ever have a need for anything. This ring would spring back on my hand before I ever need anything!"

The captain had no choice but to do what she ordered. He took the ship to the entrance of the harbour and ordered his crew to empty all the wheat into the sea. All the townspeople of Staveren were watching. The captain vowed never to return to Staveren again, he was so upset.

That evening the Lady of Staveren held a huge feast for all the wealthy people in Staveren. The main course was a huge fish caught that day. It was served on a big silver platter to her table. Just as she was cutting a portion, she saw something shining in the fish's mouth. She pulled open the mouth and held up her ruby ring. The whole room went quiet!

Many weeks later all the ships that tried to enter the harbour were getting stuck at the entrance. The wheat had sprouted and was binding the sand together. A sand bar was developing and no one could stop it. Very soon, no ships at all could enter; the merchants lost everything, including the Lady of Staveren.

Staveren became a poor city. To this day big ships cannot land properly at Staveren. The sand bar that can be clearly seen sticking up right in the entrance to the harbour, is called 'Lady's Sand'. This reminds everyone in Staveren of how the Lady of Staveren turned her nose up at the most precious thing in the world.

Prayer / Reflection

Think about some of the most precious things in the world. Keep one in your head.

Will it always be there forever?

Does everyone think it is precious?

Why is it so special?

The Jealous Moon

Origin

Indonesian folklore.

Theme

This story focuses on arrogance, jealousy, and appreciating individual qualities.

The moon and stars shone brilliantly in the sky, lighting up the darkness. They shone beautifully. They felt happy because they could also see the magnificence of the earth from the sky. They could see all the land and seas. Everything looked tiny, just like ants.

On earth, everyone used to look at the night sky in wonderment. They would sit and chat, grateful for the light at night. The moon felt really happy.

"Look! They are admiring me," moon said to star.

"Admiring you! I don't think so! It's us they are admiring, the sparkling stars."

"From the earth I am the biggest light in the sky, they'll be looking at me not you!"

"You're so arrogant," grumbled the stars to each other. They hated it when the moon was arrogant. He had quite a good opinion of himself.

"Let him be as arrogant as he likes, he'll never beat the sun," said one of the quieter stars.

"What do you mean?" shouted the moon, shocked.

"All the people on earth wait for the sun to rise each day, they go out and enjoy the sun's rays. People love the sun, they never grumble about the sun," uttered the quiet star rather timidly. He was a little scared of the moon.

"She dries all the clothes on the lines, people think she's wonderful," butted in another star.

The moon was feeling very threatened, he wanted to be the most loved.

"And she isn't arrogant either," piped up another rather brave star.

The moon went quiet; he was very upset by now. All night long, he was thinking about the sun, and how to win people over, he wanted to be the best. By the time morning came, he had thought of an idea.

It was a very bright morning; the sun was doing her best.

"Good morning moon, it's time for me to work now, off you go and rest," the sun sang happily.

"No! I want to work in the day too."

"Daytime is my time, you need your rest, ready for the night," the sun explained, a little puzzled by moon's eagerness to work.

"I want to challenge you. The stars said you were better than me, and I want to find out if that is true."

"Compete! How?" The sun was totally confused by now.

The moon asked the sun to stay put, he would stay too. Then they'd see who was the best. Moon was sure he would win, he had no real doubts. The sun laughed, she thought moon's proposal was quite funny.

"My light is stronger than yours, no one can see you in the daytime."

Moon wasn't listening, he stayed all day. All day he stayed high in the sky, trying the hardest he could to light the sky next to the sun. Nobody could see him, he felt so disappointed.

He cried, "Nobody loves me, they only love the sun."

Some of the more caring stars started circling the moon, being as sympathetic as they could.

"Rest, rest, you must rest before it's dark," they urged the moon.

The moon wouldn't listen; he was still determined to be best.

"You're just being arrogant!" shouted over a very brave star.

"You're both special, but in different ways," whispered the shyest star to the moon.

Moon stopped crying, he realised that the shy star was absolutely right, and he had been a little arrogant, hadn't he?

That night the moon was too tired to work. He tried, but he just couldn't stay awake. The stars tried really hard to light up the sky, sparkling their strongest. What was important was that the moon had realized he was arrogant, and had decided to change. The moon would be loved even more now, and he never again missed a single night working high up in the sky.

Prayer / Reflection

Think of this proverb.

'Love is not jealous'.

Think about a time you've felt jealous of someone.

Why is it bad to feel jealous?

Is jealousy a good feeling?

Honesty Does Pay

Origin

A Chinese tale

Theme

This story shows how honesty pays in the end.

Once there was a very poor man called Yo. Not only was he honest, but also he was poor. Everyone around him seemed to be making lots of money, often with dishonest tricks, but Yo still remained poor.

Yo used to like resting at an inn in his village, where all the local people went for a rest and a chat. He would always sit alone in a corner. The rest of the noisy villagers would forget he was there.

This one day was different! The door opened and a giant of a man, as tall as oak trees, stooped down to avoid the ceiling and came and sat next to Yo. He looked very unhappy; neither of them spoke for a while. They were both strangers, occupied with their own thoughts.

After a while Yo asked the stranger if he was hungry. He pushed across his own plate and offered to share it. The man ate as if he hadn't eaten before, finishing off the plate. He didn't leave a scrap. Yo was astonished, he ordered another plate from the landlord. Again the man ate the whole lot, licking the plate absolutely clean. Yo spent all the money he had, until the stranger was full.

The giant man had eaten enough for twelve men, shoulder of pork, two dozen dumplings, three loaves of bread. He sat back when he had finished eating and said, "Thank you."

His voice boomed and shook the building. All the tables and plates rattled.

"I haven't eaten a meal like that in three long years."

"Why is that?" asked Yo.

"I can't talk about the will of the Gods." Yo could see it was no good asking questions, so he kept quiet about that.

"Where are you from?" he asked.

"I have no one home, at dawn I live in the village, at night I live in the city."

Yo thought this was a very strange answer. When Yo decided to go home, the stranger asked if he could come too. Yo didn't have the heart to say no.

They walked a long way to Yo's house, getting to know each other. The stranger was full of knowledge and wisdom. He knew an awful lot about the clouds, rain, rivers, the sea, in fact anything to do with water.

He stayed for many weeks eating poor Yo out of house and home. The strange thing was he only ate every twelve days, but when he did eat, he ate enough for twelve men. Yo didn't begrudge the man the food, but he had very little left and no money to buy more.

He harvested two fields and very little was left of that stock now. His crops had difficulty growing; his greedy neighbours had diverted the streams to their own fields, leaving Yo's fields dry.

"If only I understood how rain begins," Yo used to say to himself, when he looked in his fields. "If only I could walk among the clouds myself."

Yo came back to his house from the fields and went for a little nap, the sun had been very hot that day. As he dropped off to sleep, he felt he was floating in the air. Everything around him was white, curling and twisting as he watched. He felt very rocky and put out his arms to help balance him. He felt his arm touch a hard object, he looked and was astonished, it was a star.

Yo picked one of the tiniest stars and put it in his pocket. He looked down and could see the sea, and the land. His house looked like a speck of dust. Just as he looked up, two dragons went past him, both pulling a cart full of water. Lots of men were gathering the water in buckets and sprinkling it on to the clouds. It was amazing.

Suddenly they all spotted Yo, and they stopped what they were doing immediately.

"Who are you?" they all said in unison.

"It's all right, he's my friend," shouted the giant man appearing as if from nowhere. "Give him a ladle so he can help."

The giant man explained to Yo how they were servants of the Thunder God, and they had to send the rain down on the earth, fairly, where possible. He told Yo how he had got it wrong three years ago and had been punished. His punishment was to walk on earth until he found an honest man.

The giant then told Yo to look down on his two fields and to water them well.

Yo filled his ladle to brimming and splashed loads on the clouds above his fields.

Suddenly he found himself being lowered on a rope from the clouds right to his house, the rope was attached to the dragon's reins, he couldn't believe what he was seeing.

The next morning he got up and walked to his fields, his crops were lush and green. His neighbours' fields were all brown and parched. When he got home later that day, he pulled out the star from his pocket and put it on to the table. It filled his house with light, a gorgeous warm light. It was Yo's greatest treasure. He only showed visitors its light when they were very honest, good people.

Prayer/ Reflection

Dear Lord

Help us to do the right thing when we need to, to be honest and truthful.
Stop us lying when we feel we want to.

Amen

Don't Change The World

Origin

Author unknown. Story retold by Alison Gardner.

Theme

Should you try to change the world or others when things upset you? Here is a story about the origin of shoes, and looking within yourself to change things, making the world a happy place to live.

Once upon a time, there was a very rich king. This king had the best of clothes, the best food and a very big and beautiful castle. He ruled over a country that was very prosperous. Everyone had employment and somewhere decent to live. It was a good place to live.

He liked going on trips to see people living in different parts of his land. He loved going to the markets. In his country, the people walked everywhere, it was the custom. Often, when he got back, his feet ached from all the walking. All the roads were rough and stony, cutting the soles of his feet with their sharpness. He would bathe his feet and rub oil in to soothe them. It would take days for them to recover.

He complained over and over to his servants. They didn't have any answers to help him. Eventually he thought of a plan, a very grand plan. He ordered the road builders in his land to cover every road in the land with leather. He knew that leather felt soft, but was also very hardwearing. His servants decided that it would take many thousands of cow's skins and this seemed terrible, as well as very expensive.

One of his loyal servants sat and thought about this huge problem. He himself, had suffered from sore feet on many of his journeys. This servant was known as a very wise servant. He came up with a plan and plucked up the courage to go and talk to the king.

"You can't kill all those cattle, I think I've got a better idea. It won't cost you much either."

The king was surprised, but he respected this servant. He knew him to be a good, honest, and wise servant.

"What could we do?" asked the king with interest.

"Why don't you just cut a piece of leather to cover your feet?"

The king thought about it for a while, and then decided to try it. He sat down and made first one 'shoe', and then another. It was a great success and before long everyone in his land had shoes. They could walk as far as they wanted and sore feet became a thing of the past.

Later that week the king was sitting talking to the wise servant. He congratulated him on the success of his idea.

"How do you manage to think of these ideas?" the king asked.

"When I look at the world and something appears to be wrong, I look at what I can change with myself. I don't try to change the world. You can always look at yourself and inside at your heart."

The king realised that the servant had taught him a very valuable lesson in life, as well as making his daily life much more comfortable.

Prayer / Reflection

I would like you to think about this proverb for a few moments.

'If you look in the water, you see your face reflected back at you. If you look in your heart, it reflects your own self.'

The Gifts of Wali Dad

Origin

This story has been retold from the "Story of Wali Dad. The Simple-hearted," found in Andrew Lang's, Brown Fairy Book (1904).

Theme

Does material wealth make you happy? What is most important, money and possessions, or happiness?

Wali Dad was a very old grass-cutter. He lived all on his own in a small wooden hut. His job was to cut and bundle up tall wild grass. When he had got enough, he would take it to the local market and sell it for animal food.

He only earned a little, just 30 coins a day. He would spend 10 coins on food and 10 coins towards clothes and his home. He would always save 10 coins in a clay pot under his bed.

One winter's evening, he decided to count the coins in the pot. The pot was nearly full to the top; he had a job carrying it.

"What am I going to do with all this money? I have everything I need," he thought to himself.
He sat thinking and thinking. At last, he had an idea. He got up early the next day and put all the coins into a very strong sack. He went to the marketplace and found a jeweller. He swapped the coins for a beautiful gold bracelet.

He then went visiting, the home of a very wise travelling merchant.

"Can you help me? Who is the noblest lady in the land?"

"Why that's the young queen of Khaistan," he said.

"Next time you go near the palace, would you give her this bracelet with my compliments?" asked Wali Dad.
The merchant agreed. A few weeks later, the merchant found himself at the palace. He did just as Wali Dad had asked. The queen was amazed, she thought it was lovely.

"You must take a gift in return for this," she insisted. "My servants will load a camel with the finest silks."

The merchant hurried back to Wali Dad's hut with the lovely gifts. Wali Dad didn't know what on earth he was going to do with such fine silks.

"Perhaps you could give them to someone else," piped up the merchant.

"Who is the noblest man in the land?" asked Wali Dad.

The merchant told him all about the young king of Nekabad. Wali Dad begged him to help him again. He asked him to give the young king the silks with his compliments. The merchant agreed, yet again.

On his next journey, he visited the king and presented the silks. The young king loved the silks.

"You must have twelve of my finest horses in return," he insisted.

Off went the merchant back to Wali Dad's hut. He didn't know what he was going to do with twelve horses. The merchant suggested that he keep two for himself and send the rest to the young queen.

"What a good idea! Will you help me?" asked Wali Dad. Of course, the merchant agreed to help.

The queen was puzzled. Why was this man sending these gifts? She had never met him. She decided to send back a gift that was so expensive that he could never match it. She sent twenty mules loaded with silver coins.

Again, Wali Dad didn't know what on earth he was going to do with such wealth. He gave two mules with their silver to the merchant and sent the rest to the young king. The merchant wasn't sure, but how could he resist? The king didn't know what to make of it. He decided to send him a gift just like the queen, a gift that he couldn't possibly match. He sent back twenty camels with golden seats on top, and twenty servants to care for them all.

The merchant took quite a while to guide all these to Wali Dad's hut. Wali Dad didn't know what to do. He told the merchant to keep two and send the rest to the young queen.

"I can't go there again," he protested.

Wali Dad insisted, and as usual he agreed.

The queen was stunned by the magnitude of the gifts. She thought that Wali Dad must want to marry her, so she decided to visit him. The merchant raced on ahead to tell Wali Dad she was coming. Wali Dad sank to his knees when he heard the news.

"I'm going to look really stupid, what am I to do?"

The merchant told him there was nothing to be done. Wali Dad could not face the shame of him, just a poor man, meeting the queen. He left his hut forever. He walked along the dusty road, head bowed in shame.

Suddenly he heard a voice.

"Where are you going?"

"I am a stupid man, let me on my way."

He looked up and saw a peris, he knew that a peris was a magical being. The peris touched him on the shoulder, and to his amazement, where his rags had been, fine clothes, now sat, a jewelled turban on his head.

"Return to your home," ordered the peris. Wali Dad looked back towards his home and saw a splendid palace, right where his little hut had been. He looked back, too late! The peris had vanished.

He went back and saw guards, servants, and riches galore. Three servants ran up to him shouting in excitement.

"Caravans coming! From the east and the west!"

A very puzzled Wali Dad looked up and saw the young queen coming from one direction and the young king coming from another direction. Wali Dad rushed to greet the queen first. She was very curious about the king she could see coming their way.

The king greeted Wali Dad, but he was curious about the young queen. Wali Dad introduced them to each other, and can you guess what happened? Of course, they both fell in love. They married a few days later, the celebrations all taking place in Wali Dad's palace. The next day Wali Dad left the palace and set off up the road. Not far along the road, the peris appeared.

" I know I'm foolish, I should be happy with all this wealth, but ...."

"Say no more, you shall have your hearts wishes," said the peris.

The peris touched Wali Dad's shoulder and immediately Wali Dad was back in his little hut, just a grass cutter. He thought very warmly of his new friends the king and queen, but he was happier than he had been in ages. He certainly didn't send any more gifts to them!

Prayer/ Reflection

Think about your most precious possession. What would happen if you didn't have it?

Do you value your friendships? Your family.

Is money the most important possession?

I Know What I Know

Origin

Adapted from I know What I Have Learned, in the Pink Fairy Book, edited by Andrew Lang, Longmans, London, 1897.

Theme

This story is about boasting and not listening, and the price you may have to pay one day, for not listening.

Once upon a time in the land of Denmark, there was a man called Ulf. Ulf had been married a long time and had three grown up daughters. Each of his daughters had married a troll and each of them had gone to live inside a hill.

They had all got married quite a while ago, lovely big weddings. The sad thing was that he had not seen any of them since their weddings. One day Ulf decided to visit his eldest daughter. He set off early and walked until he came to the hill that was her home.

As he neared the top of the hill a door set inside the hill, flew open.

"Welcome!" said his daughter. She was so happy to see him again "Husband, look!" she shouted, "my father's here! Can you go and buy some meat for the stew, quickly please?"

"Why buy what is already owned?" said the troll with confidence.

He did something amazing next. He picked up a wooden mallet and hit himself on the back of the head. His head flew off into the stew pot and as he was a troll, a new head grew on his shoulders. Ulf was shocked and amazed, he had never seen anything like it.

He rushed off home and told his wife all about their eldest daughter and her husband. He told her that he had learned something amazing.
"What have you learned?" she asked with curiosity. He was so annoying, he just smiled at her and said, "I know what I know."

A few days later Ulf's wife decided to make a stew.

"We need some meat, would you go and get me some?"

Ulf smiled and said. "Why buy what is already owned?"

And with that, he picked up a mallet and hit himself on the back of the head.

"Ouchhhhh........" he cried as he fell to the floor.

His wife looked shocked, what on earth was he doing? When he had recovered, his wife asked him why he had hit himself.

"Never you mind, I know what I know."

He spent the next few days recovering in bed. The bump on his head got smaller and smaller. When he felt better he decided to visit his middle daughter. He set off early and walked until he came to her hillside.

Just as before a door flew open and out sprang a very happy daughter. She loved her father and was so happy he was visiting.

"Welcome!" she greeted him. "Husband look! My father's here! Can you go and buy some candles for the table, it will be dark soon."

"Why go far for what is near?" he said very confidently.

Do you know what the troll did next? Well, he put his hand in the fire. Now we all know how dangerous that is. Not for the troll! When he pulled his hand out, his fingers were lit like candles and the room now seemed lovely and bright. Ulf couldn't wait to tell his wife. It was amazing.

When he got home later that evening, he told his wife he had learnt something marvellous.

"What have you learned?" she asked.

Ulf smiled as if he knew a secret, and said, "I know what I know."

A few days later his wife asked him to go shopping for more candles. They only had one left and she knew that wouldn't last for the whole evening.

"Why go far for what is near?" said Ulf.

His wife watched in horror as Ulf put his hand in the fire. He pulled it out pretty quick, screaming in pain. His wife bandaged the hand and helped him to bed. He slept for hours. When he woke up his wife said, "Why on earth did you burn yourself?"

"Never you mind, I know what I know."

He had to keep his hand bandaged for quite a few weeks, eventually his hand healed and the bandages came off. When he felt better he decided to visit his youngest daughter. He set off early and walked until he came to her hill. Just as before, out flew a door, and a very happy daughter.

"Welcome!" she shouted, so happy to see her father. "Husband, my father's here. Can you go and buy some fish for our dinner?"

"Why fetch what will soon arrive?" said the troll.

They walked outside to a well, the troll jumped in, and fish after fish came flying out of the well. It was an amazing sight. The troll sprang out of the well, and they had a wonderful dinner together. Ulf couldn't wait to go home and see his wife.

As usual, when he got home, he boasted to his wife.
"I have learned something amazing," he boasted.

"What have you learned?" she asked, very, very curious.
"I know what I know," he said very smugly.

A few days later his wife asked him to go shopping for some fish for their dinner.

"Why fetch what will soon arrive," he said.

He led her outside to the well and promptly jumped in. She couldn't believe what she was seeing, the well was so deep!

"Help! Help!" he screamed.

His wife lowered the bucket as quickly as she could. Ulf grabbed the rope and climbed into the bucket. It took ages for his wife to pull his heavy weight up. He climbed out and sat shivering on the ground.

His wife was still shocked.

"Why on earth did you jump in the well?"

"Never mind, I know what I know."

"Of course you do, but what is it you know?" she said exasperated.

"I know........, I know........."

He couldn't think what it was he knew. He tried again.

"I know....... I know..........Nothing!"

Prayer / Reflection

Help us all Dear Lord to listen when we need to and to be proud of what we do.
Help us to stop boasting to others.

Amen

The Rabbit's Judgement

Origin

Unknown, retold by Alison Gardner.

Theme

This story looks at how humans treat animals. Do animals have rights? What are they? Kindness or repaying?

Many, many hundreds of years ago, animals and plants used to talk! They talked to each other in the same way that people do nowadays. Well this one day a tiger was roaming back and forth through the forest looking for food. He was starving and all he could think about was food.

He wasn't looking where he was going at all, and in the blink of an eye, he had fallen into a deep pit. He looked up and could only just see the top; the walls were too steep to climb. He paced round and round, shouting loudly for help. After many minutes of shouting his voice went hoarse, it was obvious no one was coming. He lay down and went to sleep, hoping that someone would help him in the morning.

The next morning he called for help, over and over. His voice started to go very sore again. Hungry and exhausted, he slumped down on the ground, thinking he was doomed to die here! Suddenly, he heard footsteps above him. He listened hard, yes! Footsteps!

"Help! Help!" he cried desperately.

"Oh! A tiger!" said a man, as he peered down into the pit.

"Please! Please help me out of this pit!" pleaded the tiger. "If you help me, I won't forget you for as long as I live."

The man looked down into the deep pit, he knew he was terrified of tigers, they ate people!

"I would like to help you, but I'm scared you'll eat me. Please forgive me, I must be on my way," and off he went down the forest track.

"No! No! Please don't think that, I won't hurt you, I promise. Please help me, I'll be grateful to you forever. Please!"

The tiger sounded so desperate, the man felt really sorry for him. He walked back around the pit, looking for a large log. He found a very heavy one and heaved it with all his might into the pit.

"Here, climb up this."

The tiger quickly ran up the log and sprang out of the pit. His mouth was watering with hunger and he started circling the man.

"Hey, stop! You said you wouldn't hurt me, you promised. Is this how you show your gratitude? How you repay a kindness?"

"What do I care about promises? I haven't eaten in ages."

"Wait! Wait!" shouted the man, fear in his voice. "Let's ask that pine tree if it's right for you to eat me."

"All right, but hurry up," said the tiger exasperated. "But after you've asked, I'm going to eat you."

The tiger and the man stood underneath the pine tree and explained what had happened.

"What do human beings know about being grateful? They take our leaves and limbs to make fires to heat their houses, and cook their food."

The man paled as he listened, he knew the pine tree was right.

"It takes years for us to grow big, and when we finally do, you cut us down, and make furniture from us!

The man started to argue a little, saying he hadn't known the trees minded.

"Also, it was a human being that dug that pit. Gratefulness indeed! Don't give it another thought tiger, go ahead and eat him up!"

The tiger turned to face the man, licking his lips in anticipation.

"Now what do you think of that?" smirked the tiger.

Just at that moment, an ox wandered by.

"Wait! Wait!" cried the man, desperate to save himself. "Let's ask that ox to judge?"

The tiger agreed reluctantly, he thought he couldn't lose. They explained what had happened to the ox and asked his opinion.

"Well as far as I am concerned, there's no question about what to do," snorted the ox. "Eat him up. Human beings work oxen too hard. They make us carry heavy loads on our backs and plough the ground on farms. And what do they do when we are old, too old to work? Kill us, that's what they do. Eat our flesh and use our hides for shoes!"

The man thought his time was up, he was going to die. But then a rabbit came bouncing by.

"Wait! Wait!' shouted the man, as loud as he could. "Let's ask that rabbit to judge, just give me one more chance, please!"

"You know the answer will be the same," rattled the tiger. He was fed up now and just wanted to get on and eat him.

"Please! Please!" pleaded the man.

"Oh all right," relented the tiger.

They told their story to the rabbit. The rabbit listened very carefully, and then closed his eyes as if deep in thought.

"I understand what you have told me, but I need you to explain again over by the pit, I need to make a very wise judgement."

They all marched over to the pit and looked into its depths. The man was so scared.

"Well, it certainly is deep," said the rabbit.

He asked them to stand where they were when it happened. The tiger jumped straight into the pit, he just wanted to get it all over and done with.

"Ah, so this is how it was, a tiger stuck and the man helping him out after hearing his cries for help. Now I can judge."

The rabbit turned and looked as if he was speaking to an invisible person.

"If the man hadn't shown any kindness, well, there wouldn't be a problem, would there?"

The tiger looked up ready to hear the rest.

"Well, I think the man should continue his journey and the tiger should stay in the pit. Now a good day to you both," and off bounced the clever rabbit.

Prayer / Reflection

Why was the man kind to the tiger?

Can you think of a time when you have repaid a kindness?

Today if someone is kind to you, remember it and try to think of a way to repay it.

The King Who Hated to Have His Hair Cut

Origin

This story is an ancient tale from Ireland.

Theme

The king hides a terrible secret and is ashamed about a certain part of his body. He doesn't like being different. The story will promote discussion on difference and being proud of who you are.

Long ago in a town called Leinster, there was a king called Lab Lonsett. This king always had his hair long, even though fashions had changed and now short hair was the fashionable thing. His clothes were new and fashionable but his hair...........yuk!

He only had it cut once a year, on the first day of spring, and that was a day everyone in his kingdom feared. The king always had a new barber every year too! Can you imagine why?

Once a man cut the king's hair, he was never seen again, and soon the people suspected the king. The various barbers' disappearances couldn't be linked to anyone else.

Now there was a very poor woman in Leinster, her husband had died and she had one son whom she adored. He had looked after her as well as he could since his father had died, shining shoes, cleaning stables, cutting hair.

The king chose her son, Anton to cut his hair. Anton's mum begged the king to choose someone else. The king was so moved by her love for her son, that he promised her son would return to her. He went into the inner chamber to tell him to return home, but before he knew what was happening Anton had removed his headband ready for the haircut, all nervous and eager to please.

As soon as Anton removed the king's headband, two ears just like those of a donkey, sprang up. He didn't know where to look!

"Don't just stand there gaping at me," the king cried. "Swear that you will never tell anyone what you have seen, as long as you live, **Swear it!**"

Anton promised the king and then cut the king's hair as neatly as he could, his hands shaking with fear.

As promised the king let Anton return home, but Anton had terrible nightmares. His mother couldn't understand what had happened to him. Eventually his mother persuaded him to seek help from a priest. The priest listened carefully to what Anton told him.

"He has a secret which is killing him, he will never be well until he has told it," whispered the priest to his mother.

To Anton he said. "Your secret must be told. Follow the high road until you reach a crossroads, and then turn right. At the first tree you come to, tell your secret."

Anton did exactly as he was told and he whispered his secret very quietly to the tree trunk. He already felt much better and off he went home, looking forward to a good night's sleep.

The very next day Peter the palace musician broke his harp. He had to play for the king that very evening! He set off with his axe in search of a sturdy tree to make a new one. When he came to the crossroads he turned right and saw the strong willow tree, just the wood for a beautiful harp. He wasted no time and cut it down.

His harp was made a few hours later; he looked at it with satisfaction. He was now ready to play for the king's guests that evening.

He sat down and ran his fingers over the strings, instead of beautiful music a voice rang out!

"King Lonsett has donkey's ears!"

Peter stopped playing immediately and the king's guests all stared at their plates in embarrassment. Suddenly the king snatched off his headband and shouted.

"Now you all know my secret, but am I any different, just because you've seen my terrible secret?"

The guests sat in stunned silence for a minute, and then they started talking amongst themselves and decided that the king had always been a good and wise king and that a good and wise king with donkey ears was better than a wicked or foolish king with beautiful ears.

The king was relieved to have his secret out in the open; he didn't need to hide his ears under his hair anymore. He had his hair cut regularly by Anton and his straggly long hair was a thing of the past. No barber was ever put to death in his kingdom and the people celebrated the old hair cutting day as a National Holiday, dancing and eating all over the kingdom.

Prayer / Reflection

Sit and think for a moment about what makes you special, or different from everyone else.

The Black Snake and the Eggs

Origin

This is a tale retold from Panchatantra. Panchatantra is a collection of folk tales from different states in India.

Theme

This story is about stealing. Snake stole mercilessly, but was too sure of himself and came to a sticky end.

Did you know that snakes love to eat eggs, well they do! And they swallow them whole, down in one, shell and all.

Chicken was sitting happily on her nest. She had laid twelve eggs and was very proud of herself. This particular morning she woke up, stretched and looked around, and then as usual, she checked her eggs.

"My eggs!" she cried. "One of my eggs is missing! I had twelve yesterday, there's only eleven today."

She fled her nest to look for Rooster. What she didn't realise was that she was about to lose more eggs to a very nasty thief. Just out of sight was a thief, waiting very patiently for the chicken to leave her nest. Then he would strike! This nasty thief was a Black Snake. He crept up, slithering very quietly, very slowly, right up to the nest. He looked in and spied a tasty one right near him, and in an instant he swallowed it whole.

He smiled to himself. He knew his plan had worked. It had been a really simple plan, and it worked every time. He swallowed another egg; it slithered down his long throat with the muscles working to crush the shell, so he could enjoy the egg. He was feeling a little full now and slithered down to the ground.

"I'll be back later for another delicious egg, Chicken, a very fine meal indeed!"

During all this time Chicken had been crying to Rooster about the missing egg. She came hurriedly back, rooster in tow.

"Why would someone take my eggs?" she clucked to Rooster.

"Let's count them again, you might have made a mistake," suggested rooster.

Rooster knew he shouldn't have said that. Chicken looked really upset now.

She glared at him and said, "I can count you know, and I know how many eggs I counted. See for yourself, go on!"

Rooster began to count. "One, two, three, four, five." He frowned and stopped counting.

"What's the matter, don't you want to tell me I'm right?" asked Chicken.

"No, it's not that. I can only count nine eggs!"

"What? Nine eggs!" cried Chicken. "What's happening? Who would steal my eggs?"

Chicken was desperately upset for the next few days. She worried about the remaining nine eggs. She didn't want to leave them, but at times she had to leave to get food. Every time she left the nest, the same thing happened, one or two eggs would go missing each time.

"Someone is watching me all the time," cried the chicken. "They know exactly when I leave my nest. I've only got three eggs left."

Rooster explained to Chicken about Black Snake, how patient he is, and how he loves chicken eggs. Just the thought made Chicken shudder, but she knew Rooster was probably right. She'd heard stories about Black Snake, how he swallowed the eggs whole and slowly crushed them with his neck muscles.

"I must hurry back to my nest," shouted Chicken, worrying what was happening to her eggs, right now!

Too late! When she got back she rushed into her nest and found......... only one egg left. Two more eggs had gone!

"Come help me Rooster," she shouted. "I've only one egg left!"

Rooster hurried over. "Black Snake will steal your last egg tomorrow unless you have a plan to trap him," said Rooster sensibly.

"What can I do? How can I stop Black Snake?"

"I have a plan," whispered Rooster. "I think it will work."

The next morning Chicken sat on her nest guarding her last egg. Black Snake was watching from a distance, what he didn't realise was that a trap had been set for him. He licked his lips in anticipation. He was really hungry, and did so love chicken eggs!

Chicken left her nest for a short while, and of course, out slithered Black Snake, into the nest, egg straight down, slithering, slithering down his long throat. When his muscles tightened to crush the egg, it didn't break. Not only didn't it break, it got firmly stuck in his throat.

He twisted and turned, trying to crush it or loosen it. Nothing he did worked, he thrashed around trying to breathe. The egg was cutting off his air. By the time Rooster and Chicken returned, Black Snake was dead. Chicken knew she could have lots more eggs and they wouldn't disappear this time.

"I'm sure he died never knowing why that egg wouldn't crush," crowed Rooster.

"How could he have known," clucked Chicken, "that the egg was hard boiled?"

Prayer / Reflection

Think for a moment about a time when you thought about stealing something or you actually did steal something.

Did you feel bad afterwards?

How do you think someone feels when they have something stolen from them?

The Talkative Tortoise

Origin

Retold from the 'Panchatantra' folk tales from different states in India.

Theme

This story emphasises the importance of being able to hold your tongue when needed. It is a fun look at what could happen if you don't.

Once upon a time there was a tortoise with a beautiful shell for its home. She lived in an old farmyard right next to a pond. The pond had two ducks living on it and they had become her friends. She loved talking to them, she talked all day. She had something to say about everything and she loved the sound of her own voice.

They lived together for years, getting on quite well and staying good friends. Each year the water in the pond got lower and lower, until finally it dried up. The two ducks knew they would have to move to somewhere else, they needed lots of water to live. They went to the tortoise and told her they were leaving to find a new home.

"Don't leave me behind!" begged the tortoise.

"You can't fly," said the ducks.

They felt so sorry for her that eventually they came up with a plan. They told her that she would have to keep very still. They would each hold one end of a strong stick in their mouths. She would go in the middle and hold the stick in her mouth. They could then fly up in the air with her and carry her to a new home.

"Remember, you mustn't talk, if you open your mouth you will fall."

She promised not to say a single word, and not to move at all. She was desperate to go with them. She felt very grateful to her friends. The ducks found a really strong stick and positioned themselves ready. They reminded her again about talking. They knew how much she loved to talk.

Off they all set. What a sight they looked. They flew high above the treetops. Tortoise was dying to say. "Look how high I am."

But she remembered what would happen and just stopped herself in time.

They started to fly high above the church; she was dying to shout.

"Look at me, look at me," but she stopped herself just in time.

Next they flew over the village square, lots of people looked up at the strange sight. They shouted up into the sky.

"Look at those ducks carrying a tortoise."

She was dying to shout back,"Mind your own business!" But she stopped herself, only just in time. She could still hear the villagers shouting up.

"Look at it, look at it. Isn't it strange!"

Tortoise felt angry now and she started to forget everything she had been told. She wanted to tell them all to shut up and go away. In a flash she opened her mouth, and, well I think you know the rest of the story.

Isn't it a good thing that we can hold our tongue when we want to?

Prayer / Reflection

Think about a time when you should have held your tongue but didn't. Picture it in your mind.

Can you remember what happened?

Did it teach you a little lesson?

Perhaps we should all think before we speak.

Why the Evergreen Trees Keep their Leaves in Winter

Origin

This story is adapted from Florence Holbrook's, 'A Book of Nature Myths', Harrap Co.

Theme

This story relates to nature and could be told around Christmas. It focuses on selfishness and kindness, helping others.

Many, many years ago winter was on the way, each day was colder than the last one. Some mornings there was a smattering of frost on the trees, your breath would hang in the air, just briefly. All the birds started to fly south to warmer countries; they would be back in the spring. Just one poorly little bird was left, left all on his own.

This little bird had a broken wing and couldn't fly. He watched all his friends fly off, what could he do? He felt tears sting his eyes as the last lot of the birds disappeared from his view. He realised he'd have to look for somewhere warm to settle for the winter. The trees looked warm so off he hopped, fluttering his broken wing. He looked a sad sight.

The first tree he came to was a very tall silver birch.

"Beautiful birch tree, can I live in your warm branches until spring?"

"I have enough problems without you, my leaves disappear! Now go away!"

The little bird felt sadder than ever, no one wanted him.

He kept hopping through the trees looking for a warm spot. He came to a really strong oak tree, it was huge, its trunk wider than he had ever seen.

"Strong oak tree, can I live in your branches until spring?"

"If you stay in my branches you will eat all my acorns, now go away!"

He carried on hopping and fluttering his broken wing. His wing felt heavy and sore now. It would never heal if he keeps on hopping and not resting.

He hopped and hopped until he saw a beautiful shaped tree; its branches hanging towards the floor like a fountain. Its leaves were a lovely pale green. He hopped towards it, looked up and said.

"Oh lovely, lovely willow tree, can I live in your branches until spring?"

He looked up hopefully.

"I don't speak to strangers, now go away!"

The poor little bird didn't know where to go next. No one wanted him and winter was coming.

He hopped and fluttered along, his wing now dragging on the floor. He was so tired. He kept hopping and hopping, not really looking where he was going.

"Where are you going little bird?" said a spruce tree. It was a beautiful spruce, the Christmas kind, although a little too large for a house at Christmas.

"I don't know, no one wants me. None of the trees will let me live in them until spring."

The spruce looked down at the sad little bird. He looked so tired and worn out.

"You can live in my branches, here, this one's got the most leaves on," he said, lifting a laden branch down towards the little bird.

"Can I stay until the spring?"

"Of course, you can keep me company."

A chunky pine tree stood next to the spruce, he had been listening to what was happening.

"My branches aren't very warm but the wind can't get through me, I'll keep the wind off you in the winter."

The little bird felt so happy, he struggled up into the spruce tree, flying a little, then collapsing on a branch. The pine tree worked hard keeping the wind off him.

A juniper tree nearby had also heard what had been going on. She leant her branches towards the bird and asked if he was hungry.

"You can eat my berries in the winter, they are just the job for little birds."

The trees started talking amongst themselves.

"I wouldn't look after a strange bird," said the birch.

"I wouldn't either, he would eat my acorns," said the oak.

"I don't speak to strangers," whispered the willow.

The three trees swayed in the wind feeling quite proud of themselves.

That night the North wind came, howling fiercely around the trees. He puffed his icy breath at the trees, making them bend and toss wildly. He was determined to get all the leaves off the trees. He loved it when the trees were bare.

"Can I get every leaf?" he asked his dad, the Frost King.

"No!" shouted the Frost King. "The trees that were kind to the little bird with the broken wing must be left to keep their leaves."

North Wind had to do as he was told. He blew on all the trees apart from the Christmas spruce, the chunky pine and the juniper tree. They kept their leaves all winter, and still do right to this very day.

Prayer / Reflection

Dear Lord,
Help us to think of others,
to show kindness.
Help us to appreciate other peoples' kindness towards us.
Amen

The Little Jackals and the Lion

Origin

This story is rewritten from Stories in Old Deccan Days, a collection of orally told Hindu folk tales. In these tales the Jackal always plays the role of clever and humorous trickster and always ends up winning in any situation.

Theme

This story looks at fear and bullying. The lion also portrays very boastful characteristics, which are his undoing.

Once upon a time a huge lion ruled in a great jungle. He was king and all the animals obeyed him and were very scared of him. Whenever he was hungry he came out of his lair, looked around and roared fiercely. He could be heard for miles. All the people that lived in the jungle were terrified and ran away as fast as they could.

While they were running, the lion watched them, choosing someone for his dinner. He would lay in wait, pounce and gobble them up. Now he was a very hungry lion and he ate often. Eventually he had eaten nearly everything in the jungle, only two little jackals were left, and himself of course.

The two little jackals were a father and a mother jackal. They had run away from the lion everyday but now it seemed their luck had run out. On this particular day the mother jackal was really frightened.

"The lion will catch us this time, I know he will!"

"Nonsense, mother, come on let's run as fast as we can."

They ran for a while, until they were really tired, then they settled at the base of a tree. They had escaped for one more day.

The next day they heard the lion's roar, terror ran through them. His roar had seemed really near and a lot fiercer than usual. They knew he would be really hungry by now.

"He'll catch us today, I know he will," cried the mother jackal.

"No he won't, do just as I tell you and we'll be alright," said father jackal calmly. They could see the lion waiting for them ahead.

"Take my tail and hold tight," whispered father jackal.

They ran straight at the lion, he roared.

"Come on here, I'm hungry! Why did you take so long to answer my roar?"

The lion was used to all creatures coming for his roar, he was king of the jungle after all.

"We were going to come before, but each time a great big lion came out of the trees and roared at us," father jackal answered confidently.

"What?!!!" roared the lion, shaking all the trees near him, "I'm the only lion in this jungle, me! I'm king!" The lion was furious.

"You're wrong, the lion was bigger than you, his roar louder," shouted father jackal.

The lion insisted they take him to this lion, he was determined to eat him too. The jackals ran ahead and led the angry lion to a deep well. You could see deep clear water in it.

"He lives down there," cried father jackal excitedly.

The lion looked down and sure enough, a lion's face looked back at him. He roared and shook his mane fiercely, showing his vicious teeth. The lion in the water did the same back to him. He was furious; he was king, the biggest, and the best. Do you know what he did? He jumped straight into the well towards the other lion. We all know how foolish that was. There was no other lion, just his reflection in the water.

The jackals danced around the well.

"The lion is gone! The lion is gone!"

Prayer / Reflection

In this story the lion wanted to always be the boss. He loved roaring and scaring others.

Can you think of people you know who behave like this?

Some people behave like this to their friends.

How do you think friends feel when they are constantly bossed around?

The Boy who Cried Wolf!

Origin

This story has been retold from Aesop's Fables.

Theme

Telling lies gets you labelled as a liar; eventually no one will believe anything you say.

There was once a young shepherd boy who had hundreds of sheep to look after. He would take them up on the hills for a few days, then bring them back down when the weather looked bad. His wasn't the only flock of sheep in the village, so he had to share the land wisely.

Now, the village he lived in was quite small. Everyone knew each other. Everyone in the village knew the shepherd boy; they had watched him grow to nearly a teenager. On this one particular day he decided to play a trick on the villagers. He thought it was always fun to play tricks on others.

He thought for a while, he wanted a really good trick. He had it! He ran as fast as he could towards the village shouting.

"A wolf! A wolf! Help! It's getting my lambs!"

The villagers were a kind group of people and of course, they ran immediately out of their homes to help the shepherd boy. They ran as fast as they could towards the shepherd boy and his flock. When they got there, well you can imagine how they felt when they knew they had been tricked. There they were, nearly all the villagers, young and old, and a shepherd boy running around laughing.

About a week later the boy did the trick again. He couldn't resist, he had had so much fun last time. He tried to shout even louder this time.

"A Wolf! Help! Help!"

Of course all the villagers ran out to help him. They knew his family and how important the flock was to them. Wolves could eat quite a few sheep if they were really hungry. They all got there, and again, no wolf. They were furious; he had wasted their time and worried them all for nothing, yet again. Worst of all, there he was, running around laughing.

Then one day, in the middle of winter, can you imagine what happened? A wolf did find the flock and started to attack the sheep. The boy ran as fast as he could towards the village. His lungs were bursting.

"A Wolf! Help! He's attacking the flock!"

The villagers all heard his shouts, but this time they thought it was another of his tricks. They ignored his shouts and went about their business. Not one person went to help him.

The shepherd boy shouted and shouted, but it was no use. He ran back to the flock and saw that he had lost lots of sheep. And that is the kind of thing that happens to people who lie, eventually, even when they are telling the truth, no one believes them.

Prayer / Reflection

Dear Lord,

Please help us to tell the truth, even when it will get us into trouble.

Help us to find the courage and the words.

Amen

MENTAL MA
A MASTER FILE
KEY STAGE 1

Compiled by

D C Perkins, BA (Hons), MEd, PhD (Wales) and **E J Perkins,** BSc (Hons), MEd

Illustrations **Anthony James**

Educational Adviser **Alison John, BEd**

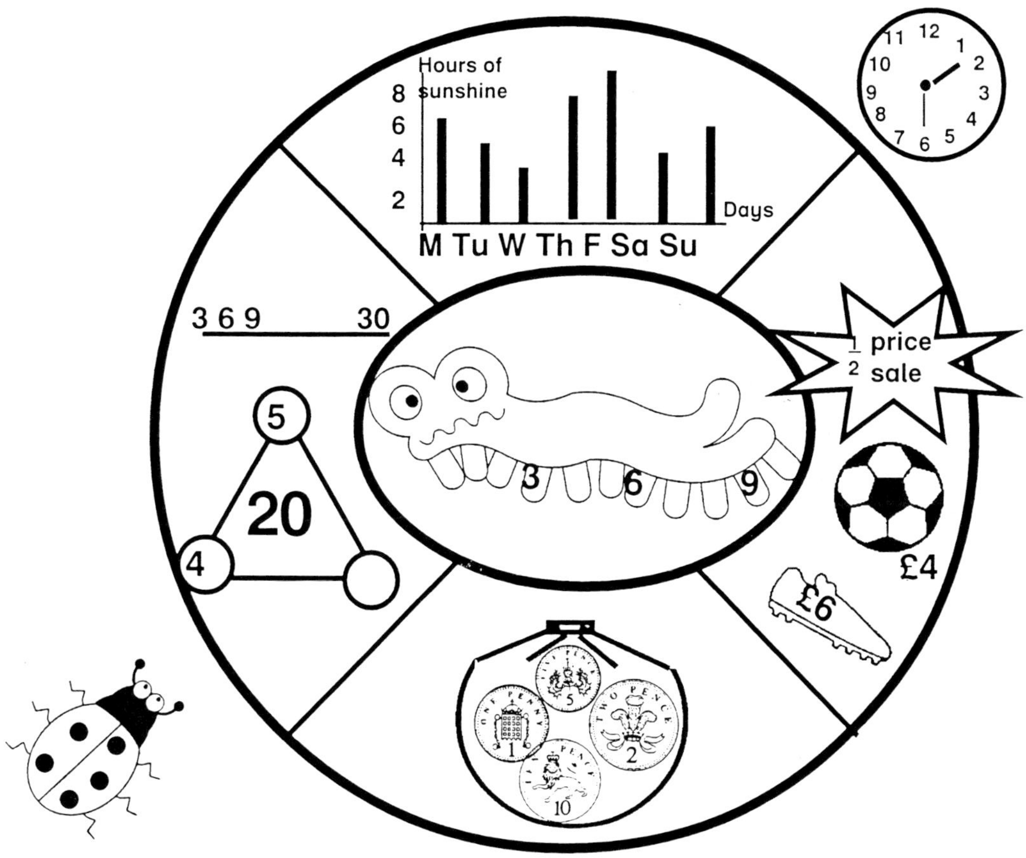

DOMINO BOOKS (WALES) Ltd

Swansea SA1 1FN

Tel: 01792 459378 Fax: 01792 466337

Mental Maths KS1 Master File © EJP & DCP 2000

ISBN 1 85772 154 3

CONTENTS 1

PUPILS' RESOURCE/WORKSHEETS

Subjects are listed at the bottom of each activity sheet

Teachers Notes and Resources Contents on next page

CONTENTS 2

TEACHERS' NOTES AND RESOURCES

HOW TO USE YOUR MASTER FILE

For many experienced teachers these few lines will seem superfluous. This book is intended to help children begin to learn to handle numbers and the concepts of number. The development of mental skills is essential for children to develop numeracy skills. Work in the National Numeracy Project shows that giving time to oral and mental maths leads to a raising of standards in numeracy. It is important for children to be able to explain and discuss the ways in which they arrive at answers although if a child says that he or she just 'knows', then usually this should be accepted. It soon becomes clear if the child really understands or not.

The activities in this book have been planned with the concepts underlying ***the Framework of Objectives of the National Numeracy Project.*** Obviously, the ways in which the activities are used depends on the age, ability and experience of the children and the resources available. We do not envisage any problems choosing appropriate material.

1. All the material in this book is photocopiable as defined on the first page. This means that all the material can be used in any way you wish. Drawings can be photocopied and adapted for further work.

2. Covering sections of the master copies with plain paper enables resource material to be used in different ways. This is useful when it is felt that the material on one sheet should be used at different times especially with children who are slower at learning.

3. The master copies can be enlarged to A3 making it easier for several children to work on them at the same time.

4. Some of the photocopies can be cut to make additional puzzles and games.

5. It is intended that the material should be used selectively depending on the ages and abilities of the children.

6. Much of the completed work may be used as visual aids around the classroom.

7. Remember, there are often several ways in which problems can be tackled.

8. Mathematics is important in most subjects and these links underpin some of the reasons for learning the subject. There is latitude and longitude and navigation in geography, dating discoveries in history and archaeology, computer work and information technology. Concepts learned now are essential later in engineering, architecture, economics, all the sciences ... Where practical, links with other subjects should be used.

The photocopiable activity sheets are based on recent research into the most commonly used mental strategies. They can be used as

the basis for the discussion of mathematical activities and strategies.

the basis for mathematical activities.

the basis of oral work.

illustrated answer sheets to reinforce what the children are being asked to do orally.

the basis of assessment and understanding of work done.

Sessions for oral and mental maths usually last for about five to ten minutes, not including the time needed to organise the children. It is important to go fast enough to keep the interest of the children but at this stage the emphasis is on understanding the work and not on the time taken. Allow a reasonable, generous time.

The activities in this book encourage children to use and build upon the information they already have and to develop the application of maths in everyday situations. Good counting practices underpin much of mathematics: methods and strategies acquired now will develop good habits. Often problems in quite advanced work stems from poor understanding of basic work. Throughout, the work is planned so that the children can think about the ways and means for solving the problems.

Strategies are discussed in detail in the Teachers' Notes at the end of the book.

Name______________________________

Shadows

Match the animals and their shadows.
Draw lines or cut out the cards.

Name ____________________

Teapots and Teacups

Match the teapots and teacups
Draw lines or cut them out.

Name____

Patterns

Add two more to these patterns.

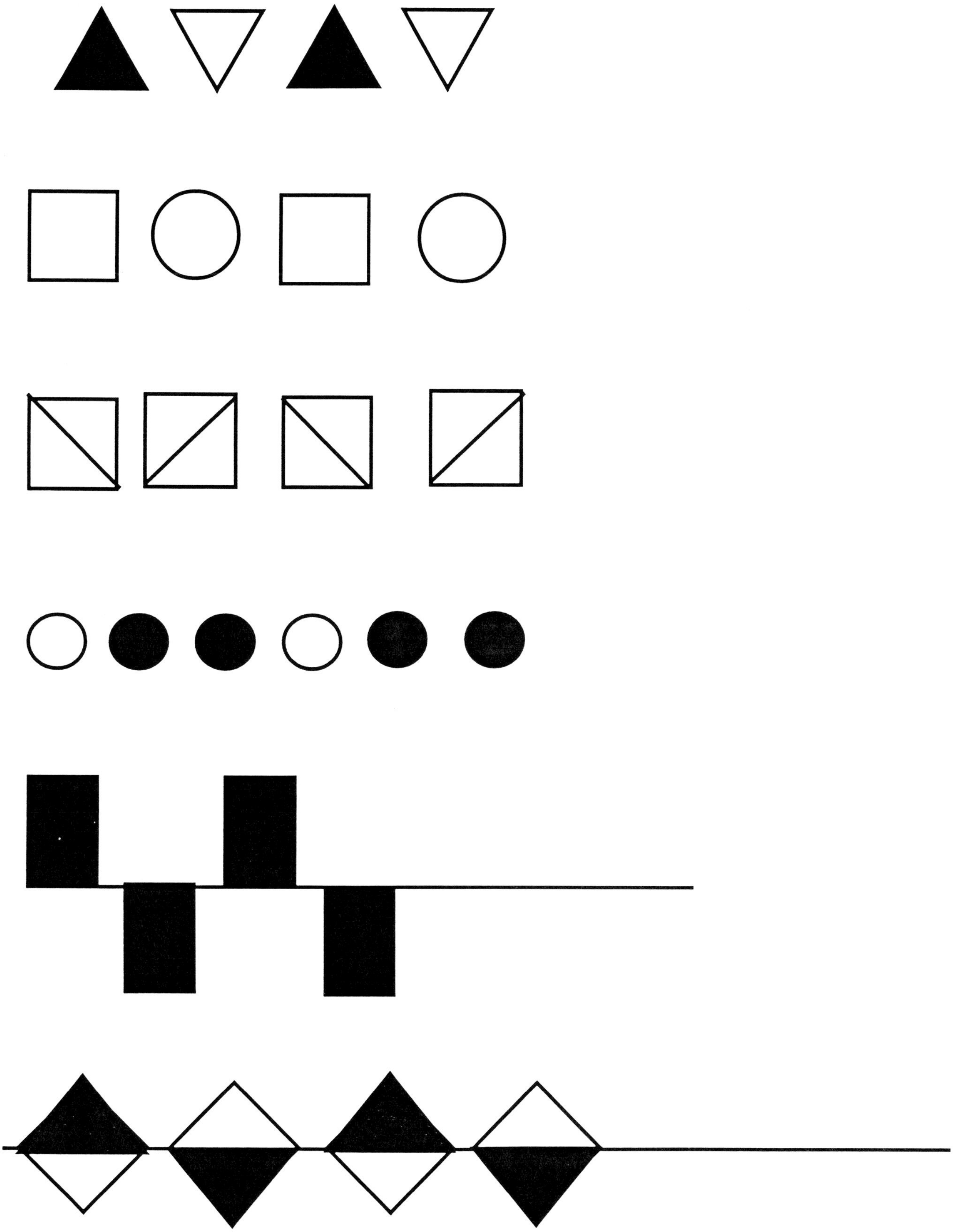

Name ______________________________

Find the Next Number

What number comes next?

1 ____

1 2 ____

1 2 3 ____

1 2 3 4 ____

Find the missing numbers.

1 ☐ 3 ☐ 5

Name ______________________________

How Many?

How many rabbits in this set?

rabbits

How many mice in this set?

mice

How many tigers in this set?

tigers

How many dogs in this set?

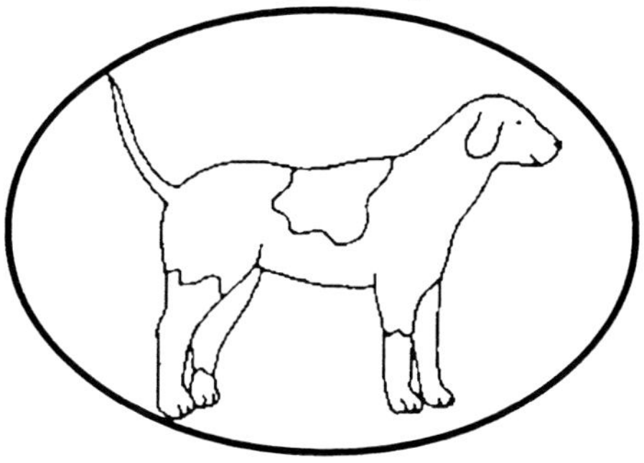

dog

How many swans in this set?

swans

Name ______________________________

Colour the Animals

Colour 2 teddies brown.

Colour 5 pigs black.

Colour 3 tigers red.

Colour 1 snail green.

Colour 4 mice pink.

Name____________________

Count the Spots

How many spots on each ladybird?

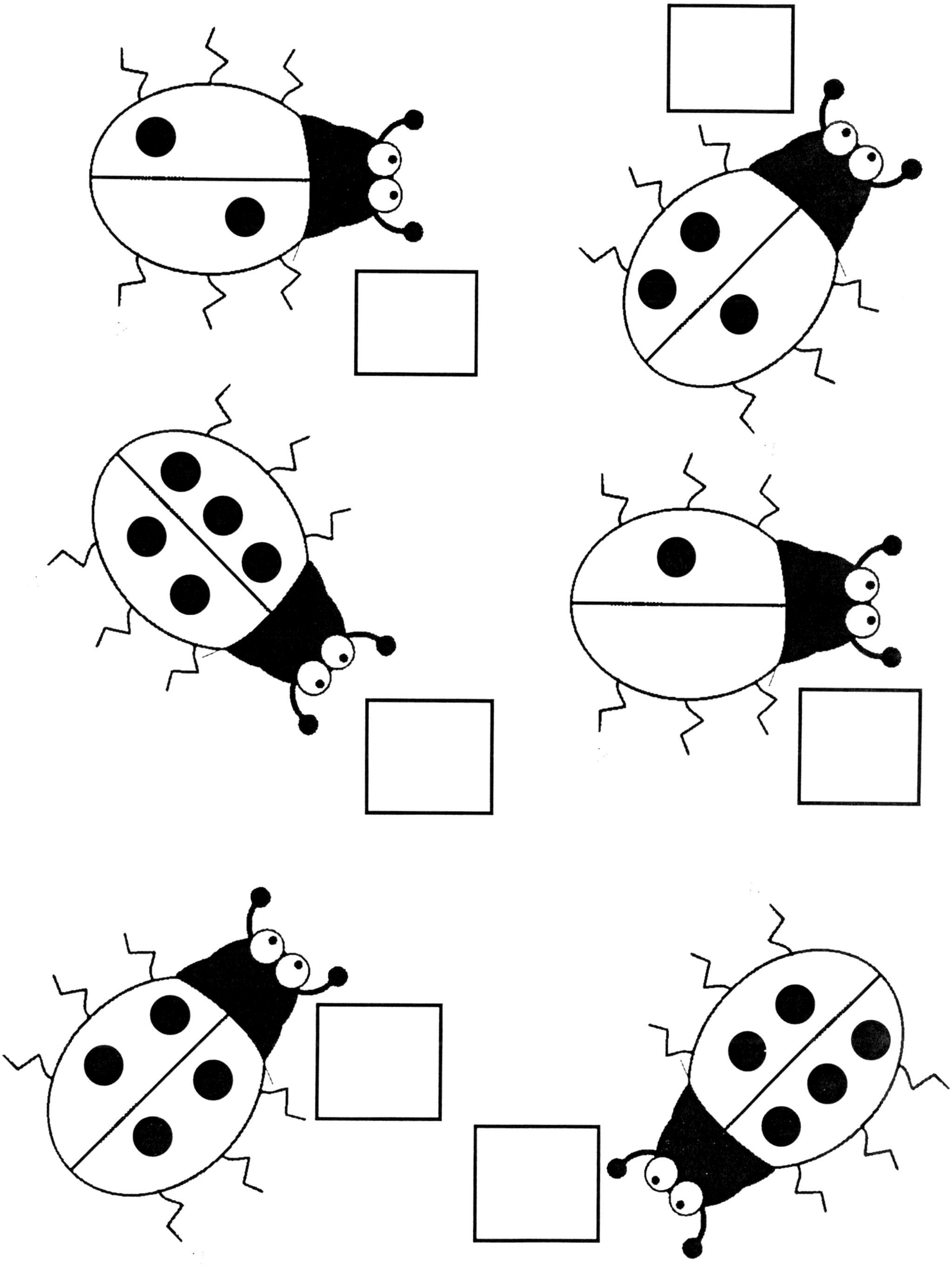

Name____

Zero Sets

Tick (√) the sets that have zero in them.

Name____

Sets

Colour the sets of 1 red.
Colour the sets of 3 blue.
Colour sets of 5 green.

Name ____

Sets

Colour the sets of 1 purple.
Colour the sets of 2 green.
Colour the sets of 4 orange.

Name_______________________________________

Sets

There are sheep in this field.
Draw rings to make 5 sets of 2 sheep.

This is a swarm of bees.
Draw rings to make 4 sets of 3 bees.

Name ______________________________

Missing Numbers

Find the missing numbers.

1		3	4	5
1	2	3		5
1	2		4	5
	2	3	4	
1		3		5
	2		4	

Name____

Counting to 10

Write the next two numbers.

1 2 ______________

1 2 3 ______________

1 2 3 4 ______________

1 2 3 4 5 ______________

1 2 3 4 5 6 ______________

1 2 3 4 5 6 7 ______________

1 2 3 4 5 6 7 8 ______________

Name ______________________________

Sets

How many in each set?

cats

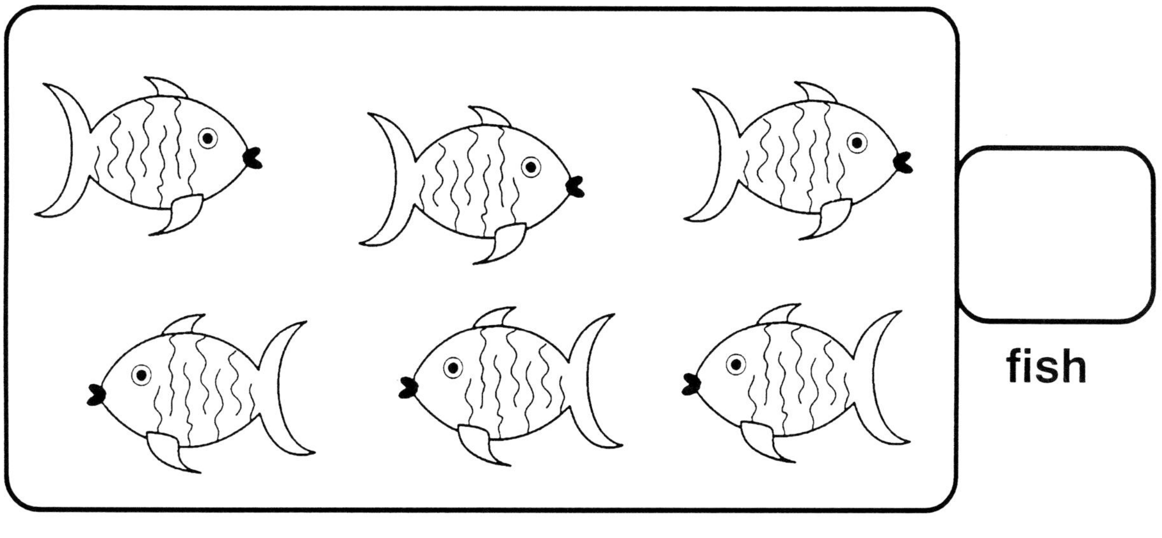

fish

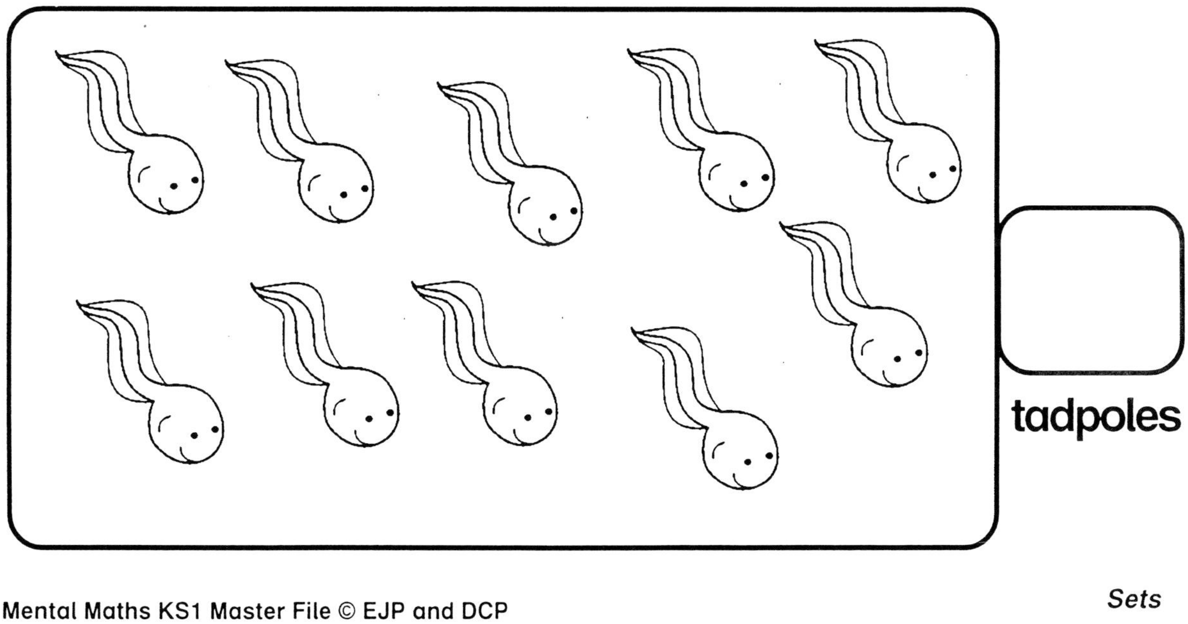

tadpoles

Name________________________________

Counting to 5

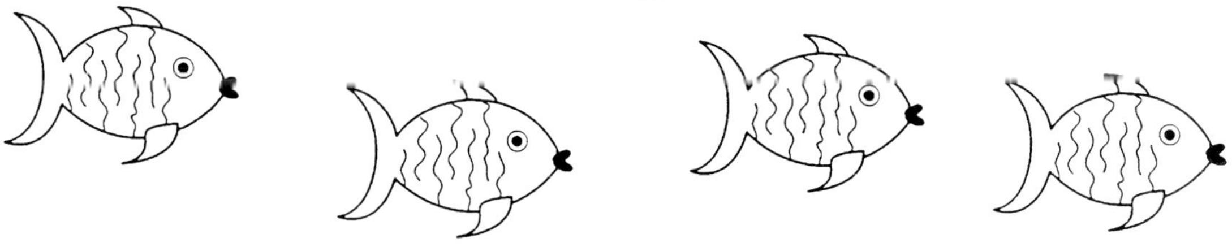

I only want 2, cross out the fish I don't want.

I only want 1, cross out the snowmen I don't want.

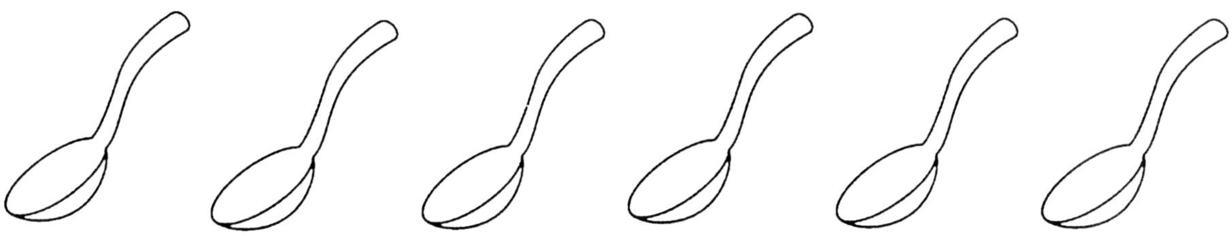

I only want 5, cross out the spoons I don't want.

I only want 3, cross out the lions I don't want.

I only want 4, cross out the teddies I don't want.

Name ______________________________

Counting to 10

I only want 6, cross out the bees I don't want.

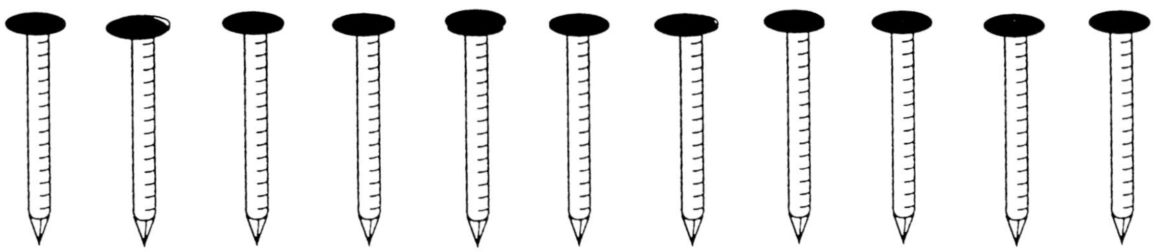

I only want 10, cross out the nails I don't want.

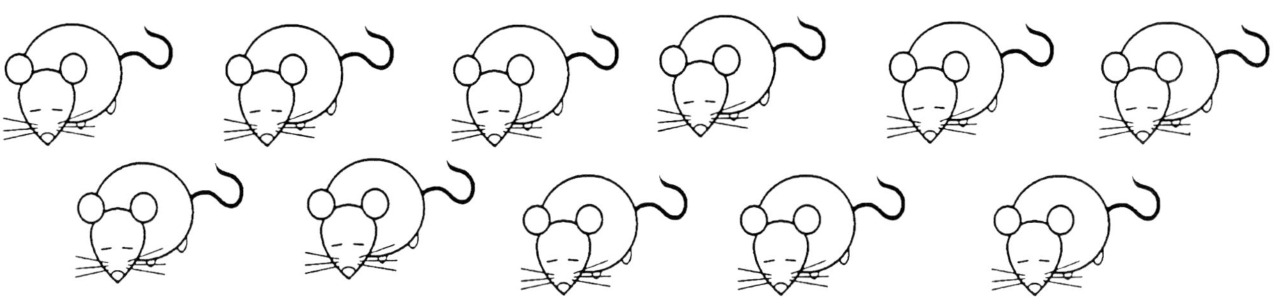

I only want 8, cross out the mice I don't want.

I only want 7, cross out the bottles I don't want.

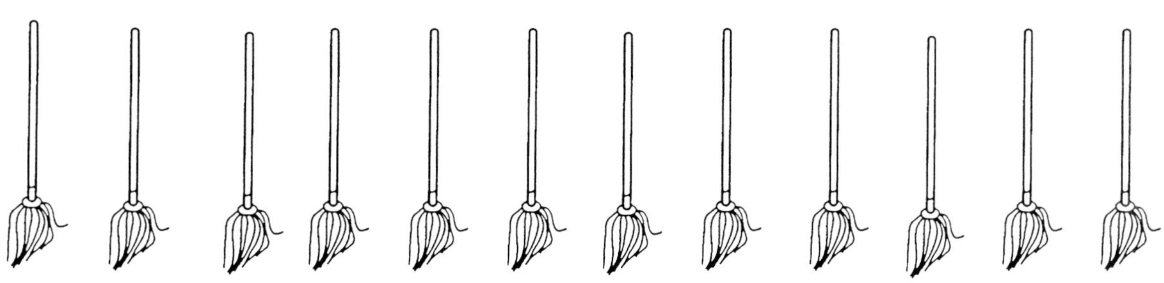

I only want 9, cross out the mops I don't want.

Name____

Make 10

Draw more spots to make 10 spots on each ladybird.

How many did you draw?

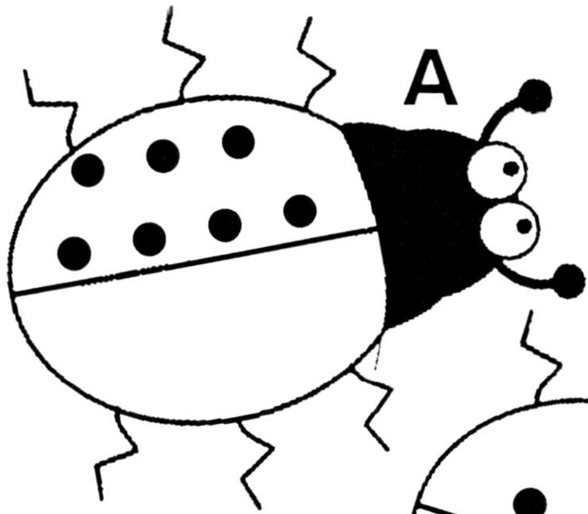

A __________

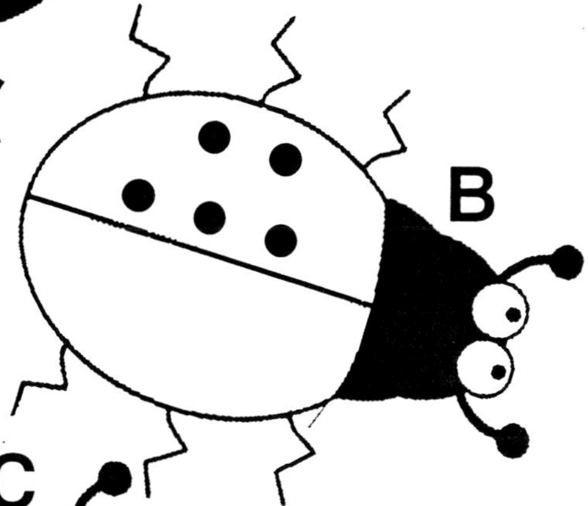

B __________

C __________

D __________

E __________

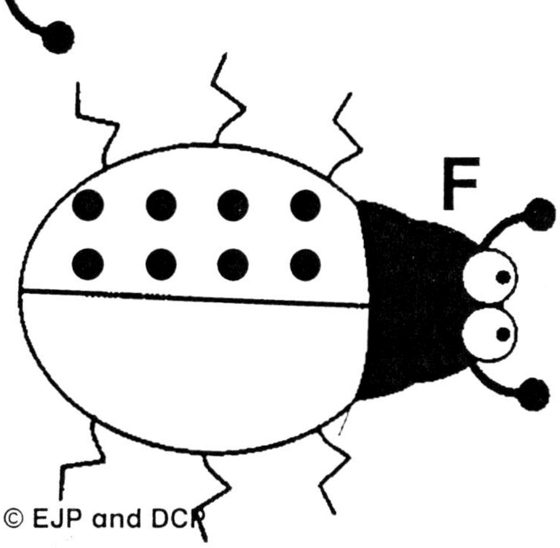

F __________

Name ________________________________

Counting On

Say then write the three numbers that come next.

1 ______ ______ ______

6 ______ ______ ______

4 ______ ______ ______

2 ______ ______ ______

5 ______ ______ ______

3 ______ ______ ______

7 ______ ______ ______

Name ______________________________

Numbers in Between

Say then write the number that comes between 1 and 3.

1 ____ 3

Say then write the number that comes between 7 and 9.

7 ____ 9

Say then write the number that comes between 2 and 4

2 ____ 4

Say then write the number that comes between 5 and 7.

5 ____ 7

Say then write the number that comes between 8 and 10.

8 ____ 10

Say then write the number that comes between 3 and 5.

3 ____ 5

Say then write the number that comes between 6 and 8.

6 ____ 8

Say then write the number that comes between 4 and 6.

4 ____ 6

Name ______________________________

Missing Numbers

Fill in the missing numbers.

A

B

C

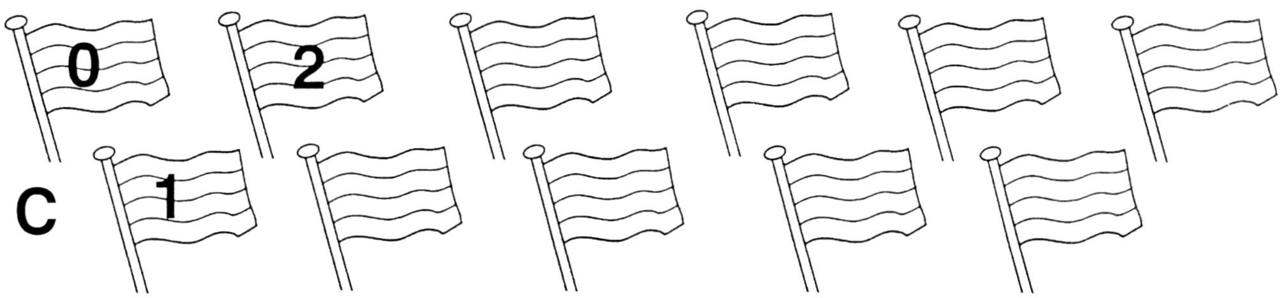

D

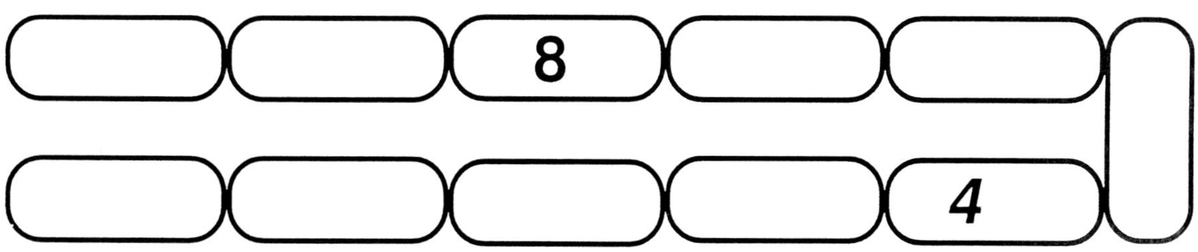

E

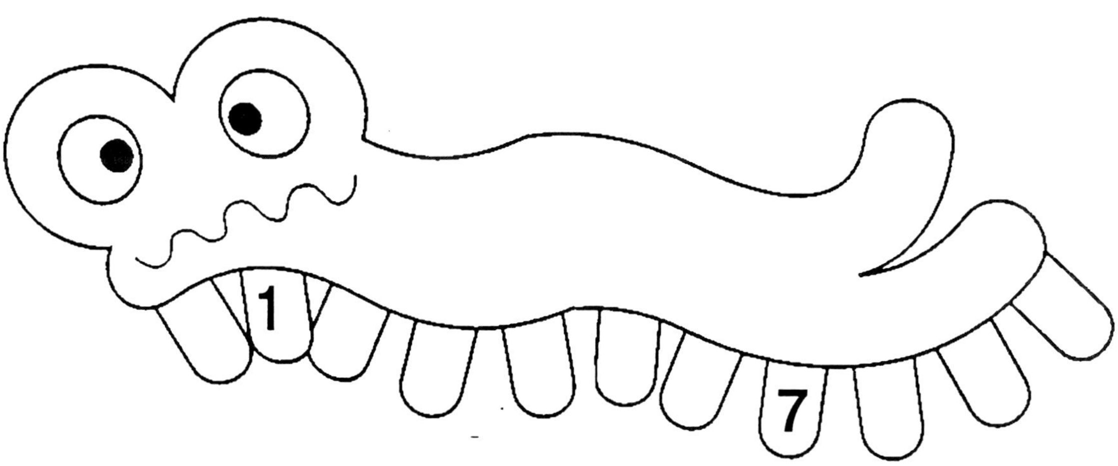

Name______________________________________

Number Pairs to 5

Join the pairs of numbers that add up to 5.

3 1 4 2 5 Write these numbers in the correct order.
1

Name ____________________

Number Pairs to 10

Join the pairs of numbers that add up to 10.

6 3 7 10 2 9 5 1 4 8 Write these numbers in the correct order beginning with 1

Name___________________________________

Counting to 10

Jane and her mother went shopping for her birthday party. Colour the things they bought.

They bought

9 cakes,

a birthday cake with 4 candles,

7 packets of sweets,

and 5 surprise parcels.

Name ______________________________

1p Coins

Colour the coins you would use to buy each of these.

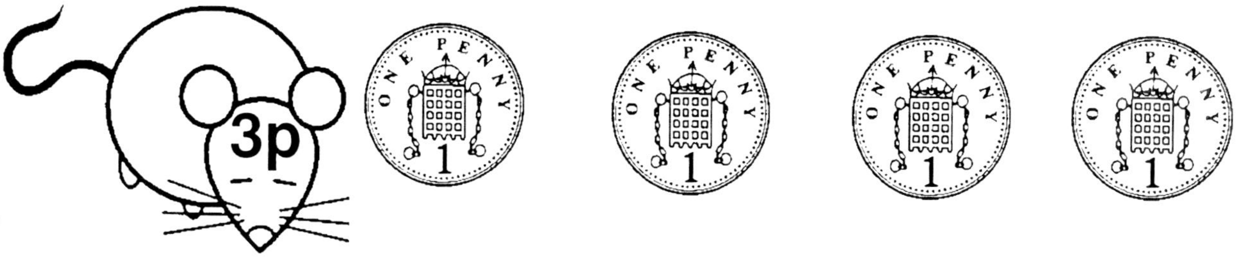

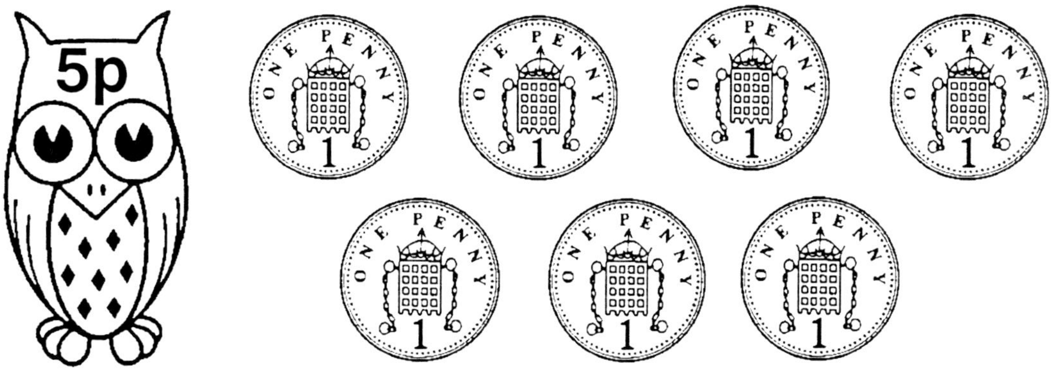

Name ____________________

Boot Sale

Jim has 7p to spend.

Look at the prices and colour the items he could buy.

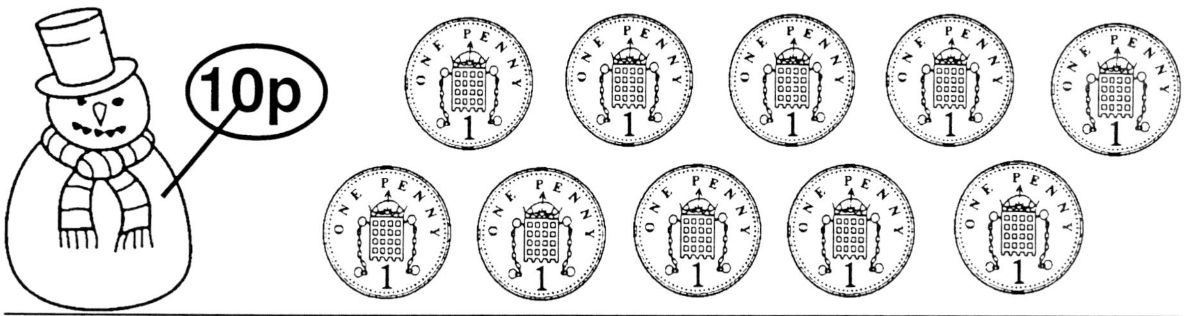

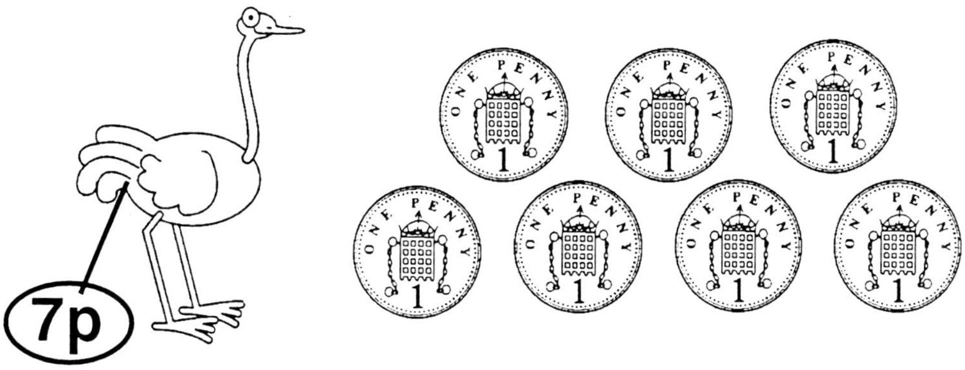

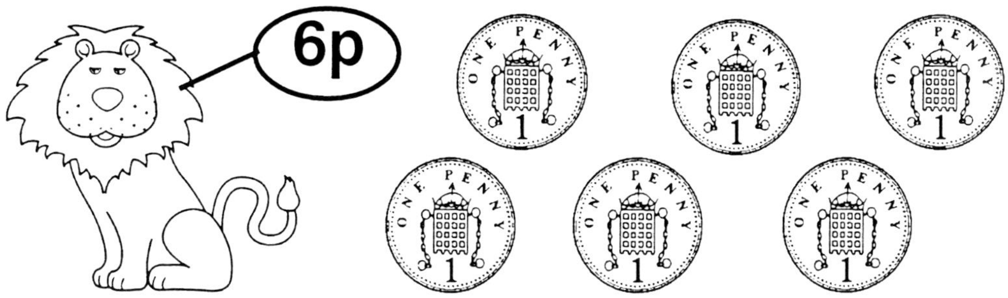

Name____

Numbers and Words

Match the dots, numbers and words.

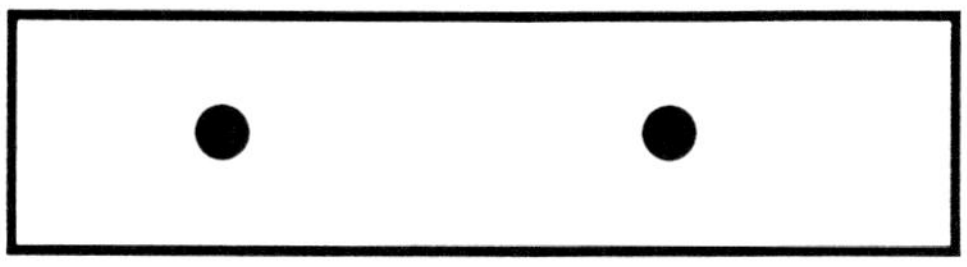	0	one
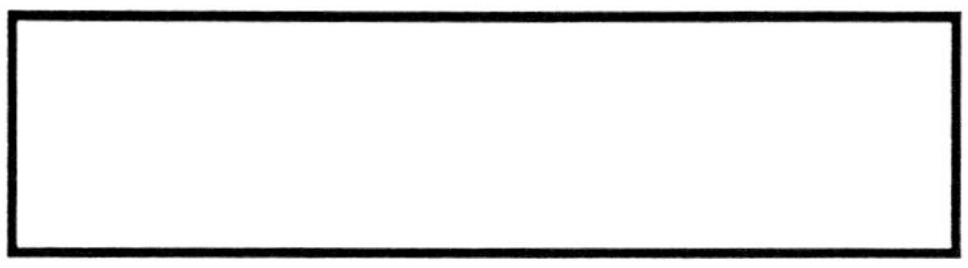	1	three
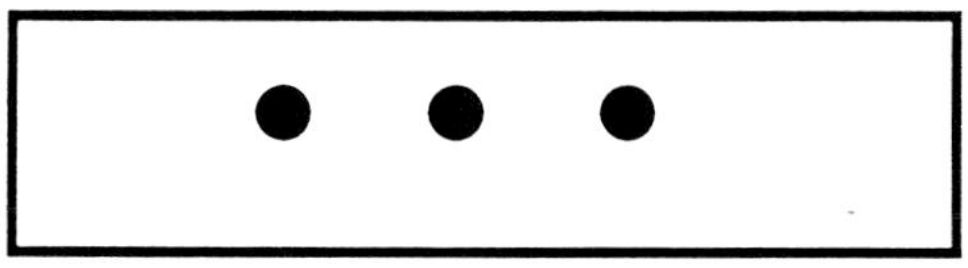	2	zero
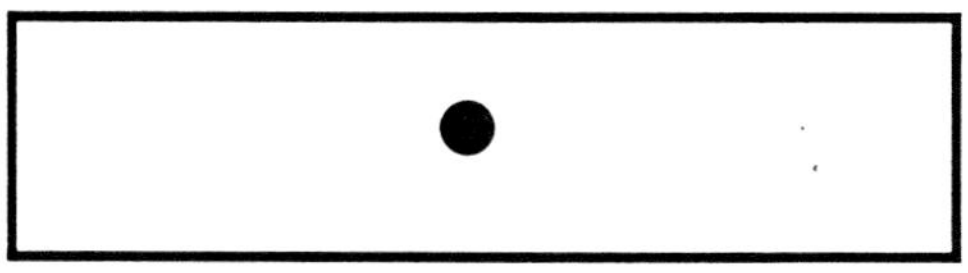	3	six
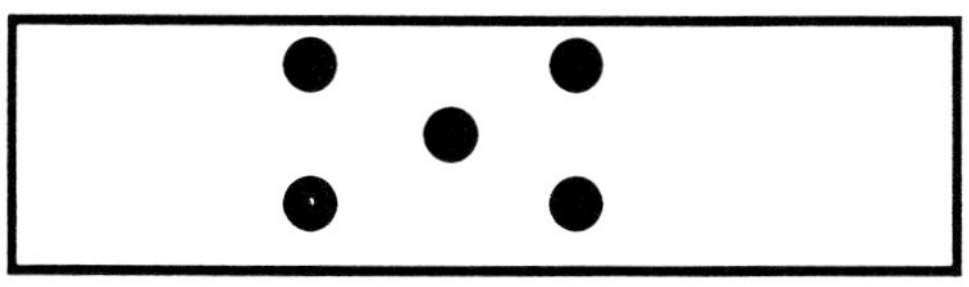	4	nine
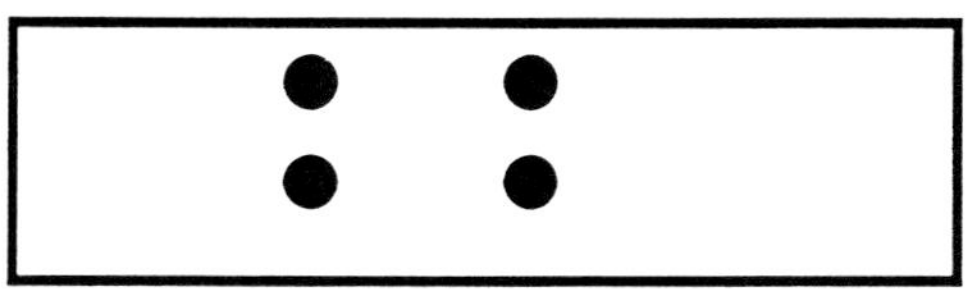	5	four
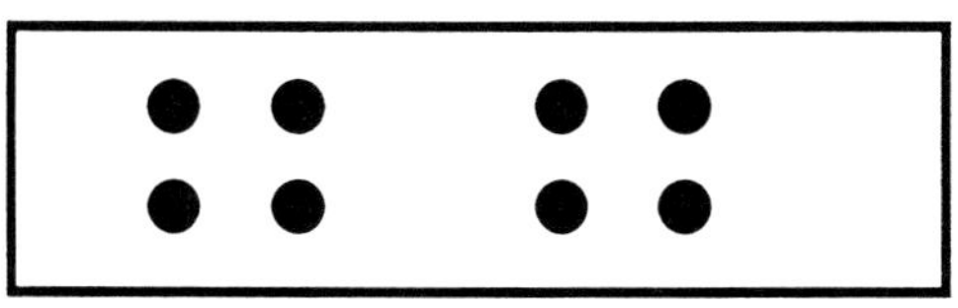	6	two
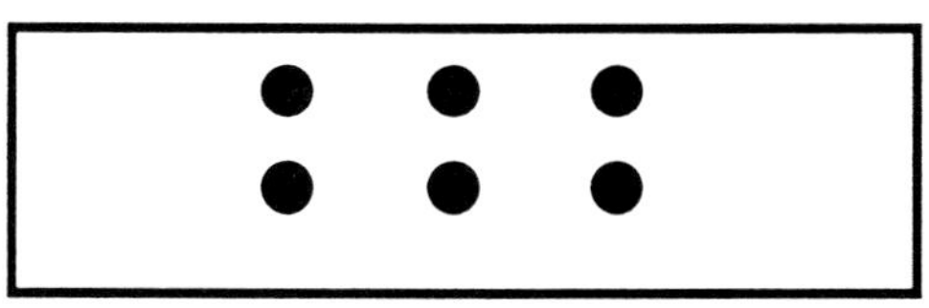	7	seven
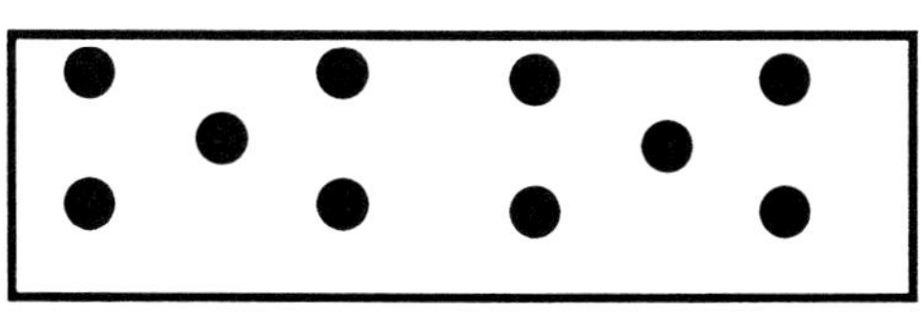	8	ten
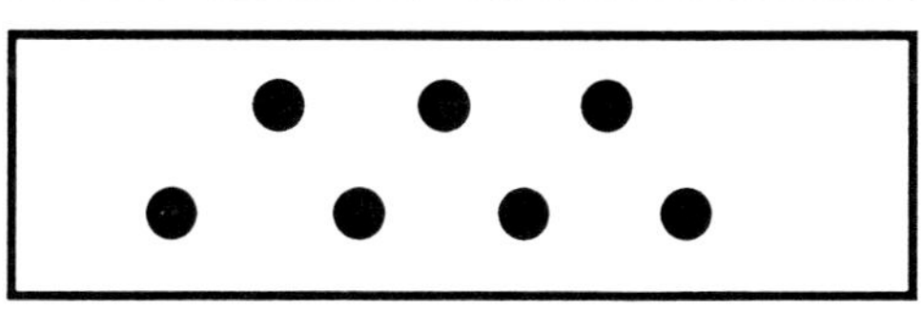	9	five
	10	eight

Name ______________________________

Add 1

Draw another one. How many now?

apples

cats

frogs

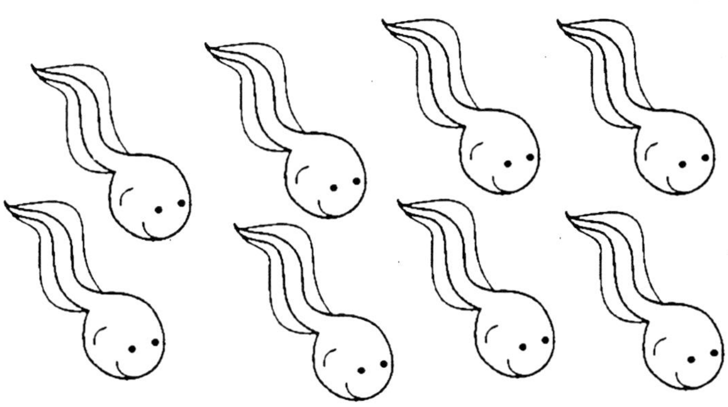

tadpoles

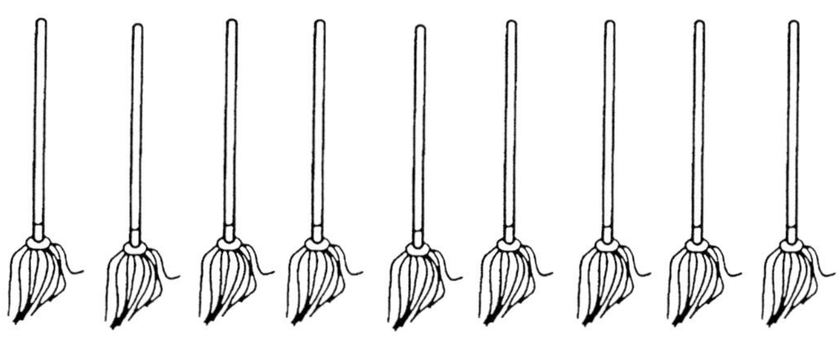

mops

Name ____________________

Add 1

Add 1. How many now?

hens

dolphins

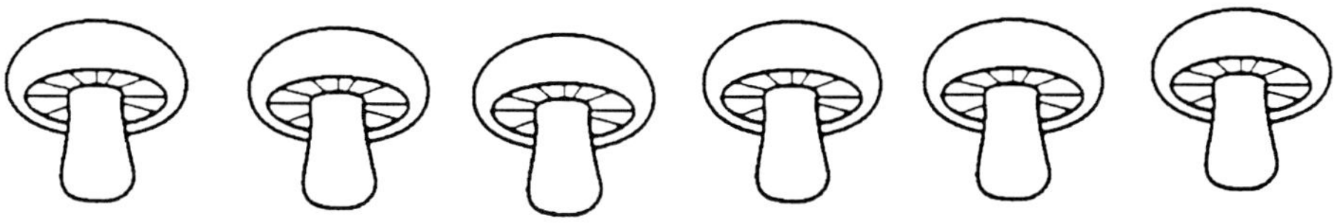

mushrooms

rabbits

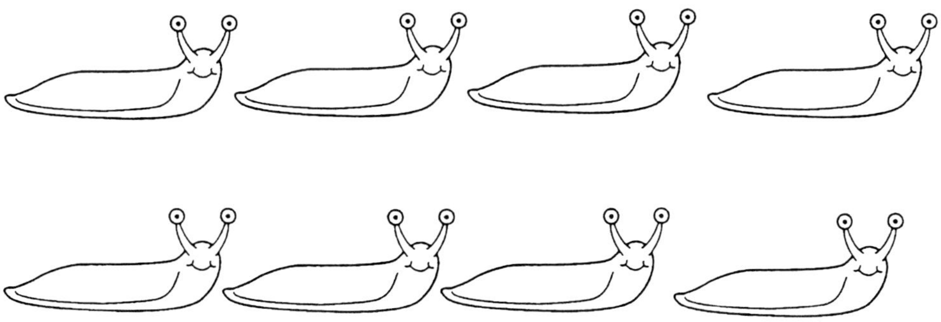

slugs

Name____________________

How Many?

Add 1. How many now?

☐ cats

☐ horses

☐ owls

☐ dogs

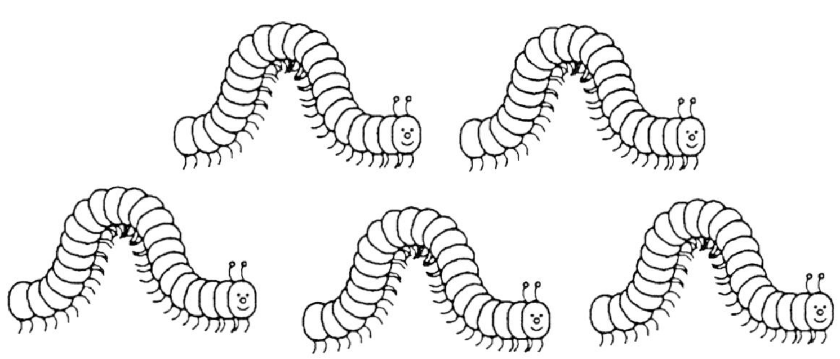

☐ centipedes

Name ______________________________

Counting On

3 count on 2.

How many chicks altogether? chicks

4 count on 3.

How many fish altogether? fish

6 count on 3.

How many sheep altogether? sheep

5 count on 5.

How many bees altogether? bees

6 count on 4.

owls

How many owls altogether?

Name ______________________________

1 More Than

Write 1 more than

2 swans 1 more is _____

5 dogs 1 more is _____

6 birds 1 more is _____

8 goats 1 more is _____

9 snails 1 more is _____

Name ______________________________

Add 1

A

Write 1 more than

1. 7 ____
2. 5 ____
3. 3 ____
4. 8 ____
5. 1 ____
6. 0 ____
7. 4 ____
8. 9 ____
9. 6 ____
10. 2 ____

B

Add 1

1. 4 + 1 = ____
2. 5 + 1 = ____
3. 3 + 1 = ____
4. 8 + 1 = ____
5. 7 + 1 = ____
6. 9 + 1 = ____
7. 1 + 1 = ____
8. 2 + 1 = ____
9. 0 + 1 = ____
10. 6 + 1 = ____

Name ______________________________

Add On

0	1	2	3	4	5	6	7	8	9	10

Work out the answers in your head.

A

Add 2

1. 0 + 2 = ____
2. 1 + 2 = ____
3. 2 + 2 = ____
4. 3 + 2 = ____
5. 4 + 2 = ____
6. 5 + 2 = ____
7. 6 + 2 = ____
8. 7 + 2 = ____
9. 8 + 2 = ____

B

1. 3 + 2 = ____
2. 4 + 0 = ____
3. 1 + 1 = ____
4. 7 + 3 = ____
5. 6 + 3 = ____
6. 4 + 5 = ____
7. 4 + 3 = ____
8. 8 + 2 = ____
9. 2 + 7 = ____
10. 5 + 3 = ____
11. 0 + 8 = ____
12. 9 + 1 = ____

Name ____

Counting Back

Write the two numbers that come next.

1. 4 3 2 ______ ______

2. 5 4 3 ______ ______

3. 6 5 4 ______ ______

4. 7 6 5 ______ ______

5. 8 7 6 ______ ______

6. 9 8 7 ______ ______

7. 10 9 8 ______ ______

Name____

1 Less Than

What is 1 less?

3 fish — 1 less is _____

5 chicks — 1 less is _____

4 slugs — 1 less is _____

6 owls — 1 less is _____

8 bees — 1 less is _____

10 penguins — 1 less is _____

Name ______________________________

1 Less Than

A

Write 1 less than

1. **3** ____
2. **5** ____
3. **7** ____
4. **2** ____
5. **4** ____
6. **6** ____
7. **1** ____
8. **9** ____
9. **8** ____
10. **10** ____

B

Subtraction

1. **1 - 1 =** ____
2. **2 - 1 =** ____
3. **3 - 1 =** ____
4. **4 - 1 =** ____
5. **5 - 1 =** ____
6. **6 - 1 =** ____
7. **7 - 1 =** ____
8. **8 - 1 =** ____
9. **9 - 1=** ____
10. **10 - 1 =** ____

Name______________________________

Subtraction

Work these out in your head.

A	B
1. 4 - 1 = ___	1. 3 - 1 = ___
2. 5 - 2 = ___	2. 7 - 2 = ___
3. 6 - 3 = ___	3. 4 - 3 = ___
4. 9 - 7 = ___	4. 6 - 4 = ___
5. 10 - 4 = ___	5. 5 - 3 = ___
6. 3 - 1 = ___	6. 7 - 4 = ___
7. 7 - 3 = ___	7. 9 - 7 = ___
8. 8 - 5 = ___	8. 8 - 8 = ___
9. 2 - 2 = ___	9. 8 - 5 = ___
10. 10 - 3 = ___	10. 10 - 6 = ___

Name ____

1p and 2p Coins

Colour the coins to make 3p.

Colour the coins to make 4p.

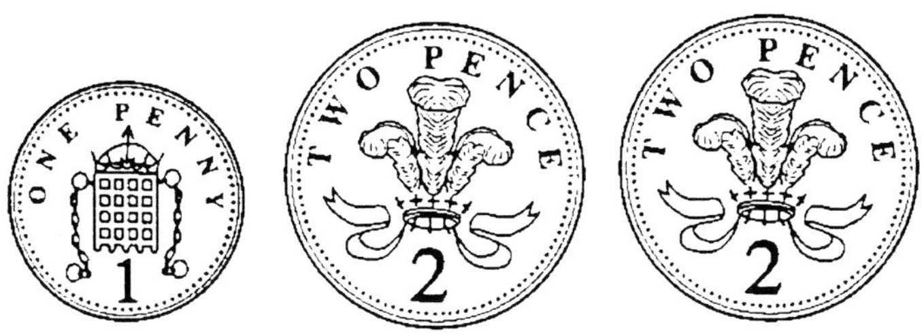

Colour the coins to make 4p.

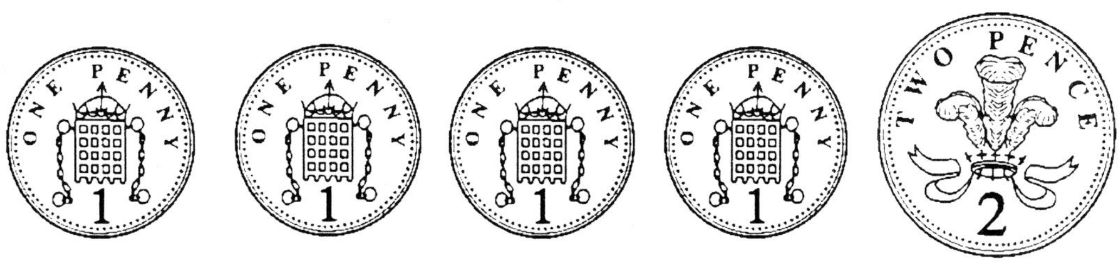

Colour the coins to make 5p.

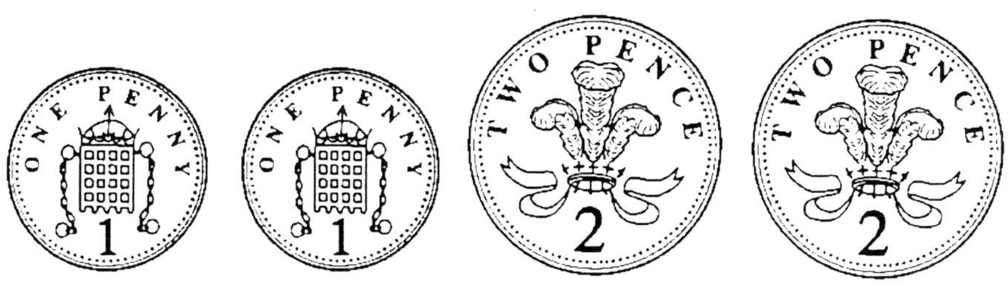

Colour the coins to make 5p.

Name______________________________

The Toy Shop

Colour the coins needed to buy these toys.

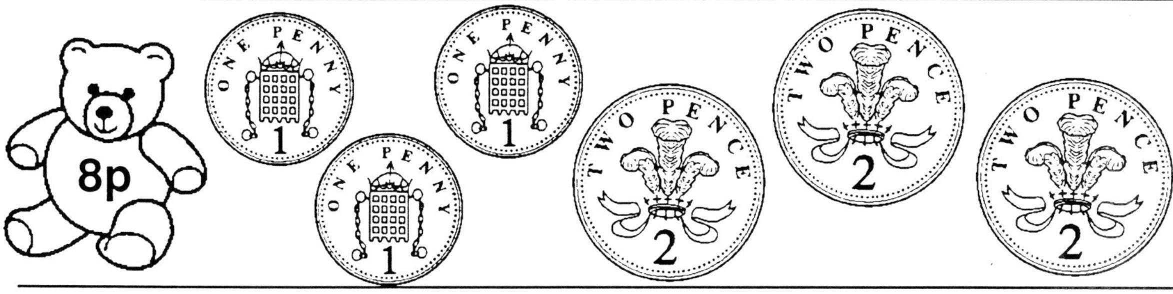

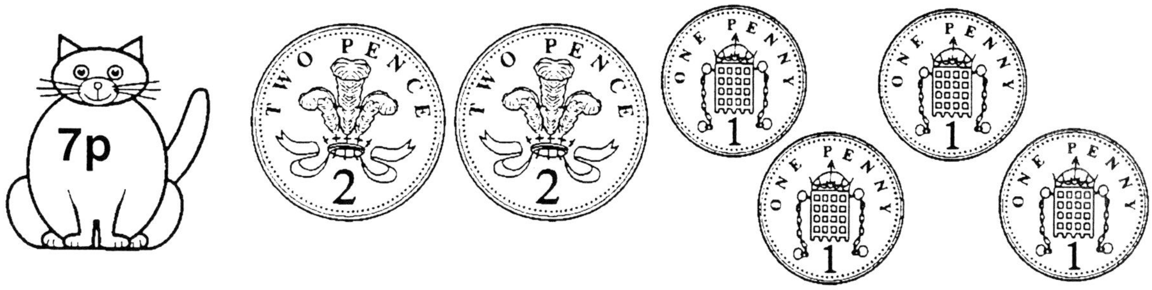

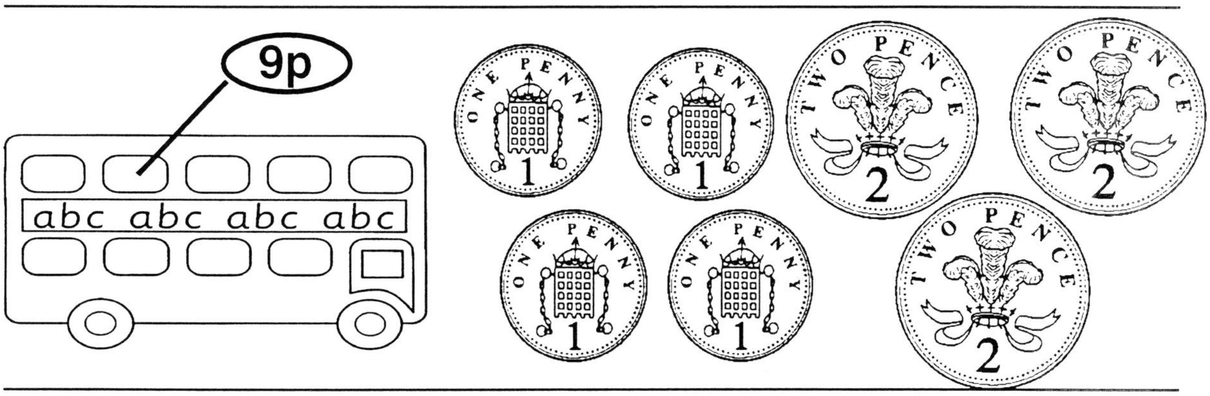

Name ______________________________

Coins

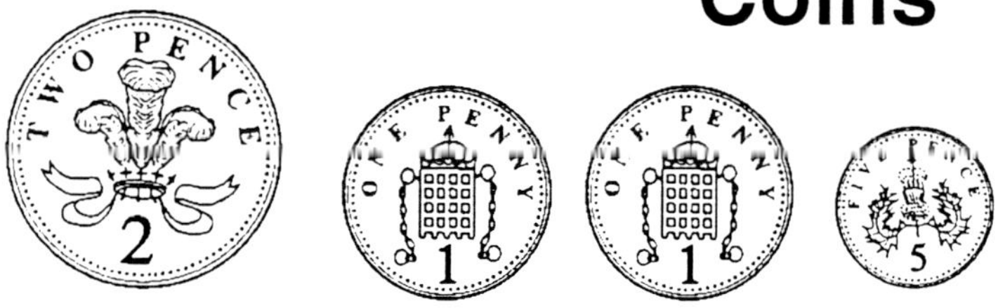

Colour the coins to make 6p.

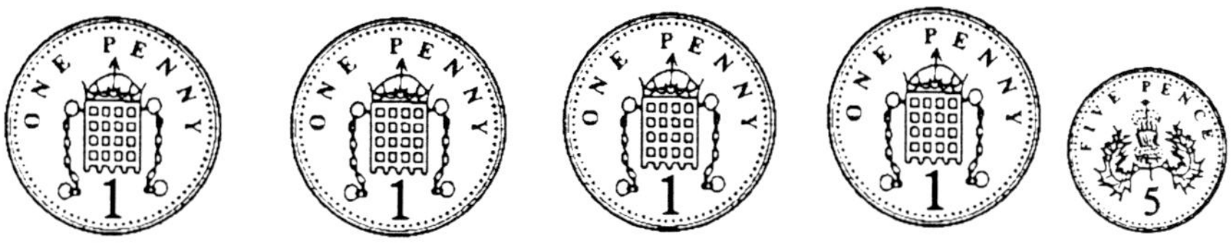

Colour the coins to make 7p.

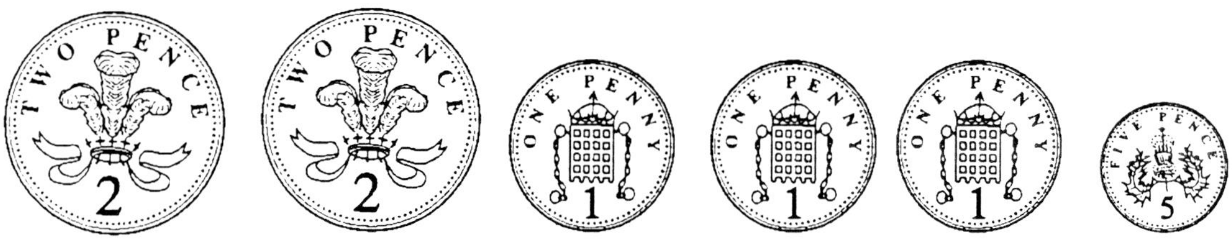

Colour the coins to make 8p.

Colour the coins to make 9p.

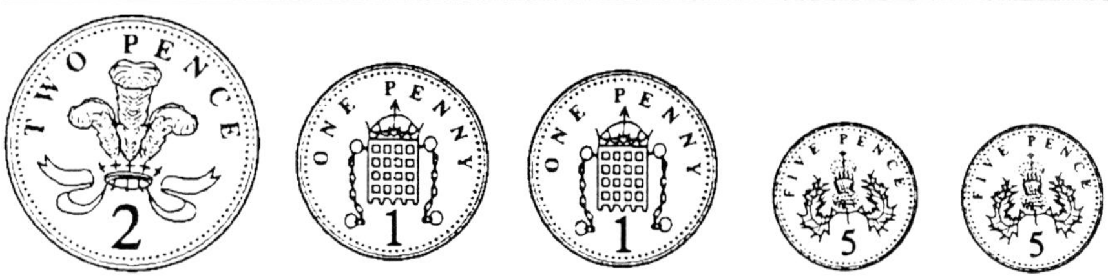

Colour the coins to make 10p.

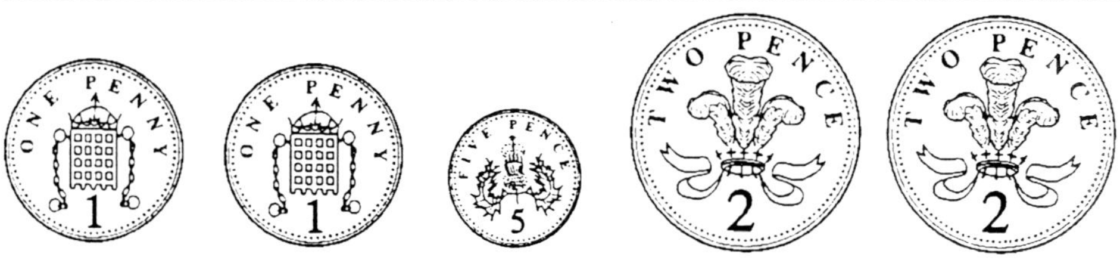

Colour the coins to make 10p.

Name________________________________

Change from 10p

Ali has 10p to spend. How much change does he have if he buys any of these toys?

Change

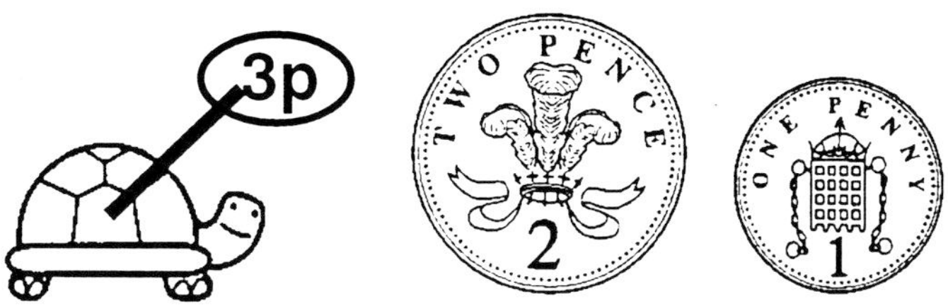

Change

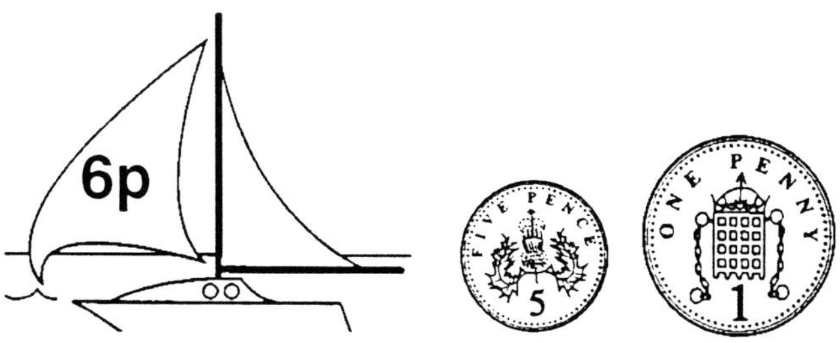

Change

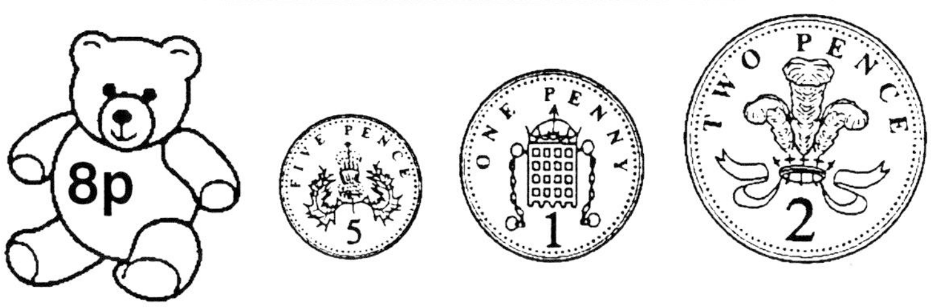

Change

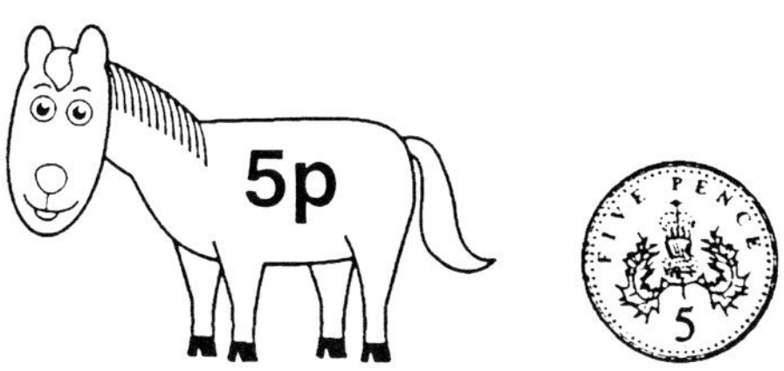

Change

Name ____________________

Missing Numbers

Find the missing numbers and complete the sums.

A	B
1. 1 + □ = 2	1. 3 + □ = 7
2. 2 + □ = 4	2. 2 + □ = 9
3. □ + 2 = 5	3. □ + 2 = 8
4. 4 + □ = 7	4. 1 + □ = 7
5. 9 + □ = 10	5. □ + 7 = 9
6. 6 + □ = 8	6. 2 + □ = 10
7. □ + 7 = 10	7. 7 + □ = 10
8. 5 + □ = 8	8. □ + 2 = 7
9. 7 + □ = 9	9. 4 + □ = 10
10. 8 + □ = 10	10. 1 + □ = 9

Name____

Missing Numbers

Find the missing numbers.

A

10		12	13	14		16	17			20

B

10	11		13		15			18	19	20

C

10		12				16		18		

D

20	19		17		15	14		12		10

E

20			17	16			13		11	10

F

	19	18			15			12		

G

20					15					10

Name ______________________________

Addition

0 1 2 3 4 5 6 7 8 9 10

Work out the answers in your head. Use the number line when you need to.

A		B	
1.	2 + 1 + 3 = ___	1.	1 + 2 + 3 = ___
2.	1 + 4 + 1 = ___	2.	0 + 3 + 2 = ___
3.	3 + 2 + 3 = ___	3.	3 + 4 + 2 = ___
4.	5 + 2 + 1 = ___	4.	1 + 2 + 0 = ___
5.	7 + 0 + 2 = ___	5.	4 + 1 + 4 = ___
6.	1 + 2 + 6 = ___	6.	1 + 5 + 3 = ___
7.	3 + 3 + 2 = ___	7.	2 + 3 + 4 = ___
8.	5 + 2 + 1 = ___	8.	0 + 1 + 5 = ___
9.	5 + 1 + 3 = ___	9.	3 + 1 + 3 = ___
10.	2 +7 + 0 = ___	10.	2 +5 + 3 = ___

Name ______________________________

Make 10

Find the numbers to make these triangles add up to 10.

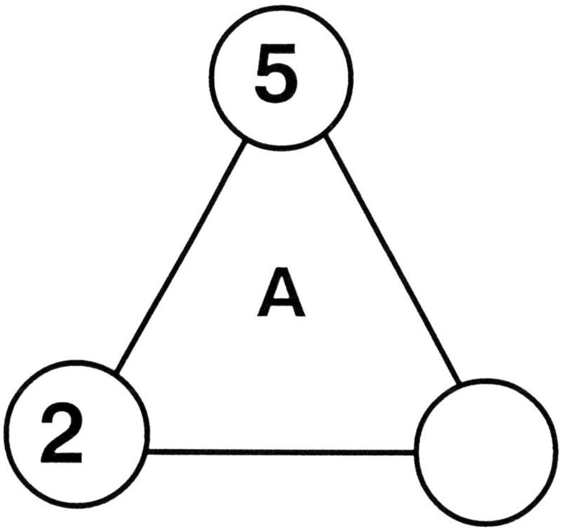

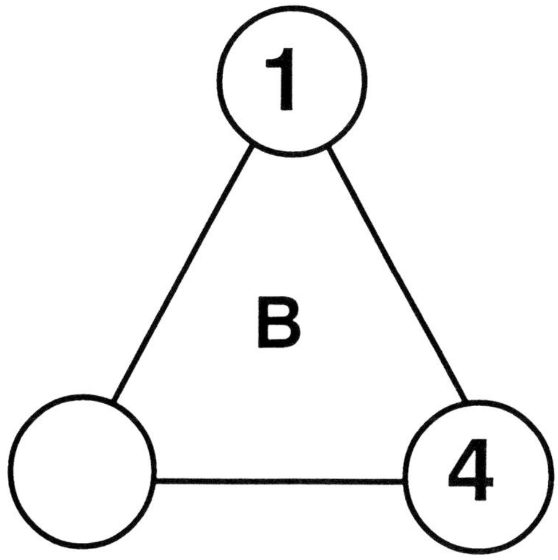

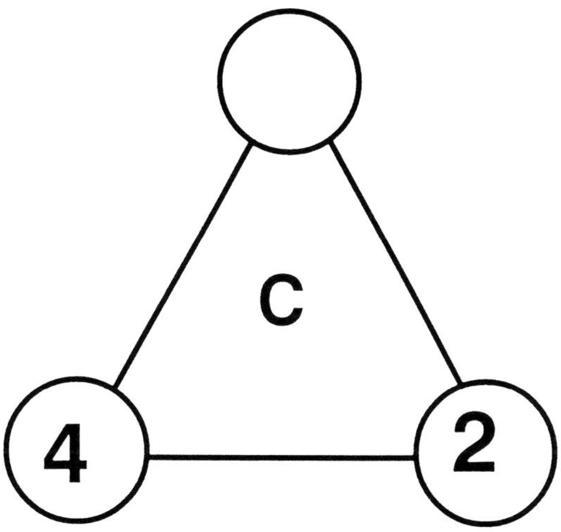

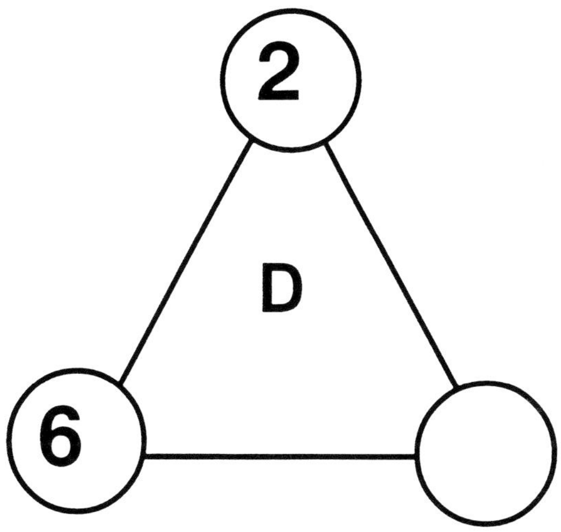

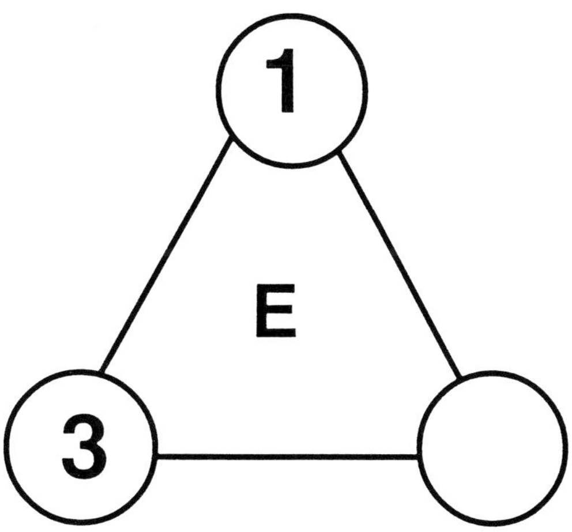

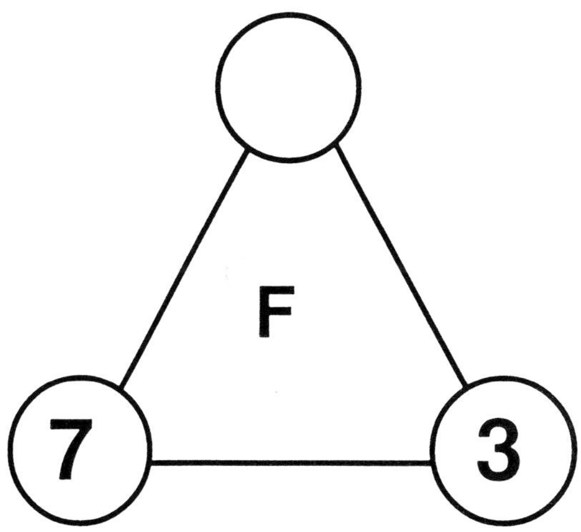

Name

Number Stories

1. There are 4 paintbrushes in a box and 3 more are put in. How many paintbrushes are now in the box?

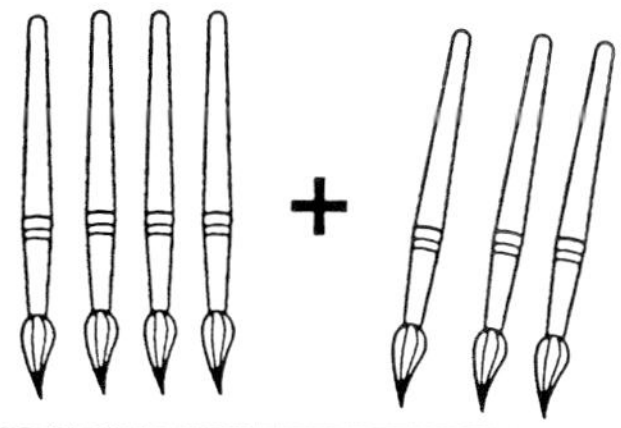

paintbrushes

2. There are 5 tulips in one bunch and 4 tulips in another. How many flowers are there altogether?

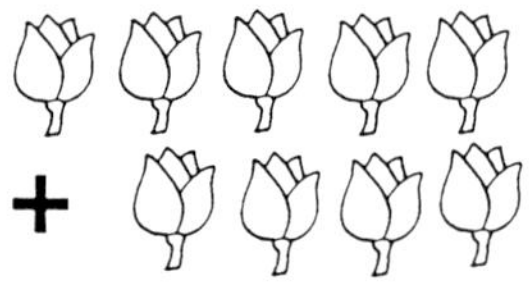

tulips

3. There are 6 apples in one basket and 3 in another. How many apples are there altogether?

apples

4. 

If I buy a cake, an apple and a banana, how much do I spend?

p

5. There are 3 dots on one ladybird and 5 dots on another. How many dots altogether?

dots

6. In a football match, John scores 3 goals in the first half and Jim scores 4 goals in the second half. Who scores the most goals and how many goals are scored altogether?

scores most

goals

Name ____________________

Addition

0 1 2 3 4 5 6 7 8 9 10

11 12 13 14 15 16 17 18 19 20

Work out the answers in your head. Use the number line when you need to.

A

1. 5 + 4 = ______
2. 7 + 5 = ______
3. 8 + 6 = ______
4. 9 + 11 = ______
5. 13 + 4 = ______
6. 5 + 11 = ______
7. 3 + 15 = ______
8. 2 + 13 = ______
9. 11+ 6 = ______
10. 9 + 8 = ______

B

1. 5 + 3 + 2 = ______
2. 4 + 6 + 5 = ______
3. 3 + 11 + 4 = ______
4. 0 + 12 + 5 = ______
5. 2 + 5 + 13 = ______
6. 1 + 8 + 11 = ______
7. 15 + 0 + 3 = ______
8. 2 + 13 + 1 = ______
9. 1 + 17 + 2 = ______
10. 9 + 5 + 3 = ______

Find the numbers to make these triangles add up to 20.

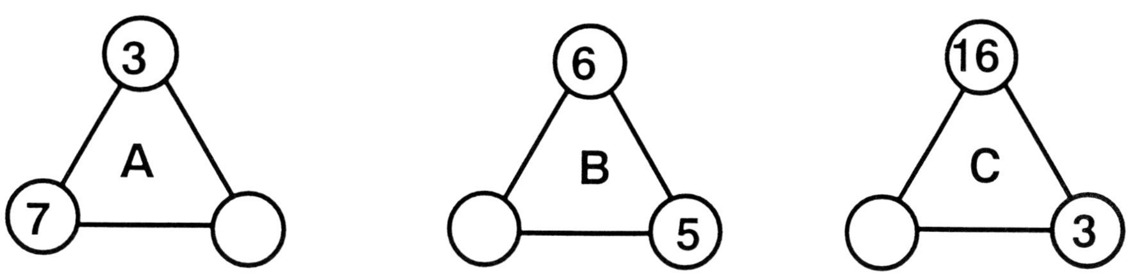

Name

Number Stories

1	2	3	4	5	6	7	8	9	10
11	12	13	14	15	16	17	18	19	20

Use the number line when you need to.

1. 

There are 7 bees on one bush of flowers and 5 bees on another.
How many bees are there altogether? ☐ bees

2. There are 10 ladybirds on one leaf and 5 on another.
How many ladybirds altogether? ☐ ladybirds

3. In a field there are 11 brown rabbits and 6 grey rabbits.
How many rabbits are there altogether? ☐ rabbits

4. There are 13 players in a team and 4 reserves.
How many players altogether? ☐ players

5. 

Find the cost of buying a frog, a dinosaur and 2 mice. ☐ p

6. John buys a pen for 3p, a pencil for 2p and a book for 11p.
How much does he spend? ☐ p

Name ______________________________

Number Stories

1 2 3 4 5 6 7 8 9 10

Work out the answers in your head. Use the number line when you need to.

1. 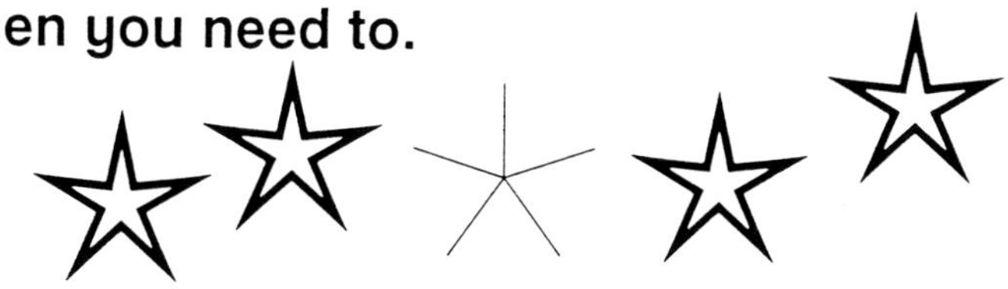

Mary the witch makes 5 spells and 1 goes wrong.
How many work?

[ ] spells

2. A squirrel stores 8 nuts for the winter but 3 are stolen.
How many are left?

[ ] nuts

3. Ali has 10p to spend.
He buys a pen for 6p.
How much change does he have?

[ ] p

4. Ted has written 9 letters but he only has 4 stamps. How many more stamps does he need?

[ ] stamps

5. In a match, the Swans score 3 goals and the Cygnets score 5 goals.
Who wins and by how many goals?

[ ] win

[ ] goals

6. There are 9 holes in the ice and 5 penguins waiting by them for fish. Each penguin has his own hole in the ice.
How many holes do not have penguins beside them?

[ ] holes

Name ____________________

Subraction

0 1 2 3 4 5 6 7 8 9 10

11 12 13 14 15 16 17 18 19 20

Work out the answers in your head. Use the number line when you need to.

A

1. 11 - 1 = ____
2. 12 - 2 = ____
3. 13 - 3 = ____
4. 14 - 4 = ____
5. 15 - 5 = ____
6. 16 - 6 = ____
7. 17 - 7 = ____
8. 18 - 8 = ____
9. 19 - 9 = ____
10. 20 - 10 = ____

B

1. 10 - 10 = ____
2. 11 - 10 = ____
3. 12 - 10 = ____
4. 13 - 10 = ____
5. 14 - 10 = ____
6. 15 - 10 = ____
7. 16 - 10 = ____
8. 17 - 10 = ____
9. 18 - 10 = ____
10. 19 - 10 = ____

Name ______________________________

Subtraction

0 1 2 3 4 5 6 7 8 9 10

11 12 13 14 15 16 17 18 19 20

Work out the answers in your head. Use the number line when you need to.

A	B
1. 11 - 1 = ___	1. 13 - 4 = ___
2. 12 - 3 = ___	2. 14 - 5 = ___
3. 16 - 4 = ___	3. 11 - 8 = ___
4. 18 - 6 = ___	4. 18 - 9 = ___
5. 15 - 2 = ___	5. 19 - 11 = ___
6. 19 - 5 = ___	6. 12 - 7 = ___
7. 14 - 3 = ___	7. 16 - 9 = ___
8. 15 - 2 = ___	8. 18 - 0 = ___
9. 17 - 5 = ___	9. 19 - 13 = ___
10. 20 - 7 = ___	10. 20 - 14 = ___

Name ______________________________

Find the Missing Numbers

1 2 3 4 5 6 7 8 9 10

Work out the answers in your head. Use the number line when you need to.

1. 4 - ☐ = 1
2. 5 - ☐ = 3
3. 2 - ☐ = 2
4. 8 - ☐ = 3
5. 10 - ☐ = 6
6. ☐ - 2 = 4
7. ☐ - 4 = 3
8. ☐ - 3 = 5
9. ☐ - 8 = 2
10. ☐ - 7 = 2

Name ____________________

Sums to 20

Work these out in your head.

A

1. 3 + 1 + 5 = ______
2. 7 + 6 + 5 = ______
3. 5 + 0 + 7 = ______
4. 4 + 2 + 6 = ______
5. 9 + 4 + 2 = ______
6. 5 + 0 + 12 = ______
7. 2 + 9 + 0 = ______
8. 15 + 0 + 5 = ______
9. 13 + 5 + 2 = ______
10. 0 + 12 + 7 = ______
11. 10 + 4 + 3 = ______
12. 12 + 5 + 2 = ______
13. 16 + 1 + 3 = ______
14. 4 + 0 + 13 = ______
15. 15 + 2 + 2 = ______
16. 0 + 8 + 9 = ______
17. 4 + 7 + 6 = ______
18. 2 + 15 + 3 = ______
19. 4 + 3 + 9 = ______
20. 5 + 2 + 8 = ______

B

1. 6 + 2 - 3 = ______
2. 7 + 6 - 2 = ______
3. 8 + 7 - 5 = ______
4. 9 + 4 - 3 = ______
5. 8 + 0 - 6 = ______
6. 0 + 7 - 3 = ______
7. 2 - 1 + 8 = ______
8. 9 - 5 + 3 = ______
9. 8 - 3 + 4 = ______
10. 11 - 3 + 0 = ______
11. 0 - 5 + 10 = ______
12. 14 - 10 + 8 = ______
13. 3 - 0 + 15 = ______
14. 6 + 3 - 7 = ______
15. 2 + 5 - 3 = ______
16. 14 + 6 - 16 = ______
17. 5 - 7 + 9 = ______
18. 8 - 9 + 12 = ______
19. 16 - 12 + 7 = ______
20. 18 - 20 + 3 = ______

Name

Numbers to make 10

1 2 3 4 5 6 7 8 9 10

Find the numbers to make these triangles add up to 10. Work out the answers in your head. Use the number line when you need to.

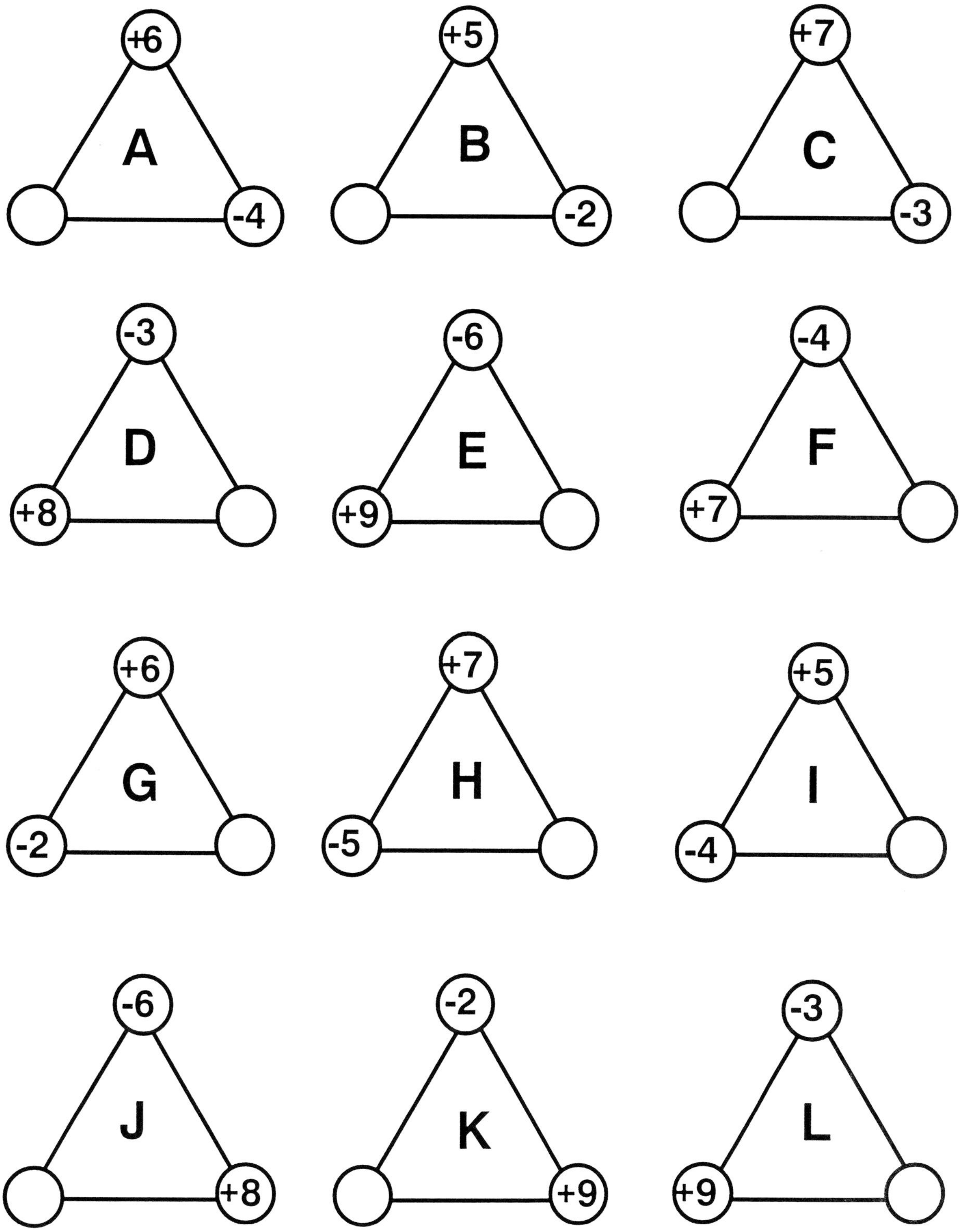

Name ___

More Number Stories

Work out the answers in your head. Make your own number line when you need to.

1. In a cricket match, Jaz makes 9 runs and Ali makes 8 runs.
   How many more runs does Jaz score than Ali? ___
   How many runs are made altogether? ___

2. Jane is 4 years younger than her brother who is 18.
   How old is Jane? ___

3. Jack needs £20 to buy a computer game. His mother gives him £3 and his father gives him £12.
   How much money does he have now? ___

   How much more does he need to buy the game? ___

4. Ali and his friend each eat 2 cakes and there are 9 left on the plate.
   How many were on the plate to start with? ___

5. These are the prices in a boot sale.

Find the cost of

a football and a flower. ___

a frog and a football. ___

a frog and a flower. ___

a football, a frog and a flower. ___

Name ______________________________

Change from 20p

Jane has 20p to spend. How much change does she have if she buys any of these toys?

1.

p

Change from 20p

2.

p

Change from 20p

3.

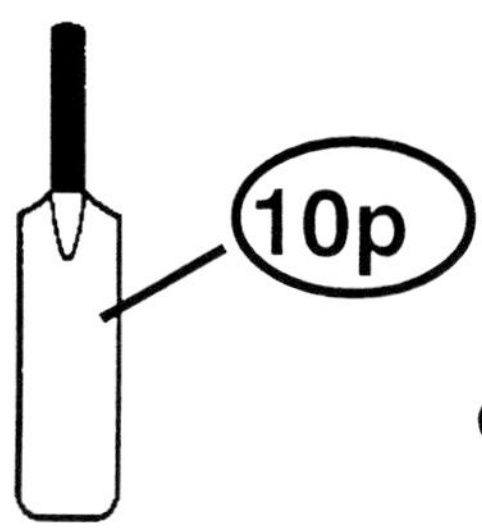

and

p

Jane spent ________ altogether.

Change from 20p

4.

and

p

Jane spent ________ altogether.

Change from 20p

5.

and

p

Jane spent ________altogether.

Change from 20p

Name ____________________

Counting to 100

1	2	3	4	5	6	7	8	9	10
11	12	13	14	15	16	17	18	19	20
21	22	23	24	25	26	27	28	29	30
31	32	33	34	35	36	37	38	39	40
41	42	43	44	45	46	47	48	49	50
51	52	53	54	55	56	57	58	59	60
61	62	63	64	65	66	67	68	69	70
71	72	73	74	75	76	77	78	79	80
81	82	83	84	85	86	87	88	89	90
91	92	93	94	95	96	97	98	99	100

A Use the 100-number square to add 10 in these sums.

1. 20 + 10 = ______
2. 35 + 10 = ______
3. 72 + 10 = ______
4. 41 + 10 = ______
5. 90 + 10 = ______
6. 56 + 10 = ______
7. 77 + 10 = ______
8. 89+ 10 = ______
9. 65 + 10 = ______
10. 19 + 10 = ______

B Use the 100-number square to subtract 10 in these sums.

1. 34 - 10 = ______
2. 29 - 10 = ______
3. 19 - 10 = ______
4. 47 - 10 = ______
5. 56 - 10 = ______
6. 71 - 10 = ______
7. 68 - 10 = ______
8. 91 - 10 = ______
9. 83 - 10 = ______
10. 18 - 10 = ______

C Use the 100-number square to find the next 3 numbers in each series.

1. 14 24 34 ___ ___ ___
2. 29 39 49 ___ ___ ___
3. 8 18 28 ___ ___ ___
4. 67 57 47 ___ ___ ___
5. 55 45 35 ___ ___ ___

Name ______________________________

Place Value

A Write the value of

1. the 5 in 65 ________
2. the 4 in 47 ________
3. the 7 in 71 ________
4. the 4 in 40 ________
5. the 7 in 735 ________
6. the 4 in 437 ________
7. the 7 in 371 ________
8. the 3 in 453 ________
9. the 9 in 392 ________
10. the 8 in 580 ________

B Write the following numbers.

1. 60 + 8 = ________
2. 20 + 6 = ________
3. 300 + 40 + 5 = ________
4. 600 + 50 + 9 = ________
5. 200 + 40 = ________
6. 700 + 7 = ________

C Write these numbers in order, beginning with the smallest.

1. 9 3 7 6 ______________________
2. 8 10 0 3 ______________________
3. 19 13 16 12 ______________________
4. 42 25 33 17 ______________________

D Write these numbers in order, beginning with the biggest.

1. 7 9 6 5 ______________________
2. 8 48 16 0 ______________________
3. 14 10 16 19 ______________________
4. 16 29 30 51 ______________________

Name

The Craft Shop Sale

Jane has £1 to spend.
What change does she have if she buys any one of the following items?

1. 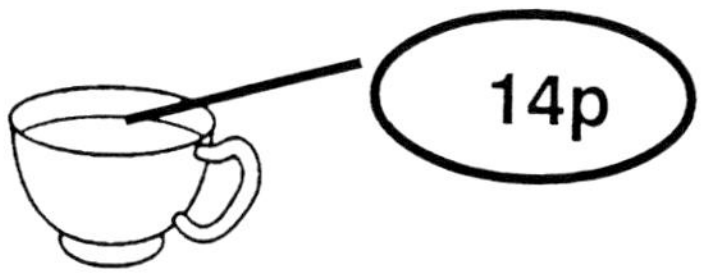

Change from £1

2. 

Change from £1

3. 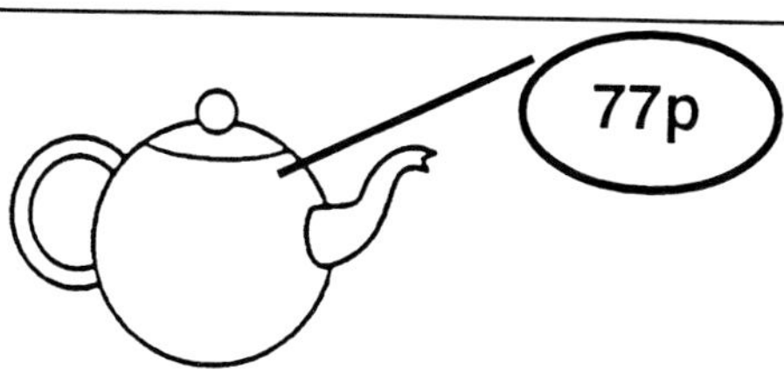

Change from £1

4. 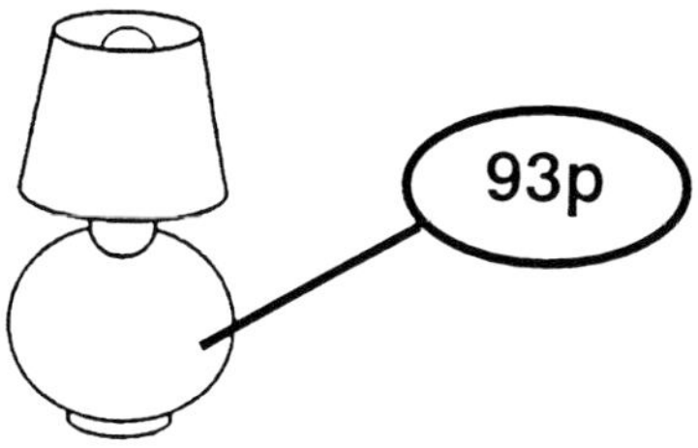

Change from £1

5. 

Change from £1

6. 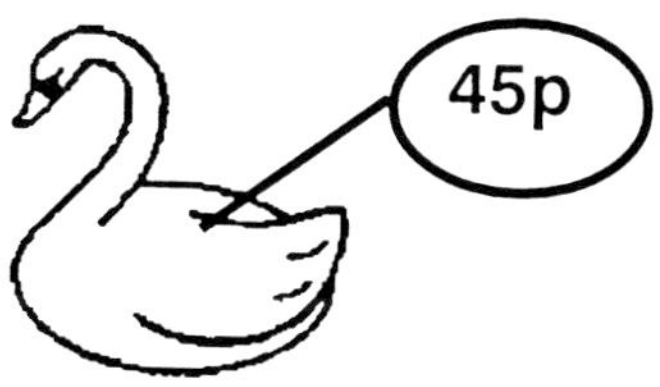

Change from £1

7. Which 2 items could Jane buy that would cost £1 altogether?

_______________ and _______________

Name ______________________________

Money

A

How much when you spend?

1. 6p + 5p = ______
2. 7p + 4p = ______
3. 3p + 2p + 7p = ______
4. 4p + 7p + 3p = ______
5. 11p + 3p + 2p = ______
6. 9p + 4p + 5p = ______
7. 10p + 10p + 10p = ______
8. 6p + 4p + 10p = ______
9. 30p + 20p + 10p = ______
10. 60p + 20p + 10p = ______
11. 8p - 3p = ______
12. 13p - 5p = ______
13. 13p + 2p - 4p = ______
14. 21p + 12p - 3p = ______
15. 35p - 6p + 11p = ______

B

How much change from 20p?

1. 20p - 2p = ______
2. 20p - 5p = ______
3. 20p - 10p = ______
4. 20p - 18p = ______
5. 20p - 9p = ______
6. 20p - 11p = ______
7. 20p - 7p = ______
8. 20p - 14p = ______

How much change from £1?

9. £1 - 10p = ______
10. £1 - 20p = ______
11. £1 - 30p = ______
12. £1 - 50p = ______
13. £1 - 75p = ______
14. £1 - 80p = ______
15. £1 - 99p = ______

Name ____________________

Counting Sets of 2

A Count in 2s to 20 and write the missing numbers.

2 4 6 ______________________________ 20

Work these out.

B	C
2 x 3 = ____	4 x 2 = ____
2 x 5 = ____	5 x 2 = ____
2 x 7 = ____	7 x 2 = ____
2 x 8 = ____	8 x 2 = ____
2 x 10 = ____	10 x 2 = ____

D

1. How many eyes do 4 owls have? ______
2. How many wheels on 5 bicyles? ______
3. There are 6 hens in the coop.
   How many legs do they have altogether? ______
4. There are 7 friends in Tom's football team.
   How many boots do they need? ______
5. Tom scores 2 goals in each of 3 matches.
   How many goals does he score altogether? ______
6. Tom saved 50p a week.
   How much does he save in 2 weeks? ______
7. Jane buys 6 sweets costing 2p each.
   How much does she spend? ______

Name

Counting Sets (3s and 4s)

Count in 3s to 30 and write the missing numbers.

3 6 9 ... 30

There are 3 legs on a stool.

How many legs on the following?

2 stools ☐ 3 stools ☐ 4 stools ☐

5 stools ☐ 6 stools ☐ 7 stools ☐

Count in 4s to 40 and write the missing numbers.

4 8 12 ... 40

A sheep has 4 legs.

How many legs do the following have?

2 sheep ☐ 3 sheep ☐ 4 sheep ☐

5 sheep ☐ 6 sheep ☐ 7 sheep ☐

Name ______________________

Counting Sets (5s and 10s)

Count in 5s to 50 and write the missing numbers.

5 10 15 ______________________ 50

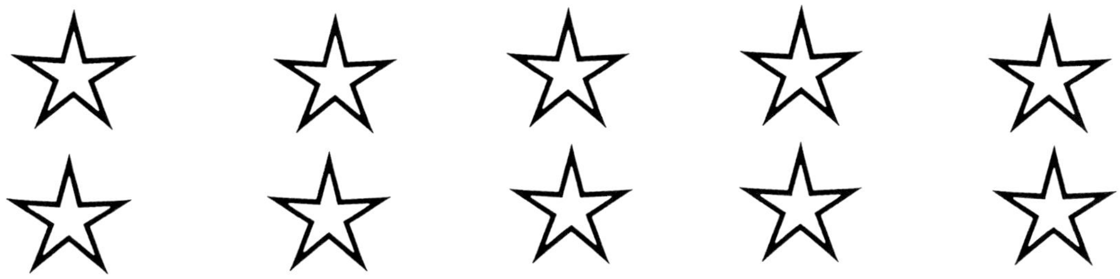

There are 5 points on a star.
How many points do the following have?

2 stars ☐ 3 stars ☐ 4 stars ☐

5 stars ☐ 6 stars ☐ 7 stars ☐

Count in 10s to 100 and write the missing numbers.

10 20 30 ______________________ 100

Write the missing numbers.

1 x 10 = ☐ 6 x 10 = ☐

2 x 10 = ☐ 7 x 10 = ☐

3 x 10 = ☐ 8 x 10 = ☐

4 x 10 = ☐ 9 x 10 = ☐

5 x 10 = ☐ 10 x 10 = ☐

Name ____________________

How Many?

1. There are 4 wheels on a car.
   How many wheels on 3 cars? ______

2. There are 3 legs on a stool.
   How many legs on 6 stools? ______

3. How many toes on 2 feet? ______

4. Jane had four 5p coins.
   How much money does she have? ______

5. Ali has 6 pairs of socks.
   How many socks does he have altogether? ______

6. John saves £3 a week.
   How much does he save in 8 weeks? ______

7. Wendy has twice as much money as her sister.
   If her sister has 50p, how much money
   does Wendy have? ______

8. There are 10 leaves on the stem of a plant.
   How many leaves on 6 stems? ______

9. A lollipop costs 3p and a cake costs five times as much.
   What is the cost of a cake? ______

10. The Cygnets have scored 5 goals and the Swans have scored four times as many goals.
    How many goals have the Swans scored? ______

Name ______________________________

Dividing

1. How many groups of 2 in 10? _____

2. How many groups of 4 in 12? _____

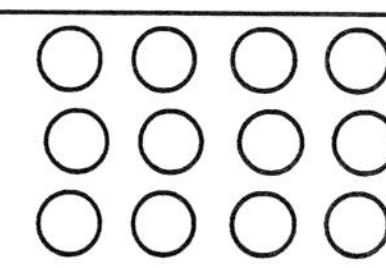

3. How many groups of 3 in 6? _____

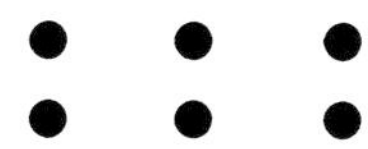

4. How many groups of 10 in 20? _____

5. How many groups of 5 in 20? _____

6. 12 ÷ 3 = _____

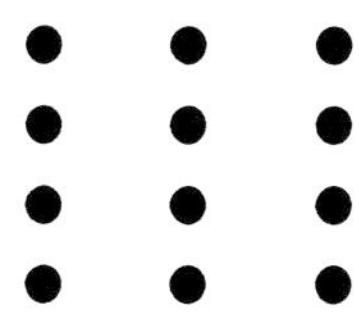

7. 15 ÷ 5 = _____

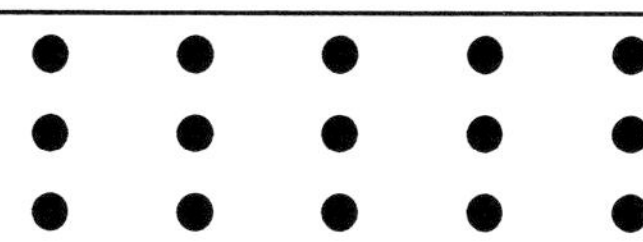

8. 12 ÷ 2 = _____

9. 10 ÷ 5 = _____

10. 8 ÷ 4 = _____

11. 20 ÷ 4 = _____

12. 15 ÷ 3 = _____

13. 18 ÷ 2 = _____

14. 50 ÷ 5 = _____

15. 70 ÷ 10 = _____

16. 16 ÷ 4 = _____

17. 21 ÷ 3 = _____

18. 25 ÷ 5 = _____

19. 30 ÷ 3 = _____

20. 18 ÷ 3 = _____

21. 12 ÷ 4 = _____

22. 35 ÷ 7 = _____

23. 20 ÷ 2 = _____

24. 60 ÷ 10 = _____

25. 20 ÷ 5 = _____

Name ______________________________

Dividing

1. 8 cakes are shared between 2 friends. How many cakes does each have? ______

2. How many 5p coins make 25p? ________

3. Three pens cost 12p. How much does one pen cost? ________

4. A gardener plants 10 flowers in 2 rows. How many flowers in each row? ______

5. How many packets are needed to pack 40 bars of chocolates if each box holds 10 bars? _______

6. 30p is shared equally between 3 boys. How much money does each boy have? _______

7. £1 is shared equally among 5 girls. How much money does each have? _______

8. How many 10p coins make 50p? _______

9. Ali has saved 4 times as much as his sister. If Ali has saved 80p, how much has his sister saved? _________

10. A car carries 4 people. How many cars are needed to take 20 people? _______

11. A bus carries 30 people. How many buses are needed to carry 50 people? _________

12. 12 sweets are shared equally amongst 5 boys. How many does each boy have? _______

    How many sweets are left over? ________

Name ______________________________

Dividing with Remainders

Use r = remainder

1. 7 ÷ 3 = _____ r =
2. 15 ÷ 2 = _____ r =
3. 19 ÷ 4 = _____ r =
4. 18 ÷ 5 = _____ r =
5. 33 ÷ 10 = _____ r =
6. 17 ÷ 3 = _____ r =
7. 32 ÷ 5 = _____ r =
8. 22 ÷ 4 = _____ r =
9. 19 ÷ 3 = _____ r =
10. 53 ÷ 10 = _____ r =

11. Share 17p amongst 3 boys.
    How much does each boy have? ______

    How much money is left over? ______

12. How many 20p stamps can you buy for 70p? ______

    How much change is there? ______

13. Share 18 cakes amongst 4 boys.
    How many cakes does each boy have? ______

    How many cakes are left over? ______

14. Jane needs 7 buttons for a jacket. They are sold in packs of 6.
    How many packs does Jane buy? ______

    How many spare buttons does she have? ______

15. Liz cooks 24 biscuits. The trays each hold 5 biscuits. How many trays does she use? ______

    How many biscuits on the last tray? ______

16. Jane packs eggs in boxes of 6. How many boxes does she need to pack 11 eggs? ______

    How many eggs are in the last box? ______

Name ____________________

Half ($\frac{1}{2}$)

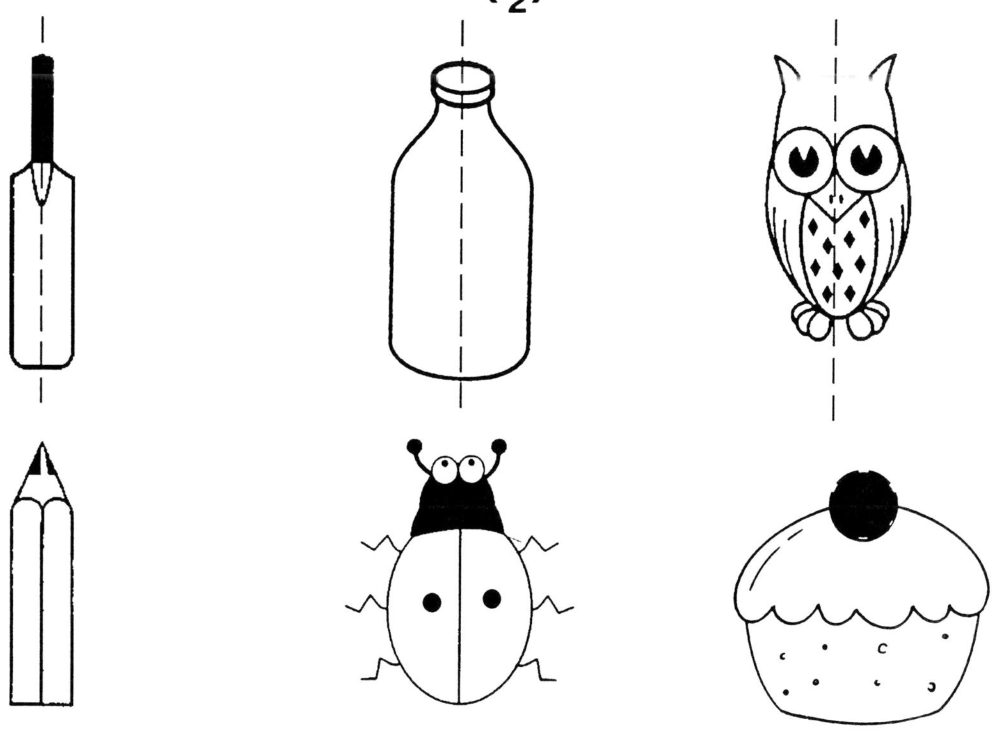

Colour half of each shape red.

Draw a line to divide this star into two halves.

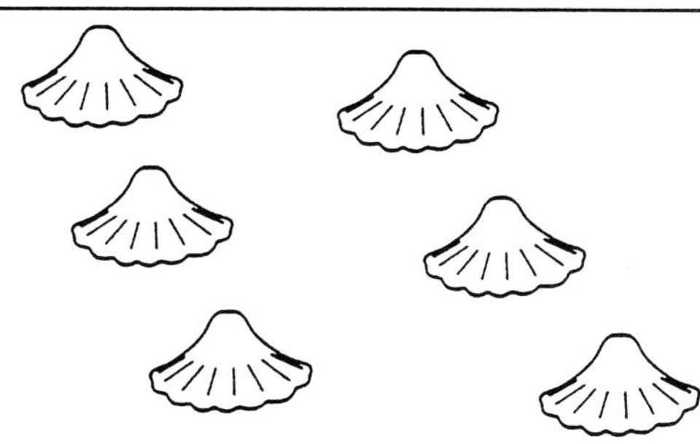

Draw a line to divide these shells into two equal groups.
Colour each group a different colour.

How many shells in each group? ______

How many shells altogether? ________

Draw a line to divide these mice into two equal groups.
Colour each group a different colour.
How many mice in each group? ________
How many mice altogether? ________

Name ________________________________

Quarter ($\frac{1}{4}$)

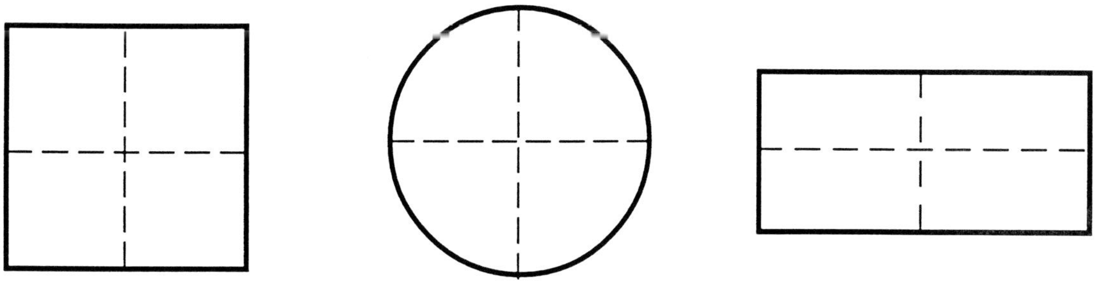

Colour a quarter of each of these shapes red.

Divide these apples into 4 equal groups.
Colour each group a different colour.

How many apples in each group? ________

How many apples altogether? ________

Divide these frogs into 4 equal groups.
Colour each group a different colour.

How many frogs in each group? ________

How many frogs altogether? ________

Name ______________________________

Fractions

1. What fraction of each rectangle is shaded?

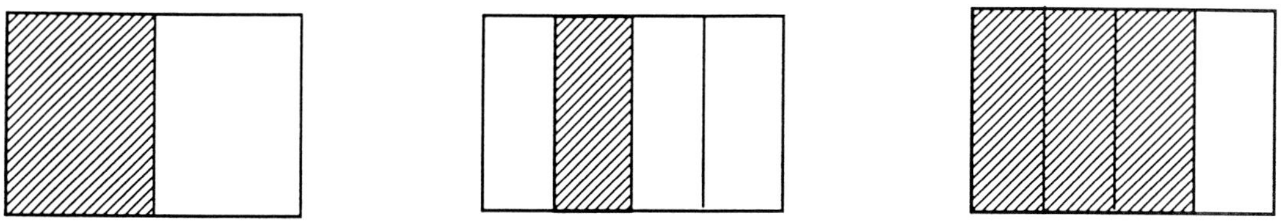

(a) __________ (b) __________ (c) __________

2. Colour these fractions in the squares below.

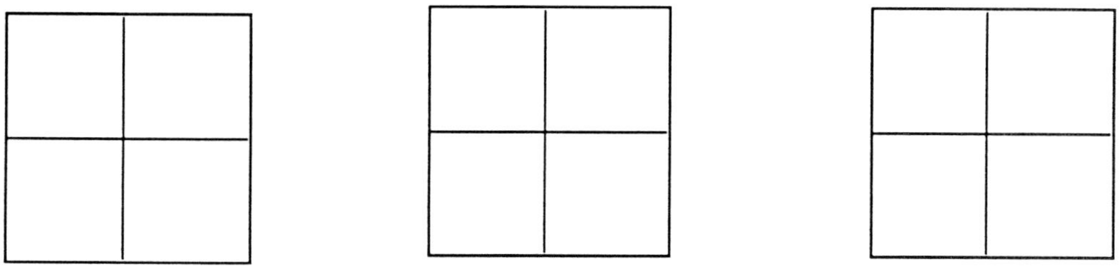

(a) $\frac{1}{4}$ (b) $\frac{3}{4}$ (c) $\frac{1}{2}$

3. What fraction of each tiled floor is shaded?

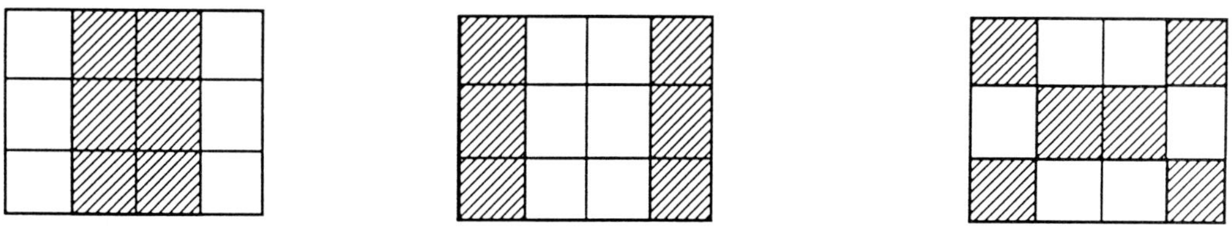

(a) __________ (b) __________ (c) __________

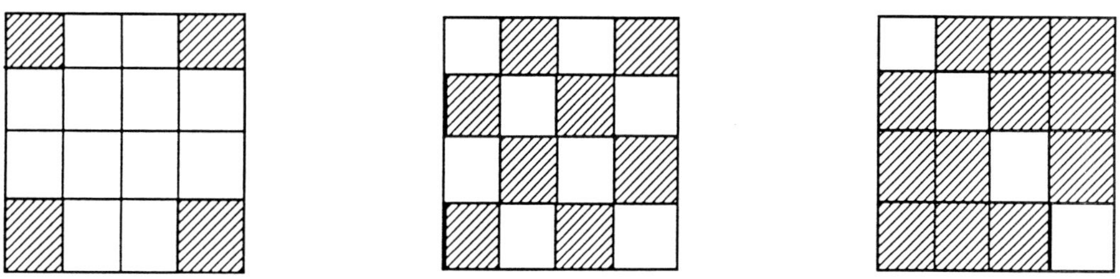

(d) __________ (e) __________ (f) __________

Name ______________________________

Halves and Quarters

Work these out.

A

1. $\frac{1}{2}$ of 4 = ______

2. $\frac{1}{4}$ of 4 = ______

3. $\frac{1}{2}$ of 6 = ______

4. $\frac{1}{2}$ of 8 = ______

5. $\frac{1}{4}$ of 8 = ______

6. $\frac{1}{2}$ of 10 = ______

7. $\frac{1}{2}$ of 12 = ______

8. $\frac{1}{4}$ of 12 = ______

9. $\frac{1}{2}$ of 16 = ______

10. $\frac{1}{4}$ of 16 = ______

B

1. $\frac{1}{2}$ of 20 = ______

2. $\frac{1}{4}$ of 20 = ______

3. $\frac{1}{2}$ of 40 = ______

4. $\frac{1}{4}$ of 40 = ______

5. $\frac{1}{2}$ of 60 = ______

6. $\frac{1}{4}$ of 60 = ______

7. $\frac{1}{2}$ of 80 = ______

8. $\frac{1}{4}$ of 80 = ______

9. $\frac{1}{2}$ of 100 = ______

10. $\frac{1}{4}$ of 100 = ______

Name ______________________________

Doubles and Halves

A Double each number.

2 ------>	5 ------>	7 ------->
8 ------->	10 ----->	20 ------->

B Halve each number

6 ------>	16 ------>	30 ------->
40 ------->	18 ----->	100 ------->

C

1. Jane has 15p. Her mother doubles the money. How much does Jane have now?

   ____

2. John has £1. He spends half of his money. How much does he have left?

   ____

3. A pencil costing 35p is half the cost of a pen. How much does the pen cost?

   ____

4. There are 7 golf balls in one box and twice as many in another box. How many golf balls are in the two boxes altogether?

   ____

5. A book costs £1 and a pen half as much. What is the cost of the book and pen altogether?

   ____

6. John saves twice as much as his sister. If his sister saves £5.00 how much do they save altogether?

   ____

Name ______________________________

Negative Numbers

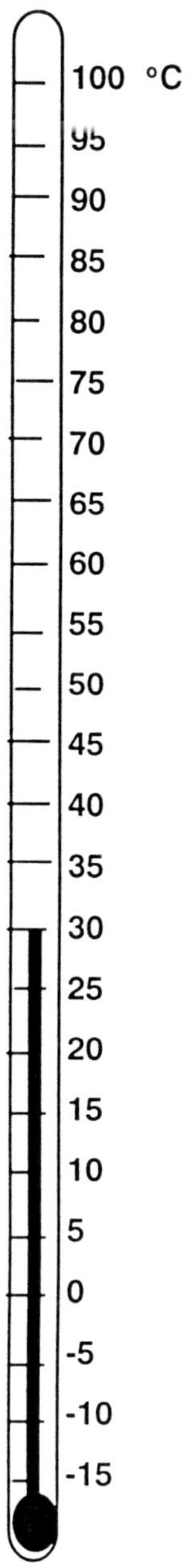

What is the temperature on this thermometer?

If the temperature rises by 10 degrees, what will the new temperature be?

If the temperature falls by 10 degrees, what will the new temperature be?

If the temperature falls by 40 degrees, what will the new temperature be?

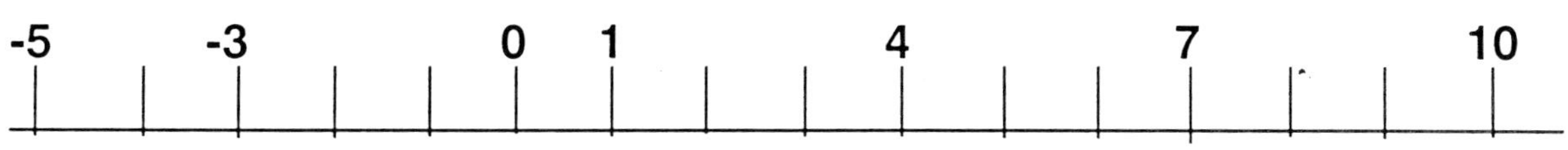

Write the missing numbers in this number line.

Use the number line to work out

the number that is 4 more than 1 ________

the number that is 5 less than 10 ________

the number that is 3 less than 1 ________

the number that is 3 more than -5 ________

the number that is 2 less than -1 ________

Name

Time

1. Write these times.

(a) ____________ (b) ____________ (c) ____________

2. Draw these times on the clocks.

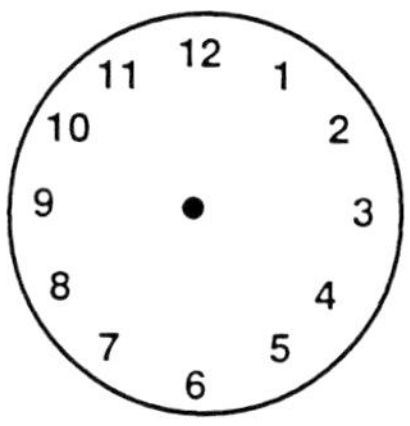
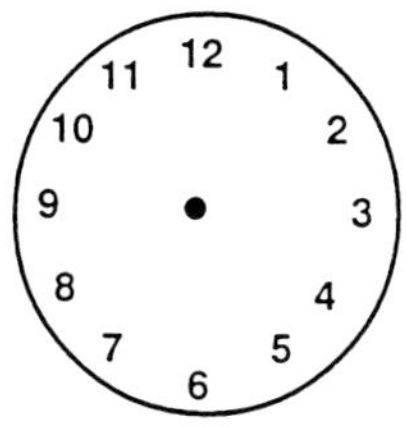
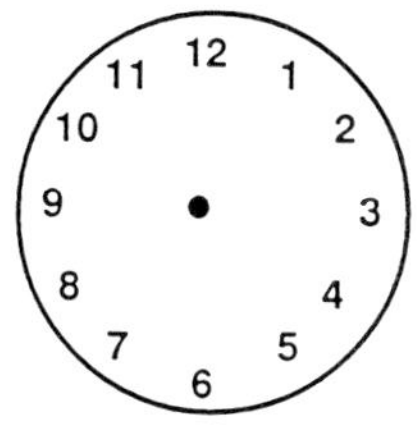

(a) 4 o'clock (b) half past 1 (c) quarter to 8

3. Write the digital times in the watch faces.

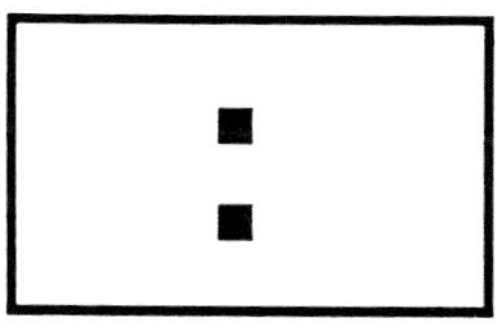
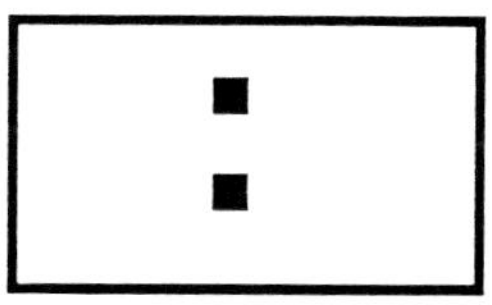
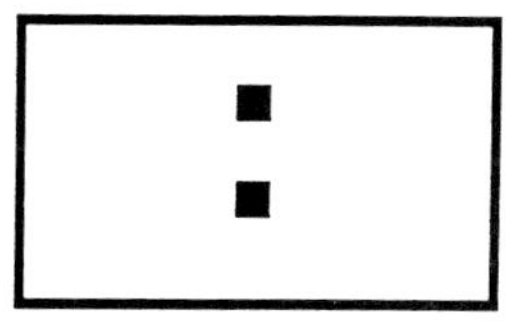

7 o'clock half past 2 quarter to 4

4. How long is it from 2:15 to 2:45? ________

5. Ali takes half an hour to walk to school. What time must he start out if he is to arrive at 8.45?

____

Name ______________________________

The Leisure Centre

The manager of a leisure centre records the number of people using the swimming pool each day. Complete the tally sheet he makes.

Day		Number of swimmers
Mon	///// ///// ///// ///	18
Tues	///// ///// ///// ///// //	
Wed		6
Thurs	///// ///// /	
Fri	///// ///// ////	
Sat		12
Sun	///// ///// ///// ///// ///// ////	

1. How many people swam on Tuesday? ________

2. On which day did the fewest people swim? _______

   How many people swam on this day? ________

3. On which day did most people swim? ________

   How many people swam on this day? _______

4. How many people swam in a week? ________

5. If the manager wanted to cut down the number of hours he opened the swimming pool, on which day would he probably do this?

   ____

Name ____

Sunshine

A

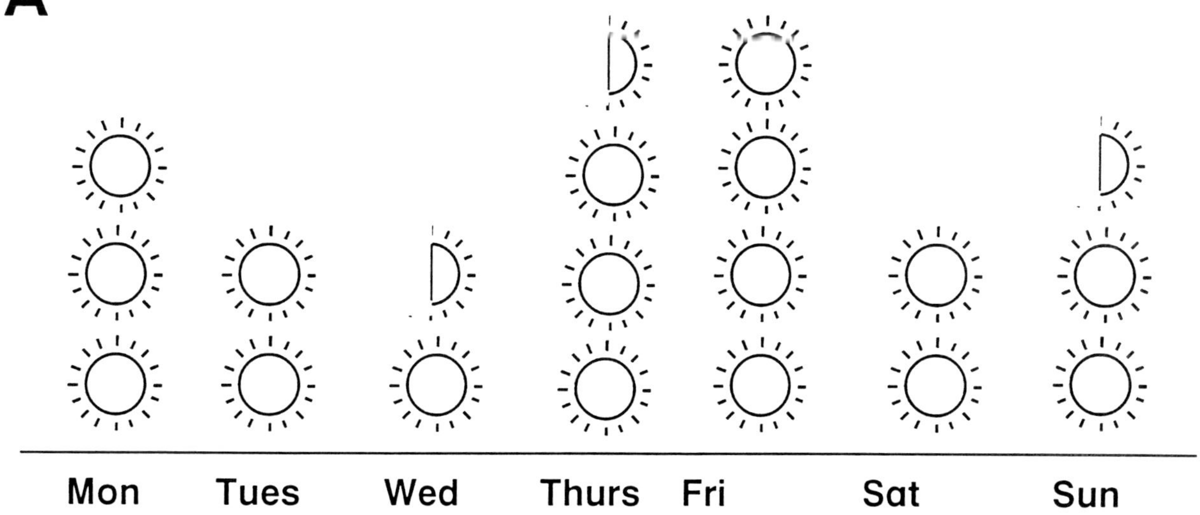

 represents 2 hours of sunshine.

B

The number of hours of sunshine on Monday is ________

The number of hours of sunshine on Sunday is ________

Which two days have the same amount of sunshine?

____

C

The number of hours of sunshine in a week in June are recorded on this chart. The results are represented on the bar chart below. Complete this chart.

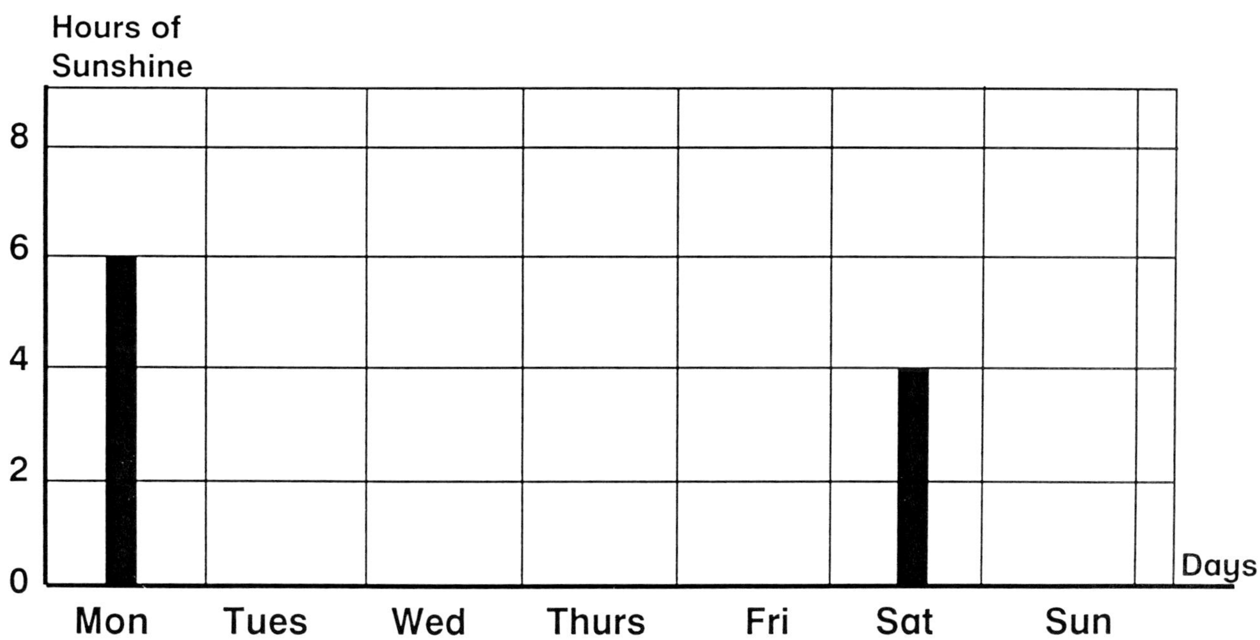

Name ____

Paper 1

1. 7 - 4 = _____

2. Three add one = ______

3. 6 ÷ 3 = ______

4. 9 plus 0 = ______

5. Half of 8 = _____

6. 5 x 2 = _____

7. Which is more: 5 or 9? _____

8. Is 7 even or odd? _____

9. 10 more than 6 is ______

10. Two coins which make 7p. and

11. Find the sum of 3 and 5. _____

12. 11 take away 3. _____

13. How much of the square is shaded? _______

14. How many boots in 5 pairs? ______

15. What is the third letter in the word, SCHOOL? _______

16. Ali saved 10p a week for 5 weeks.
How much money does he have? ______

17. Choose two numbers from 1, 2, 3, 4 and 5
which add up to 4. _______

18. Today is Thursday. What day is it tomorrow? ______

19. Jim spends 13p. How much change does she
have from 20p? ______

20. Quarter of 20 is _______

Name ______________________________

Paper 2

1. Which 2 coins make 12p? _______

2. 9 + 10 = ______

3. The difference between 13 and 9 = _______

4. Write the numbers 1, 2, 3, 4, 5 in the circles so that each side adds up to 9.
   Write each number once only.
   The number 5 has already been written for you.

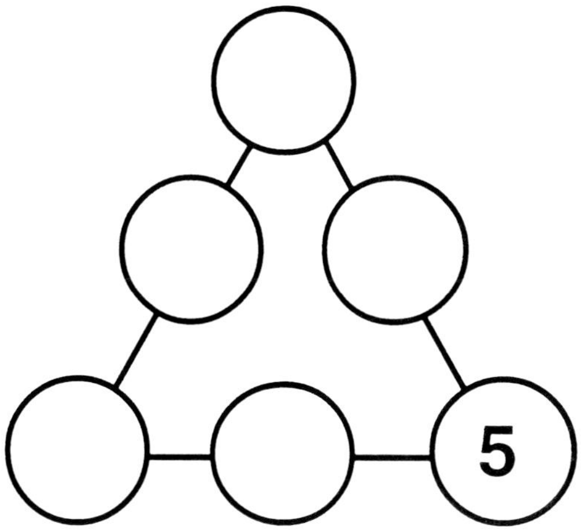

5. Half of 14 = ________

6. 9 minus 0 = _______

7. Which is bigger, 7 mm or 7 km? ________

8. There are 8 pencils in a box.
   How many pencils are in 10 boxes? _______

9. Find the whole number between 17 and 19. _______

10. How much money is in each purse?

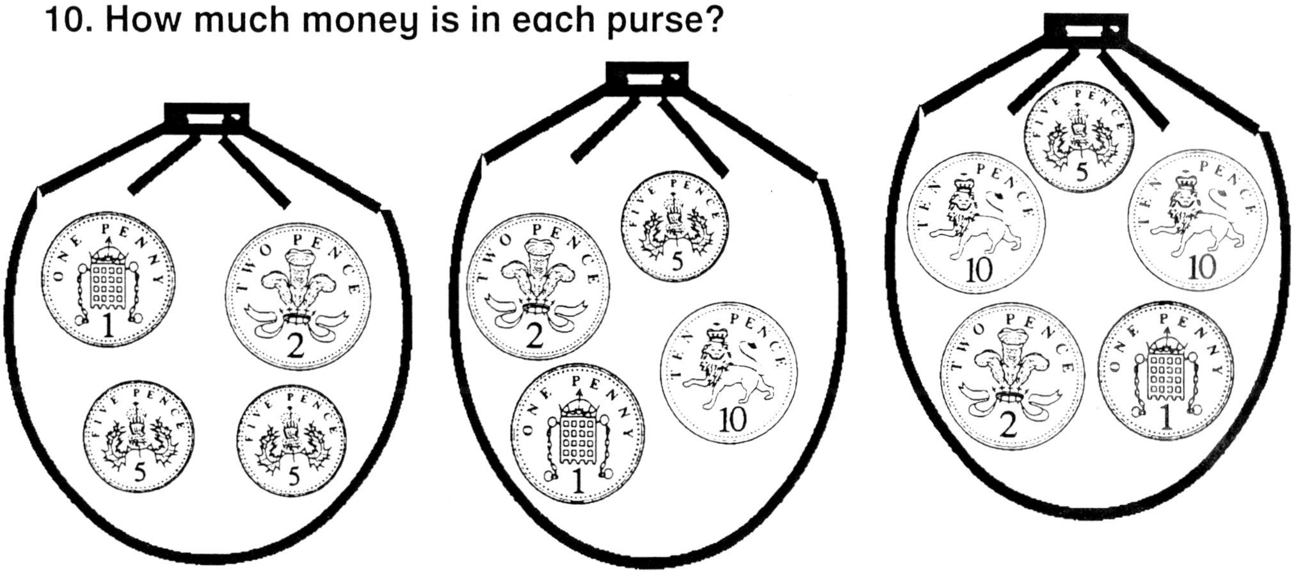

A ________ B _________ C ________

Name ____________________

Paper 3

1. Write thirty-four in figures. _______

2. Jim buys a book using a 10p coin.
He receives 4p in change.
How much does the book cost? _______

3. 9 add 5 = _______

4. 2 + 3 + 6 = _______

5. How many
triangles can you see? ________

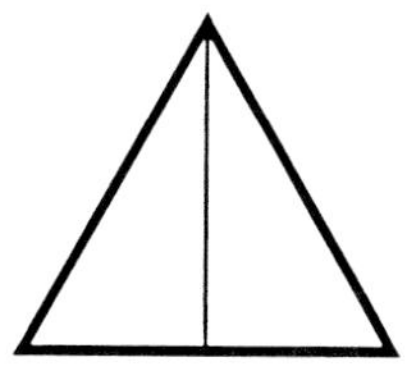

6. Double 7 = _______

7. How many wheels on 3 cars? _______

8. Today is Thursday.
What day was it yesterday? _______

9. Write the numbers shown by the
arrow heads on the number line ______ ______ ______

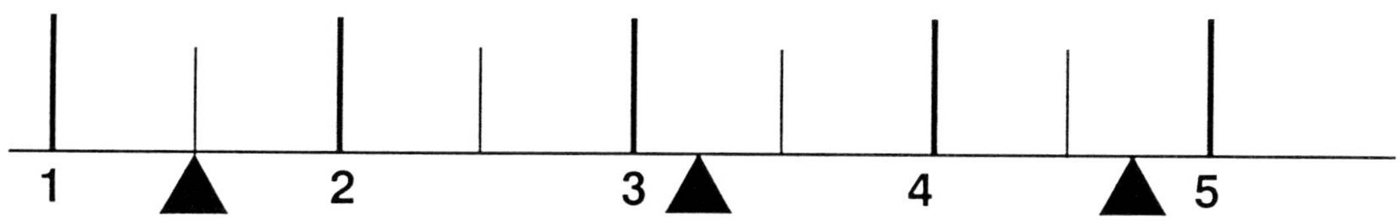

10. How many ducks are in
the pond? _______

How many ducks are
outside the pond? _______

How many ducks are
there altogether? _______

What fraction of the ducks is outside the pond? _______

What fraction of the ducks is inside the pond? _______

Name ______________________________

Paper 4

1. John is 9 years old. His sister is 4 years younger. How old is his sister? ________

2. How many 10p coins make £2? ________

3. Tick the correct answer. David rides his bike to school.

   He takes ☐ 5 seconds ☐ 5 hours ☐ 5 minutes.

4. What must be added to 7 to make 11? ______

5. A mini bus carries 16 passengers. How many buses are needed to take 45 students on an outing? ________

6. Count in 2s to 30.

   2 4 6 ______________________________ 30.

Colour these numbers in the square.

1	2	3	4	5	6	7	8	9	10
11	12	13	14	15	16	17	18	19	20
21	22	23	24	25	26	27	28	29	30

7. Count in 5s to 30.

   5 10 ______________________________ 30.

Colour these numbers in the square.

1	2	3	4	5	6	7	8	9	10
11	12	13	14	15	16	17	18	19	20
21	22	23	24	25	26	27	28	29	30

8. Write the numbers that are coloured in both squares.

   ____

9. Write the next three numbers in this series.

   ____

10. Write three numbers that divide exactly into the numbers in answer 9. ______________

Name ________________________________

Paper 5

1. There are twice as many girls in a class choir as boys. There are 4 boys.
   How many children are in the choir? ________

2. You have 2 dice, each with sides numbered 2, 4, 6, 8, 10, 12. When the two dice are thrown the numbers are added together.

   The highest possible score is ________

   The lowest possible score is ________

   The difference between
   the highest and lowest scores is ________

3. 10p + 30p + 40p = ________

4. 27 ÷ 6 = ________ Remainder ________

5. 23p = ________5p coins and ________ 1p coins.

6. $\frac{1}{2}$ of £1 = ________

7. $\frac{1}{4}$ of 20p = ________

8. Write the time shown on the clock.

____

Write the time digitally. [:]

9. A teacher divides a class of 27 children into teams of 5.

   How many teams are there? ________

   How many children are reserves? ________

10. How many sides on 7 triangles? ________

Name ______________________________

Paper 6

1. There are 7 pencils in a box.
   How many pencils are in 10 boxes? _______

2. 24 + 50 = _______

3. 5 tens and 7 units = _______

4. 36 + 20 = _______

5. How much less than £1 is 85p? _______

6. Ali leaves school at 3.45 pm and arrives home at 4.30 pm.
   How long does his journey take? _______

7. A television programme lasts for $1\frac{1}{4}$ hours.
   It starts at 7.00 pm. What time does it finish? _______

8. 3 pens and 2 pencils cost 42p.
   3 pens and 4 pencils cost 54p.

   The cost of a pencil is _______

   The cost of a pen is _______

9. Write the missing signs.

5	☐	4	=	9
12	☐	7	=	5
20	☐	5	=	4
6	☐	2	=	12

10. The temperature of a greenhouse is 3 °C.
    It falls by 5 °C.
    What is the lower temperature? _______

Name ______________________________

Paper 7

1. There are 9 sweets in half a packet.
   How many sweets are in a full packet? _______

2. Write the even number between 10 and 14. _______

3. Write the odd number between 17 and 21. _______

4. What is 20 more than 59? _______

5. What is 40 less than 67? _______

6. Write seventeen in figures. _______

7. A dog has 8 puppies. 3 are black and the
   rest are brown. How many are brown? _______

8. There are 3 fewer girls in a class than boys.
   There are 15 girls, how many boys are in the class? _______
   How many children are in the class altogether? _______

9. Today is Thursday.
   What day is it tomorrow? _______

10. Write the next three letters. H I H I H __________

11. Write these numbers in order, beginning with the smallest.

    42, 17, 350, 9, 1000 ________________________

12. Write the numbers on these abacuses.

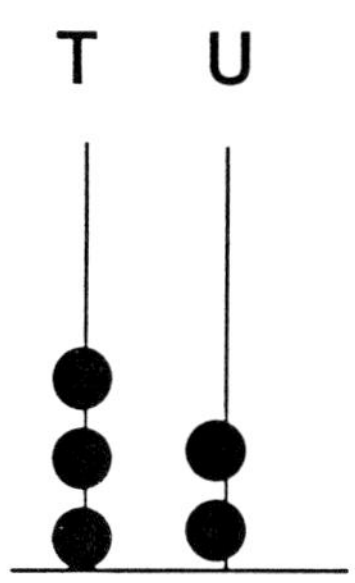

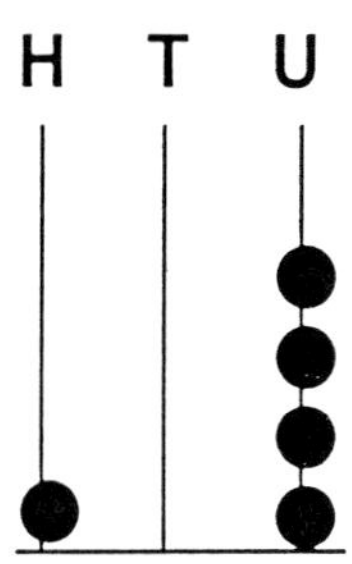

_________ _________

Name ______________________________

Paper 8

1. Circle the even numbers: 4 2 1 5 6 9

2. Draw a line which is half as long as the line AB.

A ———————————— B

3. Jane has 64p. How many pens can she buy if each pen costs 6p? ________

   How much money does she have left? ________

4. 14 + 26 + 3 = ________

5. 43 - 17 = ________

6. 13 ÷ 2 = ________ Remainder _____

7. Ali had 20p. He spent 13p. How much money does Ali have left? ________

8. Mark $-1\frac{1}{2}$, $-\frac{1}{2}$, 0, 2 and $4\frac{1}{4}$ on the number line.

9. 5 children have £10 pocket money to share equally. How much money does each have? ________

0	1	6

10. Use two of these cards to make two numbers that are less than 20. _____ and ______

    a number that is more than 60. ________

    a number that is between 61 and 59. ________

Name ______________________________

Paper 9
The School Fete

1. Visitors had to guess how many apples in a barrel. Ali guessed 111 apples, Jane guessed 100 apples, Jim guessed 106 apples. There were actually 108 apples in the barrel.
Who was nearest to the correct number? ____________

2. In a 3-legged race, team A took 85 seconds, team B took 90 seconds and team C took 96 seconds.

Which team won? ________

Which team came last? _______

3. In the competition for the biggest leek, Farmer John's leek weighed 4 kg, the vicar's leek weighed 3 kg and Farmer Jones's weighed $3\frac{1}{2}$ kg.

Whose leek won first prize? _______

Who won second prize? _______

Who won third prize? _______

4. The graph below shows the food sold at the fete.

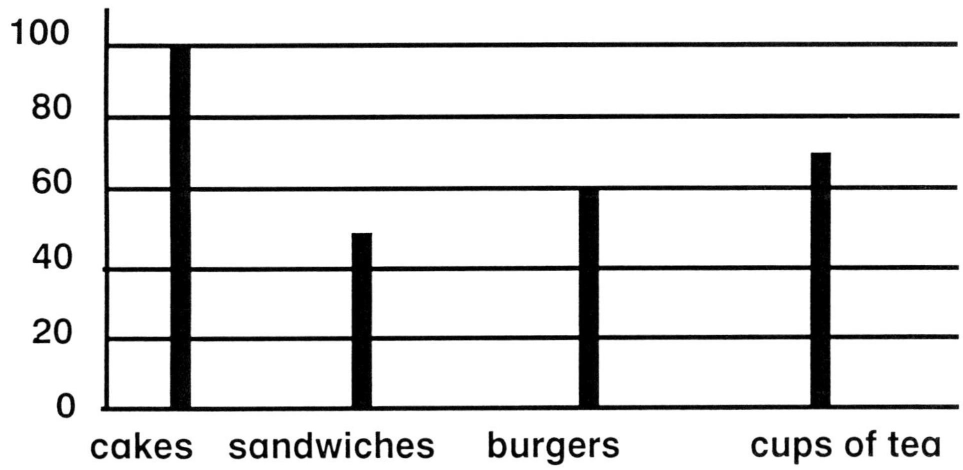

Complete the chart below.

Food	Number sold
cakes	
sandwiches	
burgers	
cups of tea	

If each cup of tea costs 20p, how much did the visitors spend on cups of tea?

____

Name ____

Paper 10

1. Ali has two chances to hit the penguin targets.
Each penguin can be hit only once.

The highest score he can make is ________

The lowest score he can make is _________

The difference between the lowest and highest scores is ________

2. Colour a quarter of this rectangle.

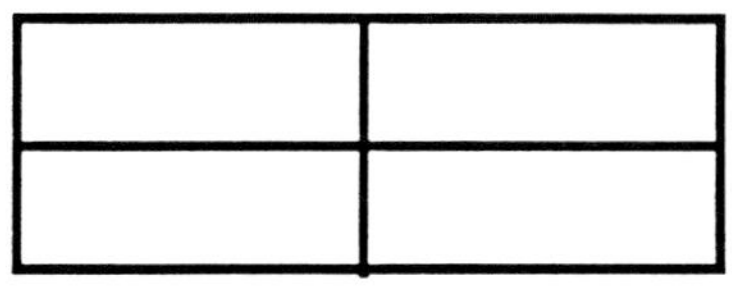

3. In a game, Sam was on square 19. He had to move 7 squares back.
He landed on square number

____

4. Write the missing number in the series 5 10 ☐ 20

5. Draw the numbers 43 and 302 on these abacuses.

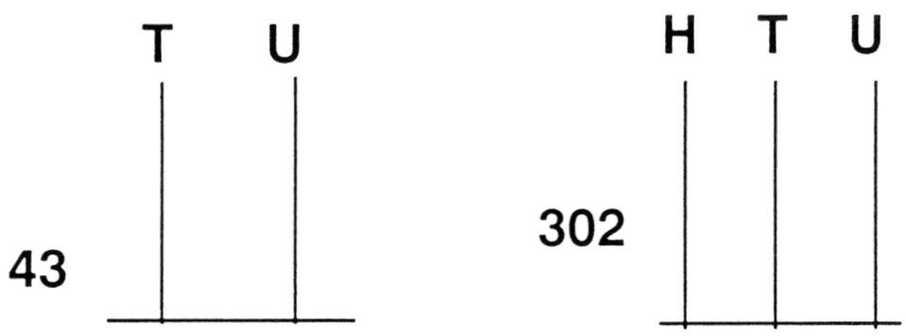

6.

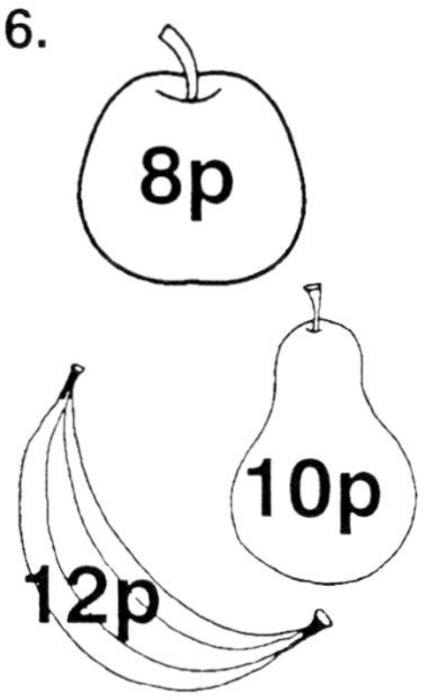

	Change from £1
Cost of an apple and a pear is ________	________
Cost of 2 apples and a banana is ________	________
Cost of 3 pears and a banana is ________	________

TEACHERS' NOTES

Her Majesty's Inspectors have called for greater attention to be paid to mental calculation. They emphasise the need to make sensible estimates, to develop language and a feel for mathematics. Much can be learned from identifying, analysing and correcting errors and misconceptions in understanding number. Discuss how answers are reached.

The Cockcroft Report (1982) pointed out that ***the decline of mental and oral work within mathematics classrooms represent a failure to recognise the central place which working done in the head occupies throughout mathematics. Even when using traditional methods of recording calculations on paper, the written record is usually based on steps which are done mentally.***

Mental maths is about the way we make calculations, the way we do calculations in our heads. It is about the methods and strategies we use. Using everyday maths, people often use their own methods which are not necessarily the same as those taught in school. Although many people develop a variety of methods, children still need to be taught to develop a variety of flexible methods which can be used in different contexts.

The following should be kept in mind:

1. Number activities in the classroom should be relevant to the children's experiences and be seen as worthwhile.

2. Whenever possible, use number activities that relate to things the children want to know. Perform number operations in theoretical and practical situations.

3. Numerical information should be presented in a variety of ways.

4. It is important for children to experience a sense of achievement in number work. Keep targets achievable and ensure you give plenty of encouragement.

5. At the same time ensure that the work stretches and challenges the children through inquiry and problem solving.

6. Encourage children to talk about numbers and make up stories using them. Relate numbers to their families.

7. Read stories containing numbers.

Early operations such as addition and subtraction which young children already experience in everyday life should be developed through activities. The giving out of biscuits or cakes or drinks involves the concepts of enough, not enough, more, fewer ... Children will also be aware of sharing (practical dividing).

Role play encourages children to become familiar with quantities used in real life. In their everyday experiences, they see very large numbers but they may not understand what they mean and be confused by them.

Worksheets

Pages 5 - 7 **Matching.** This work develops observational skills and the recognition of pattern and sequence.

Pages 8 **Counting to 5.** Practice in counting to 5.

Page 9 - 11 **Counting to 5 and sets.** This work develops the concept of sets.

Page 12 **Zero sets.** This helps children to understand and recognise the concept of empty sets and zero.

Page 13 - 15 **Sets.** More practice in counting to 5 and using sets.

Page 16 **Counting to 5 and finding missing numbers.**

Page 17 - 21 **Counting to 10 and using sets.**

Page 22 **Introduction of counting.** This develops the concept of counting on to 10.

*From the same publishers.
There are numerous worksheets on the early development of numeracy skills in ***First Steps, Beginning Mental Maths*** **(ISBN 1 85772 142 X),** ***Mental Maths 5 - 6 years*** **(ISBN 1 85772 143 8) and** ***Mental Maths 6 - 7 years*** **(ISBN 1 85772 146 2). For an introduction to the concept of number see** ***First Steps, Number and Counting*** **(ISBN 1 85772 133 0).**

Page 23 **Numbers in between.** Calculating the number in between helps to learn the order of numbers.

Page 24 **Number lines.** Practice in finding missing numbers helps the children learn to count.

Pages 25 - 26 **Number pairs to 5 and to 10.** It is useful for children to become familiar with numbers that add up 5 to 10.

Page 27 **Counting to 10.** This gives the children practice in counting in familiar situations.

Pages 28 - 29 **1p coins.** This begins the introduction of money.

Page 30 **Numbers and words.** This work relates numbers, their names and the concept of what they stand for.

Pages 31- 33 **Add 1.** The start of addition. At first the children draw the extra item, then they do the exercise in their heads.

Page 34 **Counting on.** This develops the important practice of not starting from 1 to continue a count.

Page 35 **1 more than.** Again this develops the concept of counting on in the head.

Pages 36 - 37 **Add 1.** These worksheets extend the work to use numbers and not drawings.

Page 38 **Counting back.** This work requires the children to count back as the preliminary to taking away.

Pages 39 - 41 **1 less than.** These sheets develop the concept of taking away, at first using drawings and then with numbers.

Pages 42 - 45 **Coins.** This work introduces the concept of 2p, 5p and 10p coins and idea of change.

Pages 46 - 47 **Missing numbers.** This work involves finding the numbers missing in simple sums and in number lines.

Pages 48 - 53 **Numbers to 10 and then to 20. Addition and Number Stories.** The work develops away from the early counting of objects to quicker paper work. Children need to become proficient in counting on and be able to cope with say, 2 + 8 as quickly as 8 + 2. If the children are confident then some of the worksheets are suitable for rapid calculations in the head. It is important that the children should be able to relate the work to everyday problems and understand number stories.

Page 54 - 55 **Subtraction within 10 and then within 20.** Children need practice in the concept of 'taking away'. Some of the work is particularly suitable for rapid calculations in the head. Number story problems help the children to relate the work to situations.

Page 56 - **Simple statements with missing numbers.** This work gives more practice in handling addition and subtraction within 10.

Page 57 **Sums to 20.** More practice in dealing with numbers up to 20.

Page 58 **Flexible approach to numbers that make 10.** It is important that children appreciate that 10 (and later other numbers) can be obtained in different ways including the use of zero and negative numbers.

Page 59 **More number stories.**

Page 60 **Change from 20p.** This may be done as a practical exercise or as a follow-up/test to practical work.

Pages 61 **Counting to 100.** This involves the use of the hundred square for addition, subtraction and the formation of series.

Pages 62 **Place value.** Work begins with the hundred square and continues with practice in working out place values.

Page 63 **Shopping and money.** This may be treated as practical work or as exercises to follow up and reinforce practical work done before.

Page 64 **Money.** This gives more practice in adding and subtraction using money to £1.

Page 65 - 68 **Counting in groups and sets.** This leads to the concept of multiplication beginning with 2, 3, 4, 5 and 10. There is practice in the relationship between counting in groups and multiplication as well as some simple number stories.

Pages 69 - 71 **Sharing and dividing.** The work develops the idea of sharing into dividing and includes some simple number stories. The idea of 'remainders' is explored.

Pages 72 - 75 **Halves and quarters.** The work is well illustrated with clear diagrams ending with a worksheet of numerical problems.

Page 76 **Doubles and halves.** This work explores the relationship between doubling and halving quantities.

Page 77 **Negative numbers.** This illustrates the concept of a negative number and the use of number lines.

Pages 78 **Time.** Telling the time is an essential skill. Children need to be able to read analogue and digital clocks.

Pages 79 - 80 **Handling data.** This is very important. The way in which data is presented often influences the way in which it is understood or misunderstood. It is necessary to investigate the different ways in which data can be presented from pictograms to charts. The work here involves interpreting data presented in several different ways and answering questions about it. (At a later stage children may like to investigate what happens when only part of a graph or chart is available for study - does this affect the interpretation of the results and so on.)

Pages 81 - 90 **Practice papers.** These give practice in the work already dealt with. These tests may be used as revision and consolidation work or as timed exercises.

NUMBER

Children need to develop strong mental images of the number system. They need to be able to see, show, understand and explain how the mathematics can be explained. They need to be able to use

positive whole numbers
negative whole numbers
the concept of zero
fractions.

The number line is a convenient way of representing the number system.

-100 -10 -3-2-1 0 1 2 3 10 100

Whole numbers

A number consists of digits and the value of a digit depends on its place, e.g. 5 means 5 units (U), 50 means 5 tens (T), 500 means 5 hundreds (H) and 5000 means 5 thousands (Th). Thus
ten units make one ten, 10
ten tens make one hundred, 100
and ten hundreds make one thousand, 1,000
Place value is easily shown on a counting frame or abacus, e.g the number 423.

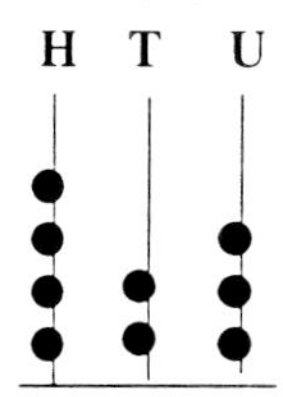

Ordering

Being able to compare different numbers is essential to understanding their values e.g. smallest, middle and biggest. Similarly, it is necessary to be able to put several numbers in order.

Approximating numbers

Children need to be able to round a number to the nearest ten. If the number is greater or equal to 5, round up to the next ten. If the number is less than 5, round down to the ten i.e.
36 becomes 40 to the nearest 10

51 becomes 50 to the nearest 10
25 becomes 30 to the nearest 10
97 becomes 100 to the nearest 10
Approximating to the nearest 100 depends on whether the number is greater, less than or equal to 50 i.e.
263 becomes 300 to the nearest 100
650 becomes 600 to the nearest 100
754 becomes 700 to the nearest 100

Negative numbers
This is easily illustrated with reference to the Centigrade scale with the temperature of melting ice being 0°C. Temperatures above are positive and temperatures below are negative. A common situation involves bank accounts when more money is spent than there is in an account, the account is overdrawn with a negative balance.

Fractions
A fraction is part of a whole number. The most common are

$\frac{1}{4}$ = a quarter $\frac{1}{2}$ = a half $\frac{3}{4}$ = three-quarters

Number Patterns and Sequencing
These are formed by repeating numbers in a regular order or sequence which can be predicted.

Even and Odd Numbers
Even numbers can be divided into two equal parts, they can be divided by 2 without any remainder. It is necessary to look at the last digit in the number. If it is even (0, 2, 4, 6 or 8), the number is even.
Odd numbers cannot be divided into two equal parts. There is always one left only as a remainder. It is necessary to look at the last digit in the number. If it is odd (1, 3, 5, 7 or 9), the number is odd.

Four Basic Arithmetic Operations

Addition
This means adding or finding the sum or total. Children should be able to recognise and deal with (+) and understand that 'and' means add up, i.e. 4 and 3 = 7 for example. They should have practice in exercises such as add 1, add 2, add 10. Some sums may require the problem to be set as HTU.

Subtraction
This means taking away, finding the difference or minus. Children need practice in taking away 1, taking away 2, taking away 10.

Multiplication
Children need to understand that this is repeated addition. They should learn the two, three, four, five and ten times tables up to 10.

Division
Children need to understand that this is repeated subtraction. Children are well aware of sharing and the concept that sometimes the number cannot be shared equally so that there is a remainder.

Relate the examples to real situations such as laying a table, buttons on clothes, busses and passengers, time ... Include games such as dominoes, dice and cards.

COMPARING

Children need to compare objects in relation to size and time.
Size: big, large, small, little, short, tall, long, thin, wide, narrow ...
Time: quick, slow, fast, a long time, a short time.
Children learn who is the tallest and the shortest, the tallest house or tree, the smallest stone. Compare the size of shoes: children can arrange them in order of size. Compare the size of books and which is heaviest or lightest. Children can make towers from building blocks of different heights.
Enough/not enough. Playing tea party introduces the concept that each person has the same, there must be enough cups, plates, pretend cakes and tea ...

ORDERING

Children need to understand first, second, third ... first, last ... Dressing is an excellent way to understand ordering. Children know what clothes go on first. Hold up the wrong item and ask if it goes on first. Ask children to plan their day: First get up, second have breakfast ... Some stories are useful such as *Goldilocks and the Three Bears*. Children can list their favourite TV programmes or different flavours of crisps in order of preference.

ZERO or NOUGHT

This is a special number. Give a child say 5 toys or buttons and tell him/her to count them. Then ask the child to give you the objects one at a time while counting back from 5. When the last one is given to you say zero or nought: there are no toys left and so zero means none.

WRITING NUMBERS

Children need as much practice as possible in writing numbers.

NUMBER CARDS

Children make towers of bricks or piles of stones and then match number cards with them. Encourage the children to arrange the bricks in groups of 2 so that they are easy to count.

PROBLEM SOLVING

Some problems may be dealt with in a short time, others may take a few days.

1. Starting a task involves understanding the problem and deciding what to do.
2. Carrying out the task may mean choosing ways and means, deciding on materials, drawing a picture and trying out different strategies to find out one that works.
3. Reporting on the task and discussing the results and other possible ways of carrying it out.

These three stages in problem solving match those in Key Stage 1, *Using and Applying Mathematics* as required by the National Curriculum, that is

1. Making and monitoring decisions to solve problems.
2. Developing mathematical language and communication.
3. Developing mathematical reasoning.

Making a plan This will be verbal but children can be encouraged to draw a picture and record numbers in whatever way they choose.

Choosing materials This may have already been decided by the nature of the problem. If not then the children can discuss and decide what is best.

Estimating Children should be encouraged to make a guess and then if possible find out how close they are by counting.

Use knowledge they have already acquired.

Discuss the progress of the task. Learning to evaluate how a task is getting on is an invaluable skill.

Evaluating the effectiveness of the work. The final work should be compared with what was planned at the outset. Learning to put forward ideas and opinions and at the same time listen to other people is an important part of education.

Throughout, children should be encouraged to try and tackle problems, suggest alternative strategies, persevere even when the going becomes difficult, learn to work with their peers and be willing to put forward and to listen to other opinions and solutions.

Books, rhymes and songs There are many action stories, rhymes and songs which are useful. Some examples are listed in this book.

Cooking At home children love to help in the kitchen and cooking contains all the concepts of mathematics and the associated language. Role play in the nursery is invaluable in this kind of activity.

Art and craft work involves paper folding, plasticine, clay, dough and painting.

Nature studies involve measurements of growth and time in plants and animals.

REPRESENTING DATA

Graphs and charts

Data and information may be represented by block or bar charts, symbols in pictograms and line graphs. Material is often presented in charts, lists and menus. Children need to consider the ways in which information is presented and decide which is the best way. They need to discuss why particular methods are chosen and if they affect the interpretation of the information presented.

PATTERNS

Children need to be able to recognise pattern in symbols and numbers. Discuss the importance of pattern in everyday life from the tiles on bathroom walls to windows in building.

SHAPES AND SYMMETRY

Two-dimensional shapes are identified according to whether they are round or have angles and sides.
Triangles have 3 sides and 3 angles.
Quadrilaterals have 4 sides and 4 right angles. If the sides are equal, the quadrilateral is a square, if the opposite sides are equal, the quadrilateral is a rectangle.
Polygons have more than 4 sides
Circles and semi-circles are the two most common circular shapes.

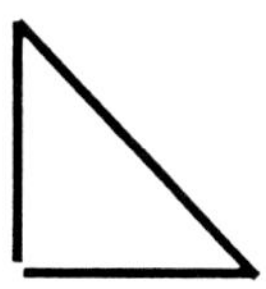

right-angled triangle

triangle with 3 equal sides

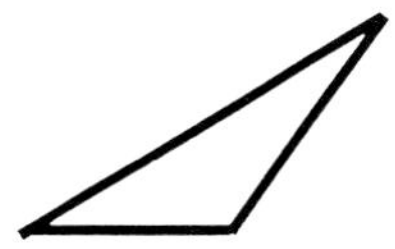

triangle with sides of different length

quadrilateral with 4 sides equal
square

quadrilateral with opposite sides equal
rectangle

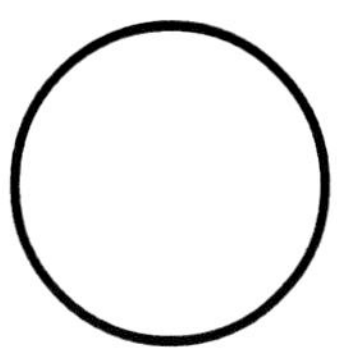

circle

semicircle

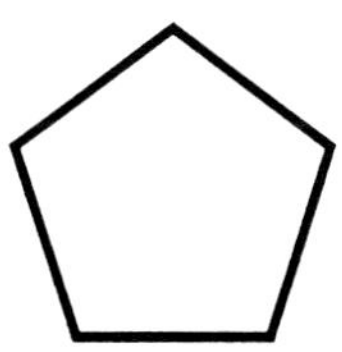

polygon - pentagon (5 sides)

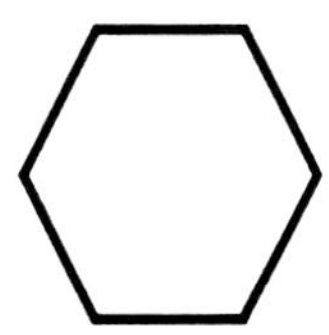

polygon - hexagon (6 sides)

Three-dimensional (3-D) shapes include the sphere, cube, cuboide and cylinder. 3-D objects have volume while 2-D shapes have area.

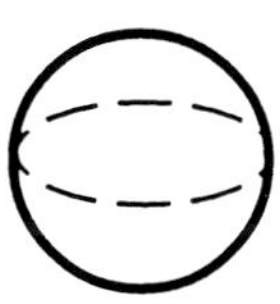

sphere

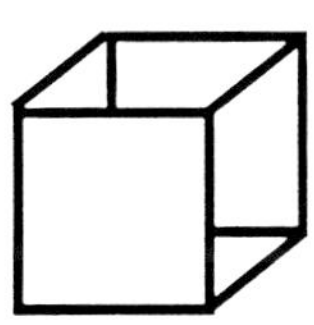

cube

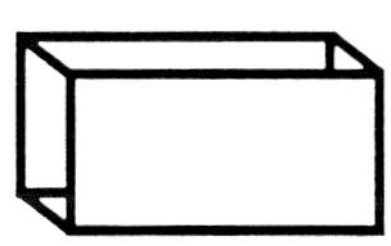

cuboid

cylinder

REFLECTION IN A MIRROR LINE

Children are used to looking at themselves in a mirror. They may not realise that their image is a left-to-right reflection. They need to imagine folding the mirror line, what the shape on the other side of the mirror line will look like and then draw the shape on the other side of the mirror line.

Reflective symmetry

When a shape can be folded exactly into two halves, the fold line is called a line of symmetry.

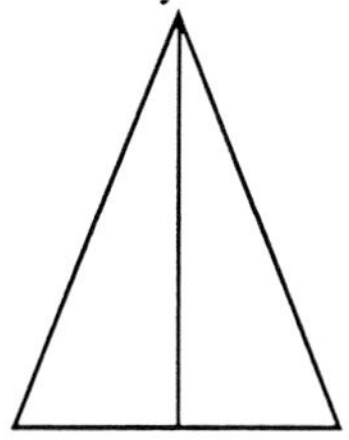

triangle with two equal sides
has one line of symmetry

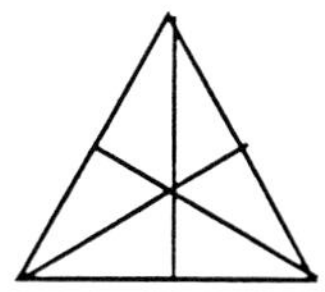

triangle with three equal sides
has three lines of symmetry

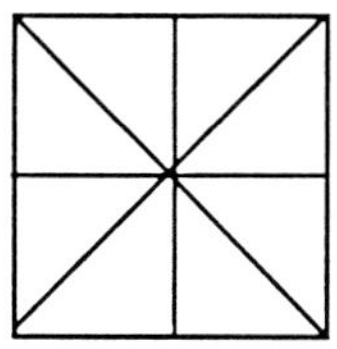

square has four lines
of symmetry

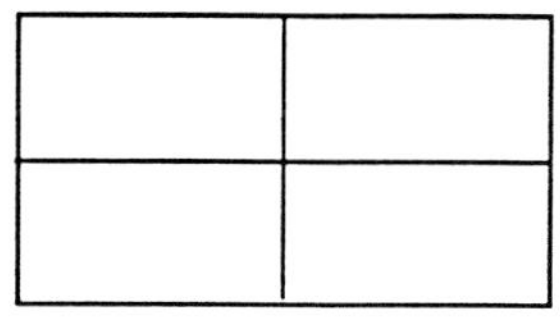

rectangle has two lines
of symmetry

POSITION

Position says where an object is. Children need to understand and use words such as by, near, under, on top of, in, next to, above, beneath, underneath ... Children need to be able to relate position to a numbered grid and read co-ordinates. They need to understand the meaning of turn left and right.

MOVEMENT

Shapes can be made to move by translation and by rotation.
Translation involves moving an object by sliding the shape in any direction.
Rotation involves turning a shape about a point. It may be rotated in a clockwise or anti-clockwise direction.

REPEATING PATTERNS

Many patterns consist of translations, rotations or a combination of these movements.

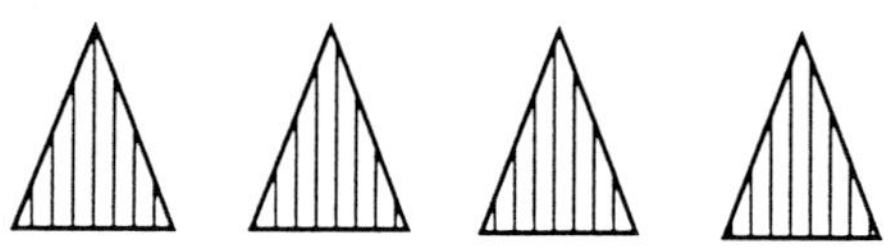

Pattern formed by translation of the triangle.

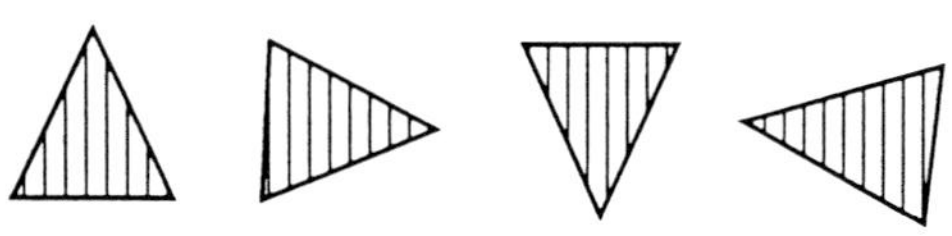

Pattern formed by rotation of the triangle.

ANGLES

An angle is a measure of the turn between two lines. Children need to know about right angles, 90°, 180°, 270° and 360°

MEASUREMENTS

Children need to know the metric and imperial units for length/distance, weight/mass, capacity/volume and time. They need to know the relationship between millimetres, centimetres, metres and kilometres; grams, kilograms and tonnes; millilitres, centilitres and litres; seconds, minutes and hours; days, weeks, months and years. They need to be able to choose the most appropriate unit and be able to estimate length, volume, weight and time.

GETTING MATHS NOTICED

Use maths displays to stimulate work and discussion.
Display numbers and information relating to mathematical situations. For example, label the shelves in the tidy cupboard with the number of items supposed to be on them.
Make maths important by sitting with the children and discussing what they are doing.
Give constructive praise, e.g. 'your tower is taller than John's. You must have used more bricks. That's very good.'
At circle time, encourage children to explain clearly what they are doing. At the same time encourage them to listen to others.
Ask the children what they have learned during the day. Writing this on the board reinforces what they say.
It is important to count something with children every day in both nursery and reception.

Methods used in mental maths are based on a sound understanding of number and a good recall of number facts. Oral sessions help to build up the speed and confidence of the children in recalling facts, using those facts and developing their awareness of the number system without worrying about formal recording. Children choose their own methods. Draw attention to the different ways of doing things by asking the children as often as possible how they worked things out.

MENTAL MATHS IN THE CLASSROOM

It is important that each child feels at ease and not under pressure to work and answer quickly.

Give children time to work out the questions.
Children should not call out answers but should use an agreed signal that they are ready with an answer.
It is important that all the children should listen to the answers given by others.
Begin with easy questions so that everyone feels able to take part.
Be sure that all the children are paying attention.
Keep the sessions short.
Keep the language simple so that the children can concentrate on the maths.
Make time 'on the carpet' interesting and fun.
Respond to all contributions so that each child feels valued.

Ask
Has anyone got a different answer?
What do the rest of you think?
Are there any other ways we could do this?

Children need lots of practice to develop mental strategies. Five or ten minutes of 'carpet time' each day to talk about mathematics is better than half-an-hour once a week. The session is usually best at the beginning of the day when the children are wide awake. Children learn best when they have an active role to play. Many answers will be given orally. This helps to build confidence and speed of the children without formal recording.

LANGUAGE FOR CALCULATIONS

Children have to learn to talk about the ways in which they perform calculations in their heads. This can be difficult. They have to learn and understand the vocabulary needed. This is done talking about counting and calculating using a wide range of equipment from cubes, number lines, cooking, shopping and number rhymes. Children find it difficult to explain how they have carried out a calculation. For example, 3 add 1 or 3, 1 more. Children may work this out quickly and easily by counting on their fingers. However, when asked what they have done, they may not understand the question or know how to tell us. They have to practice talking about their calculations and learn the vocabulary. Gradually they will begin to analyse and talk about what is going on in their heads. Explain there is more than one way of doing some calculations: e.g. use cubes, use fingers, use a number line. With older children, it is necessary to discuss different methods.

MOVING ON

Children need to learn

specific number facts such as number bonds to 5, to 10 and 20.

that once a set has been counted, it does not have to be counted again.

that it is sometimes easier to change the order of a calculation, e.g. that 1 more than 5 is easier than 5 more than 1.

Praise children and ask questions to encourage them to understand what they are doing and to extend their work.

Can you think of a quicker way of doing that?

Can you think of another way of doing that?

Put that number in your head (instead of counting again).

Be sure that your response to the work and questions of the children is positive and encouraging.

How did you do that?

That is really good but can you think of another way?

Can anyone think of a different way?

Children are not usually able to work quickly at this age. The emphasis is on

understanding the work.

being able to discuss and explain what they are doing.

extending their vocabulary.

developing the flexibility and range of the calculating methods they use.

MENTAL PICTURES

Children need help to imagine and 'see' pictures in their heads.

Describe objects/animals and then ask the children to describe what they can 'see'. e.g. a large thick book with red covers, or a small thin book with green covers, a white dog with a black spot...

Have a number of different cats on a page. Describe one and ask the children to identify the one you are thinking of.

Ask children to imagine a number line using T-shirts on a line or hats in a row ...

Use stories and rhymes e.g. ***Goldilocks and the Three Bears, Two Littly Dicky Birds ...***

Imagine a bus and different numbers of people getting on and off it.

CIRCLE GAMES

These activities are done with the children sitting in a circle on the carpet.

Sorting. The children might sort various items according to size, colour or use ...

Counting. This may be done around the circle beginning again when 5 or 10 or 20 is reached. Include zero when the children are comfortable with it.

Each child in turn holds up his or her fingers. The next child has to say the number.

Give each child in turn a group of beads of two colours. The child counts the beads.

Each child in turn counts on from 5 to a given number. Remind the children they do not need to count the 5.

Count back from 5 or 10 or 20.

Spread number cards on the floor face down. Each child in turn picks up a card and counts on (or counts back) from the number on it.

Give each child 4 beads. Ask them to arrange them in different ways and count them again. Ask if it is necessary to count them again.

Give each child a number card and then ask them to put themselves in order.

Give each child a number card. Choose two adjacent odd numbers to hold up their cards. Ask who has the card that comes between the two numbers.

Repeat choosing two adjacent even numbers.

RHYME

The importance of rhyme and rhythm for very young children cannot be overestimated. First, let them listen to rhyme and rhythm and then get them to participate. If possible give the children something to use in these 'poetry' activities such as a bell, triangle, drum, tambourine, maracas or whistle. These can be blown or shaken in time with the beat with you leading. A list of suggested rhymes is given at the end of this section.

GAMES

Elsewhere we have stressed the importance of play at this age. If the children are divided into two groups or sets, a competitive element is introduced and this can be fun. The sets should be equitable and avoid boys only and girls only

groups. Miming actions are very useful.

It is very important to keep the activities within the ability and the stage of development of the individual child. Moving too fast, unintentionally trying to do too much or extending the material too far, can cause confusion and fear. As well, we have all met the bright child who becomes bored and frustrated because he/she is not able to go fast enough. No one said teaching was easy.

STORIES AND RHYMES

Goldilocks and the Three Bears
Snow White and the Seven Dwarfs
The Three Billy Goats Gruff
The Three Little Pigs
As I was going to St Ives
Hickory, Dickory, Dock
One, Two, Buckle My Shoe
Three Blind Mice
One, Two, Three, Four, Five,
    Once I Caught a Fish Alive
One, Two, Three, Four, Mary at the Cottage Door
The First Day of Christmas
Ten Green Bottles
Two Little Dicky Birds
Five Fat Gentlemen
Five Little Soldiers
Peter Hammers with One Hammer
Ten Little Men
One Man and His Dog went to mow the Meadow

DEVELOPING NUMERACY SKILLS
CHECKLIST

√	
	Matching and recognition of pattern.
	Recognition of numbers to 3/5/10100 and 1000s.
	Numbers and words.
	Number bonds to 5/10.
	Counting, naming, numbers.
	Writing numbers.
	Zero.
	Number line.
	Missing numbers in simple additions.
	Solving numerical problems.
	Number bonds to 20.
	Addition within 20.
	Add 1.
	Add 2.
	Understand addition as counting on.
	Using + sign.
	10 + numbers.
	Holding numbers in 'your head'.
	HTU.
	Subtraction within 20.
	Subtraction as counting back.
	Missing numbers in simple subtractions.
	Using - sign.
	Sums with + and - signs.
	Number patterns.
	100-number square.
	Change from 20p.
	Counting to 100.
	Comparing numbers.
	Place value.
	Abacus.
	Odd and even numbers.
	Money and 1p, 2p, 5p, 20p and 50p coins.
	Money.
	Change from £1.
	Shopping to £1.
	Money and shopping.
	Sets.
	Counting sets of 2.
	Multiplying by 2.
	Counting sets of 3.
	Multiplying by 3.
	Counting sets of 4.
	Multiplying by 4.
	Counting sets of 5.
	Multiplying by 5.
	Multiplying by 3, 4 and 5.
	Counting in 10s.

√	
	Multiplication tables.
	Numerical problems.
	Sharing equally between two.
	Sharing amongst three.
	Dividing.
	Dividing with remainders.
	Numerical problems.
	Half.
	Quarter .
	Fractions.
	Doubling.
	Halving.
	Negative numbers.
	Time.
	Measurement and units.
	Choice of units.
	Units in everyday use.
	Presentation of data.
	Handling data.
	Use of lists and charts.
	Use of pictograms.
	Use of line graphs.
	Use of bar charts.
	Patterns.
	Position.
	Movement.
	Translation and rotation.
	Maps and position.
	Recognition of different shapes..
	Symmetry and reflection.
	Reflective symmetry.
	Characteristics of different shapes: sides, angles.
	Comparison of objects for size.
	Position words and words for movement.
	Ordering numbers.
	Ideas of 'enough', more, less ...
	Exploring children's mental strategies.
	Talking about and explaining new strategies.
	Language: tall, medium, short, wider, thinner, full, empty, holds more/less, heavy/light/weighs more than, fast/slow.
	Recognise and recreate repeating patterns.
	Conservation of number.
	Understand and use the vocabulary of comparing and ordinal numbers.
	Order and complete sequence of numbers.
	Say a number lying between two others.
	Order selected numbers.

From the same publishers
For further practice see *First Steps Beginning Mental Maths for 4 - 5 year olds* (ISBN 185772 142 X), *First Steps Mental Maths 5 - 6 year olds* (ISBN 185772 143 8) and *First Steps Beginning Mental Maths for 6 - 7 year olds* (ISBN 185772 146 2). For an introduction to the concept of number see *First Steps Number and Counting* (ISBN 185772 133 0),

ANSWERS

Of course, there may be some alternative answers or presentations which are correct and acceptable.

Page 7

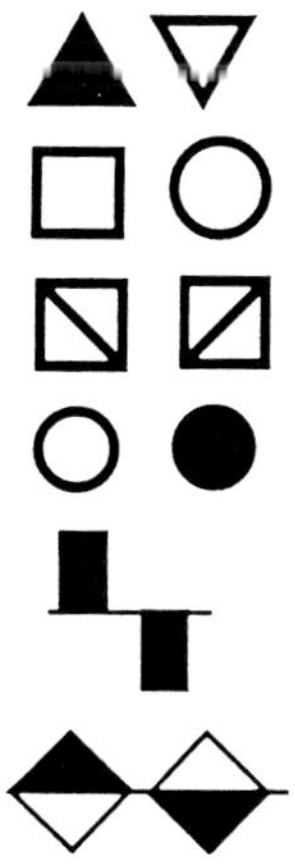

Page 8
23
4
5
2 4

Page 9
3 rabbits
4 mice
2 tigers
1 dog
5 swans

Page 11
2, 3
5, 1
4, 5

Page 13
red - cow, elephant
blue - frogs, ducks
green - tadpoles, bees

Page 14
purple - octopus, lion
green - sheep, snakes
orange - tortoises, dogs

Page 16
2
4
3
1, 5
2, 4
1, 3, 5

Page 17
3, 4
4, 5
5, 6
6, 7
7, 8
8, 9
9, 10

Page 18
8 cats
6 fish
10 tadpoles

Page 19
Cross out 2 fish
Cross out 4 snowmen
Cross out 1 spoon
Cross out 2 lions
Cross out 2 teddies

Page 20
Cross out 1 bee
Cross out 1 nail
Cross out 3 mice
Cross out 3 bottles
Cross out 3 mops

Page 21
A 3
B 5
C 1
D 4
E 6
F 2

Page 22
2, 3, 4
7, 8, 9
5, 6, 7
3, 4, 5
6, 7, 8
4, 5, 6
8, 9, 10

Page 23
2
8
3
6
9
4
7
5

Page 24
A 2, 3, 5, 6, 7, 9, 10
B 0, 1, 2 4, 5, 6 8, 9, 10
C 4 6 8 10
3 5 7 9
D 10, 9, 7, 6, 5,
3, 2, 1, 0
E 0, 2, 3, 4, 5, 6, 8, 9, 10

Page 25
0 + 5
1 + 4
2 + 3

1 2 3 4 5

Page 26
0 + 10
1 + 9
2 + 8
3 + 7
4 + 6
5 + 5

1 2 3 4 5 6 7 8 9 10

Page 29
Jim can buy the
ostrich or the lion.

Page 31
4 apples
6 cats
8 frogs
9 tadpoles
10 mops

Page 32
6 hens
8 dolphins
7 mushrooms
10 rabbits
9 slugs

Page 33
9 cats
8 horses
7 owls
10 dogs
6 centipedes

Page 34
5 chicks
7 fish
9 sheep
10 bees
10 owls

Page 35
3 swans
6 dogs
7 birds
9 goats
10 snails

Page 36

A	B
1. 8	1. 5
2. 6	2. 6
3. 4	3. 4
4. 9	4. 9
5. 2	5. 8
6. 1	6. 10
7. 5	7. 2
8. 10	8. 3
9. 7	9. 1
10. 3	10. 7

Page 37

A	B
1. 2	1. 5
2. 3	2. 4
3. 4	3. 2
4. 5	4. 10
5. 6	5. 9
6. 7	6. 9
7. 8	7. 7
8. 9	8. 10
9. 10	9. 9
	10. 8
	11. 8
	12. 10

Page 38
1. 1 0
2. 2 1
3. 3 2
4. 4 3
5. 5 4
6. 6 5
7. 7 6

Page 39
2 fish
4 chicks
3 slugs
5 owls
7 bees
9 penguins

Page 40

A	B
1. 2	1. 0
2. 4	2. 1
3. 6	3. 2
4. 1	4. 3
5. 3	5. 4
6. 5	6. 5
7. 0	7. 6
8. 8	8. 7
9. 7	9. 8
10. 9	10. 9

Page 41

A	B
1. 3	1. 2
2. 3	2. 5
3. 3	3. 1
4. 2	4. 2
5. 6	5. 2
6. 2	6. 3
7. 4	7. 2
8. 3	8. 0
9. 0	9. 3
10. 7	10. 4

Page 45
1p
7p
4p
2p
5p

Page 46

A	B
1. 1	1. 4
2. 2	2. 7
3. 3	3. 6
4. 3	4. 6
5. 1	5. 2
6. 2	6. 8
7. 3	7. 3
8. 3	8. 5
9. 2	9. 6
10. 2	10. 8

Page 47
A 11 15 18 19
B 12 14 16 17
C 11 13 14 15 17 19 20
D 18 16 13 11
E 19 18 15 14 12
F 20 17 16 14 13 11 10
G19 18 17 16 14 13 12 11

Page 48

A	B
1. 6	1. 6
2. 6	2. 5
3. 8	3. 9
4. 8	4. 3
5. 9	5. 9
6. 9	6. 9
7. 8	7. 9
8. 8	8. 6
9. 9	9. 7
10. 9	10. 10

Page 49

A 3 B 5
C 4 D 2
E 6 F 0

Page 50

1. 7 paintbrushes
2. 9 tulips
3. 9 apples
4. 8p
5. 8 dots
6. Jim 7 goals

Page 51

A	B
1. 9	1. 10
2. 12	2. 15
3. 14	3. 18
4. 20	4. 17
5. 17	5. 20
6. 16	6. 20
7. 18	7. 18
8. 15	8. 16
9. 17	9. 20
10. 17	10. 17

A 10 B 9 C 1

Page 52

1. 12 bees
2. 15 ladybirds
3. 17 rabbits
4. 17 players
5. 19p
6. 16p

Page 53

1. 4 spells
2. 5 nuts
3. 4p
4. 5 stamps
5. Cygnets win by 2 goals
6. 4 holes

Page 54

A	B
1. 10	1. 0
2. 10	2. 1
3. 10	3. 2
4. 10	4. 3
5. 10	5. 4
6. 10	6. 5
7. 10	7. 6
8. 10	8. 7
9. 10	9. 8
10. 10	10. 9

Page 55

A	B
1. 10	1. 9
2. 9	2. 9
3. 12	3. 3
4. 12	4. 9
5. 13	5. 8
6. 14	6. 5
7. 11	7. 7
8. 13	8. 18
9. 12	9. 6
10. 13	10. 6

Page 56

1. 3	6. 6
2. 2	7. 7
3. 0	8. 8
4. 5	9. 10
5. 4	10. 9

Page 57

A	B
1. 9	1. 5
2. 18	2. 11
3. 12	3. 10
4. 12	4. 10
5. 15	5. 2
6. 17	6. 4
7. 11	7. 9
8. 20	8. 7
9. 20	9. 9
10. 19	10. 8
11. 17	11. 5
12. 19	12. 12
13. 20	13. 18
14. 17	14. 2
15. 19	15. 4
16. 17	16. 4
17. 17	17. 7
18. 20	18. 11
19. 16	19. 11
20. 15	20. 1

Page 58

A 8 B 7 C 6
D 5 E 7 F 7
G 6 H 8 I 9
J 8 K 3 L 4

Page 59

1. 1 17
2. 14
3. £15 £5
4. 13
5. 14p 16p 10p 20p

Page 60

1. 3p
2. 8p
3. 19p 1p
4. 17p 3p
5. 18p 2p

Page 61

A	1. 30	6. 66
	2. 45	7. 87
	3. 82	8. 99
	4. 51	9. 75
	5. 100	10. 29
B	1. 24	6. 61
	2. 19	7. 58
	3. 9	8. 81
	4. 37	9. 73
	5. 46	10. 8

C 1. 44 54 64
2. 59 69 79
3. 38 48 58
4. 37 27 17
5. 25 15 5

Page 62

A	1. 5	6. 400
	2. 40	7. 70
	3. 70	8. 3
	4. 40	9. 90
	5. 700	10. 80
B	1. 68	4. 659
	2. 26	5. 240
	3. 345	6. 707

C 1. 3 6 7 9
2. 0 3 8 10
3. 12 13 16 19
4. 17 25 33 42

D 1. 9 7 6 5
2. 48 16 8 0
3. 19 16 14 10
4. 51 30 29 16

Page 63

1. 86p
2. 31p
3. 23p
4. 7p
5. 69p
6. 55p
7. Pot and cow

Page 64

A	B
1. 11p	1. 18p
2. 11p	2. 15p
3. 12p	3. 10p
4. 14p	4. 2p
5. 16p	5. 11p
6. 18p	6. 9p
7. 30p	7. 13p
8. 20p	8. 6p
9. 60p	9. 90p
10. 90p	10. 80p
11. 5p	11. 70p
12. 8p	12. 50p
13. 11p	13. 25p
14. 30p	14. 20p
15. 40p	15. 1p

Page 65

A 8 10 12 14 16 18

B	C
6	8
10	10
14	14
16	16
20	20

D

1. 8
2. 10
3. 12
4. 14
5. 6
6. £1
7. 12p

Page 66

12 15 18 21 24 27
6 9 12
15 18 21

16 20 24 28 32 36
8 12 16
20 24 28

Page 67

20 25 30 35 40 45
10 15 20
25 30 35

40 50 60 70 80 90

10	60
20	70
30	80
40	90
50	100

Page 68

1. 12
2. 18
3. 10
4. 20p
5. 12
6. £24
7. £1
8. 60
9. 15p
10. 20

Page 69

1. 5	14. 10
2. 3	15. 7
3. 2	16. 4
4. 2	17. 7
5. 4	18. 5
6. 4	19. 10
7. 3	20. 6
8. 6	21. 3
9. 2	22. 5
10. 2	23. 10
11. 5	24. 6
12. 5	25. 4
13. 9	

Page 70

1. 4	7. 20p
2. 5	8. 5
3. 4p	9. 20p
4. 5	10. 5
5. 4	11. 2
6. 10	12. 2 2 over

Page 71

1. 2 r = 1	6. 5 r = 2
2. 7 r = 1	7. 6 r = 2
3. 4 r = 3	8. 5 r = 2
4. 3 r = 3	9. 6 r = 1
5. 3 r = 3	10. 5 r = 3

11. 5p	2p over
12. 3	10p change
13. 4	2 over
14. 2	5 spare
15. 5	4
16. 2	5

Page 72
3 shells in each group
6 shells altogether

4 mice in each group
8 mice altogether

Page 73

2 apples in each group
8 apples altogether

3 frogs in each group
12 frogs altogether

Page 74
1. (a) $\frac{1}{2}$ (b) $\frac{1}{4}$ (c) $\frac{3}{4}$

2.

3. (a) $\frac{1}{2}$ (b) $\frac{1}{2}$ (c) $\frac{1}{2}$

(d) $\frac{1}{4}$ (e) $\frac{1}{2}$ (f) $\frac{3}{4}$

Page 75

A	B
1. 2	1. 10
2. 1	2. 5
3. 3	3. 20
4. 4	4. 10
5. 2	5. 30
6. 5	6. 15
7. 6	7. 40
8. 3	8. 20
9. 8	9. 50
10. 4	10. 25

Page 76
A 4 10 14
16 20 40

B 3 8 15
20 9 50

C 1. 30p
2. 50p
3. 70p
4. 21
5. £1.50
6. £15

Page 77
30°C
40°C
20°C
-10°C

-4 -2 -1 2 3 5 6 8 9

5
5
-2
-2
-3

Page 78
1. (a) 3 o'clock
(b) Half past 10
(c) Quarter to 4.

2. (a)

(b)

(c)

3. 7:00 2:30 3:45

4. Half an hour/30 minutes

5. 8.15

Page 79

Mon	
Tues	22
Wed ///// /	
Thurs	11
Fri	14
Sat ///// ///// //	
Sun	29

1. 22
2. Wednesday 6
3. Sunday 29
4. 112
5. Wednesday

Page 80
B Monday - 6 hours
Sunday - 5 hours
Tuesday and Saturday

C

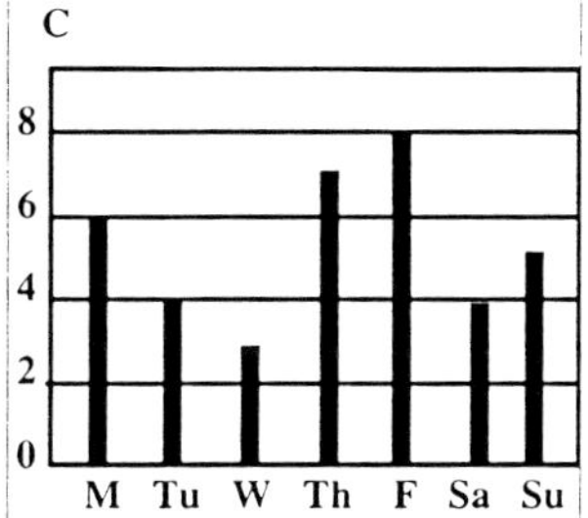

Papers

Page 81 Paper 1
1. 3
2. 4
3. 2
4. 9
5. 4
6. 10
7. 9
8. odd
9. 16
10. 5p, 2p
11. 8
12. 8
13. $\frac{1}{2}$
14. 10
15. H
16. 50p
17. 1 + 3
18. Friday
19. 7p
20. 5

Page 82 Paper 2
1. 10p + 2p
2. 19
3. 4
4.

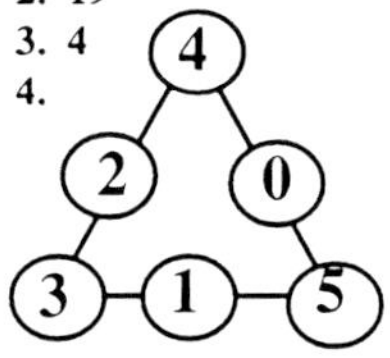

5. 7
6. 9
7. 7 km
8. 80
9. 18
10. A 13p B 18p C 28p

Page 83 Paper 3
1. 34
2. 6p
3. 14
4. 11
5. 3
6. 14
7. 12
8. Wednesday
9. $1\frac{1}{2}$ $3\frac{1}{4}$ $4\frac{3}{4}$
10. 6 in pond
2 outside pond
8 altogether
$\frac{1}{4}$
$\frac{3}{4}$

Page 84 Paper 4
1. 5
2. 20
3. 5 minutes
4. 4
5. 3
6. 8 10 12 14 16 18 20 22
24 26 28
7. 15 20 25
8. 10 20 30
9. 40 50 60
10. 2 5 10

Page 85 Paper 5
1. 12
2. 24
4
20
3. 80p
4. 4 r = 3
5. 4 3
6. 50p
7. 5p
8. Half past 2 2:30
9. 5 2
10. 21

Page 86 Paper 6
1. 70
2. 74
3. 57
4. 56
5. 15p
6. 45 minutes
7. 8.15 pm
8. 6p 10p
9. +
-
÷
x
10. -2°C

Page 87 Paper 7
1. 18
2. 12
3. 19
4. 79
5. 27
6. 17
7. 5
8. 18 33
9. Friday
10. I H I
11. 9 17 42 350 1000
12. 32 104

Page 88 Paper 8
1. 4 2 6
2. 3 cm line
3. 10 4p
4. 43
5. 26
6. 6 r = 1
7. 7p
8.

$-1\frac{1}{2}$ $-\frac{1}{2}$ 0 2 $4\frac{1}{4}$

-2 -1 1 3 4 5

9. £2
10. 10 16
61
60

Page 89 Paper 9
1. Jim
2. A won C last
3. Farmer John
Farmer Jones
the Vicar
4.

cakes	100
sandwiches	50
burgers	60
tea	70

£14

Page 90 Paper 10
1. 14 3 11
2.

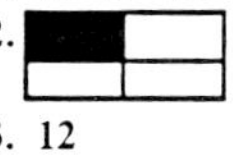

3. 12
4. 15
5.

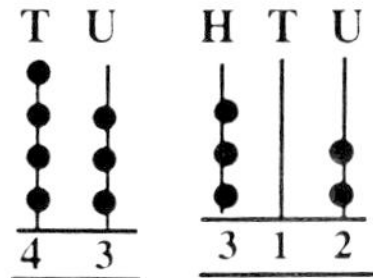

6. 18p 82p
28p 72p
42p 58p

MASTER FILE ORDER FORM

KEY STAGE 1 (Age 5 - 7) **KEY STAGE 2 (Age 7 - 11)** **KEY STAGE 3 (Age 11 - 14)**

Quantity	Title	ISBN	Price	Cost
	KS1 ENGLISH	1 85772 111 X	£20.00	£
	KS1 MATHEMATICS	1 85772 107 1	£20.00	£
	KS1 MENTAL MATHEMATICS	1 85772 154 3	£20.00	£
	KS1 SCIENCE	1 85772 108 X	£20.00	£
	KS1 DEVELOPING ICT SKILLS	1 85772 166 7	£20.00	£
	KS1 HISTORY	1 85772 112 8	£20.00	£
	KS2 ENGLISH	1 85772 085 7	£20.00	£
	KS2 MATHEMATICS	1 85772 086 5	£20.00	£
	KS2 SCIENCE	1 85772 087 3	£20.00	£
	KS2 DEVELOPING ICT SKILLS	1 85772 165 9	£20.00	£
	KS2 ICT DATA AND SPREADSHEETS	1 85772 167 5	£20.00	£
	KS3 ENGLISH	1 85772 127 6	£20.00	£
	KS3 MATHEMATICS	1 85772 126 8	£20.00	£
	KS3 SCIENCE	1 85772 128 4	£20.00	£
	KS3 ICT DATA AND SPREADSHEETS	1 85772 164 0	£20.00	£
HISTORY				
	KS2 Invaders and Settlers, The Celts	1 85772 067 9	£15.95	£
	KS2 Invaders and Settlers, The Romans	1 85772 070 9	£15.95	£
	KS2 Invaders and Settlers, The Vikings	1 85772 069 5	£15.95	£
	KS2 Life in Tudor Times	1 85772 076 8	£15.95	£
	KS2/KS3 Victorian Britain	1 85772 077 6	£15.95	£
	KS2 - KS3 Second World War	1 85772 121 7	£20.00	£
TOPICS				
	KS2/KS3 Castles	1 85772 075 X	£15.95	£
	CHRISTMAS (AGES 5 - 12)	1 85772 065 2	£20.00	£
EARLY YEARS				
	First Steps Basic Activities in the 3Rs	1 85772 130 6	£12.50	£
	First Steps Number and Counting	1 85772 133 0	£12.50	£
	First Steps Beginning to Read	1 85772 138 1	£12.50	£
	First Steps Beginning to Write	1 85772 139 X	£12.50	£
	First Steps Beginning Mental Maths	1 85772 142 X	£12.50	£
	First Steps Mental Maths, 5 - 6 years	1 85772 143 8	£12.50	£
	First Steps Mental Maths, 6 - 7 years	1 85772 146 2	£12.50	£
	First Steps Mental Maths, 7 - 8 years	1 85772 147 0	£12.50	£
	First Steps Mental Maths 8 - 9 years	1 85772 148 9	£12.50	£
	First Steps Developing Literacy Skills 4 - 5 years	1 85772 151 9	£12.50	£
	First Steps Developing Literacy Skills 5- 6 years	1 85772 152 7	£12.50	£
	First Steps Developing Literacy Skills 6 - 7 years	1 85772 153 5	£12.50	£
	Reading and Comprehension 5 - 7 years, Book 1	1 85772 144 6	£12.50	£
	Reading and Comprehension 5 - 7 years, Book 2	1 85772 145 4	£12.50	£
			Total	£

Name/Organisation/School

Address

Post Code Tel.

Contact Signature

Order Number

Date

Available from Blackwells, Foyles Bookshop, Hammicks, Ottakars, Waterstones, Welsh Books Council, WH Smith, and all good booksellers or direct from

DOMINO BOOKS (WALES) LTD, P O BOX 32, SWANSEA SA1 1 FN.
Tel. 01792 459378 Fax. 01792 466337
www.dominobooks.co.uk email: sales@dominobooks.co.uk

All official orders must have an official requisition form attached (schools, educational establishments, LEAs, bookshops, libraries). Cheques with private orders please.